T3-BNY-670

FICTION BY NINETEENTH CENTURY WOMEN WRITERS

GARLAND REFERENCE LIBRARY OF THE HUMANITIES
VOLUME 2112

LIBRARY
COLBY-SAWYER COLLEGE
NEW LONDON, NH 03257

LIBRARY
COLBY-SAWYER COLLEGE
NEW LONDON, NH 03257

Fiction by Nineteenth Century Women Writers

A New England Sampler

Volume 1

Edited by
Thomas A. Maik

Garland Publishing, Inc.
A Member of the Taylor & Francis Group
New York and London
1999

LIBRARY
COLBY-SAWYER COLLEGE
NEW LONDON, NH 03257

*PS
648
.N38
F53
1999
v. 1
c. 1*

4266176

Copyright © 1999 by Thomas A. Maik
All rights reserved

Library of Congress Cataloging-in-Publication Data
Fiction by nineteenth century women writers : a New England sampler / edited
   by Thomas A. Maik.
         p.   cm.   —   (Garland reference library of the humanities ;
   2112)
         Contents : Mis' Elderkin's pitcher / Harriet Beecher Stowe — Ann
   Potter's lesson ; Squire Paine's conversion / Rose Terry Cooke — On
   Sand Island / Sarah Johnson Prichard — The brothers ; Scarlet stock
   ings / Louisa May Alcott — Miss Moggaridge's provider / Harriet
   Prescott Spofford — A lost lover ; Tom's husband ; Marsh Rosemary /
   Sarah Orne Jewett — A gatherer of simples ; Evelina's garden ; The
   revolt of Sophia Lane / Mary Wilins Freeman.
      ISBN 0-8153-3189-4 (alk. paper)
      1. Women—New England Fiction. 2. American fiction—Women
   authors. 3. American fiction—19th century. 4. American fiction—
   New England. 5. New England—Fiction. I. Maik, Thomas A. II. Series.
   PS648.N38F53   1999
   813'.30809287'0974—dc21   99–29224
                                                                        CIP

Printed on acid-free, 250-year-life paper
Manufactured in the United States of America

LIBRARY
COLBY-SAWYER COLLEGE
NEW LONDON, NH 03257

For Linda, Kathy, and Andy

Contents

Foreword

I never knew a New England heroine beaten. I have seen her assailed by all the enemies of our race,—sickness, poverty, misfortune, disgrace, and sorrow,—and she has conquered them all. I have seen her as an export to the West, that West which *she* has made the prosperous land that it is; and I have admired her bent form, her sallow paleness, her patient mouth, from which that pearly gleam had departed, far more than the most roseate bloom, the most Venus-like outline. . . . The typical New England woman makes everything for herself, from her bonnet up to her destiny. She can be anything; there are no limitations to her ambition.

"New England Women" (234, 235)
The Atlantic Monthly, August 1878

Preface

This book grows out of many years of teaching at the University of Wisconsin–La Crosse. More than ten years ago I began having students in one of my classes do primary research for their course paper. Specifically, I asked them to research the bound volumes and microfilm for *Harper's New Monthly*, *The Atlantic Monthly*, *Galaxy*, and other newly established, nineteenth–century magazines for the purpose of "discovering" short fiction for their analysis paper. In addition, since revision of the canon was in progress, I wanted the students to focus on stories that had been published by women writers.

What they discovered were some real gems. Besides stories from established women writers, they discovered new writers. Although the stories had been published in magazines in the nineteenth century and may have later been included in collections by the author, most of the stories had languished since their publication. What started out as a project on short fiction by women writers without respect to region led over the years to a focus specifically on New England women writers.

The end result is this collection of seven New England women writers. Thanks to the reexamination of the canon in recent years, most readers will be familiar with Sarah Orne Jewett and Mary Wilkins Freeman. Readers may also have come to know Harriet Beecher Stowe and Louisa May Alcott for works beyond their classics. Others may have some familiarity with Rose Terry Cooke and Harriet Prescott Spofford; however, none will probably have heard of Sarah Johnson Prichard. Although some of these writers are now regularly anthologized, fiction included in this collection will be new to most.

Through the pages of the newly emerging magazines in the nineteenth century, these writers found a voice. As I read these women writers, some of them for the first time, I marveled at their fiction and, at the same time, the quandary of their voice being lost to readers today. I became convinced that they deserved a larger audience than just me and my class. I am grateful to Garland Publishing for feeling the way I do about the fiction and for giving these writers voice again.

Thomas A. Maik
February 1999

Acknowledgments

Thanks go to my students over the years who diligently researched writers and fiction not included in our regular texts and anthologies and "discovered" these and other stories.

To Krista Shulka I am indebted for her laborious work of "keying" the stories from the Xeroxed copies of microfilm and doing such an excellent job. Students, particularly Pete Adam and Erik Hooverson, in the University of Wisconsin–La Crosse Technology Center have been most helpful in formatting text. Phyllis Bedessem in the English department has also assisted with computer questions.

Lavonia "Moni" McCarty in Murphy Library helped so much in locating material for me on Sarah Johnson Prichard. Her assistance in interlibrary loan materials has helped me immensely.

To the University of Wisconsin–La Crosse, I am grateful for both a small research grant, which provided financial support for the assistance of Krista Shulka, and a sabbatical. The sabbatical gave me the opportunity and the time, which I have long sought, to select, edit, and introduce this collection. Without the sabbatical, I could not have completed the project.

Finally, I owe special thanks to my wife, Linda. Besides initially encouraging me to pursue this project and supporting me along the way, she has provided valuable insights, helped with editing, and just been there.

FICTION BY NINETEENTH CENTURY WOMEN WRITERS

Introduction

In the post–Civil War era, which saw the acceleration of the Industrial Revolution, the establishment of the continental railroad, the rise of robber barons, massive immigration, and westward expansion and exploration, American writers emerged in various geographic regions to observe and record the significant transformation taking place. Contributing to this development was the expansion of public education, an increasing public literacy as well as leisure time, and, most importantly, newly emerging magazines seeking material to fill their pages. *The Atlantic Monthly, Harper's New Monthly, Galaxy,* and *Putnam's* were just a few of the new magazines looking for writers. In regions such as New England, the West, and the South, writers responded. Sarah Orne Jewett and Mary Wilkins Freeman in New England; Mark Twain, Artemus Ward, Bret Harte, and Hamlin Garland in the West; and George Washington Cable and Kate Chopin in the South were some of the writers submitting and publishing fiction in various magazines.

In fact, short stories became the literature of choice for an emerging mass audience. Although the writers previously mentioned may still be familiar to readers today, numerous other writers discovered an audience through the pages of these emerging magazines. Increasingly, these writers were female. In New England, women such as Rose Terry Cooke, Sarah Johnson Prichard, and Harriet Prescott Spofford published regularly. Although unfamiliar to large audiences today, Harriet Prescott Spofford during her lifetime had avid readers, most notably Emily Dickinson. To Thomas Wentworth Higginson, critic and writer as well as mentor to Dickinson, the poet writes: "I read Miss Prescott's 'Circumstance,' but it followed me in the dark—so I avoided her." Interestingly, and despite her comment to Higginson, Emily Dickinson wrote to her sister-in-law, Sue Gilbert Dickinson: "Sue, it ["Circumstance"] is the only thing I ever read in my life that I didn't think I could have imagined myself. . . .[S]end me everything she writes" (Martha Dickinson Bianchi, *Emily Dickinson Face to Face.* [Boston: Houghton Mifflin, 1932], p. 28). Dickinson's remarks illustrate both the originality and the power of Spofford's work.

Although read widely in the late nineteenth century, increasingly these women writers—with a few exceptions—began to be marginalized early in the twentieth century. From the extensive representation of American writers in anthologies edited by Rufus Griswold and Evert and George Duyckinck in the nineteenth century, came the elevation of the few—primarily male—writers in the twentieth century. As Karen L. Kilcup points out, with the professionalization and masculinization of literary study in the early twentieth century came the aesthetics for literary "periods," "themes," and privileged male-authored texts (*Nineteenth-Century American Women Writers*. [Cambridge, Mass.: Blackwell, 1997], p. xxxix). Marginalization of women writers, in fact, became so extreme that anyone studying nineteenth-century American literature during the middle decades of the twentieth century would usually find only token representation of women: certainly Emily Dickinson and perhaps Sarah Orne Jewett and Mary Wilkins Freeman. Although the following remarks by Van Wyck Brooks, one of America's leading critics near the middle of the twentieth century, pertain specifically to Sarah Orne Jewett, they could just as easily be applied in general to women writers in that time period: "Her vision was certainly limited. It scarcely embraced the world of men, and the vigorous, masculine life of towns like Gloucester, astir with Yankee enterprise and bustle, lay quite outside her province and point of view" (*New England: Indian Summer*. [New York: E.P. Dutton, 1940], pp. 347-48). At this point in American literary criticism, the common yardstick used to measure literature was a masculine world and male writers. Women's lives, their values, friendship, nurture, and bonding took a distant second place to the rugged, individualistic, and adventurous world of men.

Only within the past fifteen to twenty years has this situation changed. Interest in the women's movement, minority literature, and multiculturalism has energized the call to reexamine and broaden the American literary canon. As a result, critics and readers have "rediscovered" writers and their fiction that had been popular in the nineteenth century, but neglected and relegated to inferior status in this century. Thankfully, these writers are again being given voice. All too often, however, the focus in American literature anthologies has rested on selective touchstone pieces. Typical selections, for example, are "The Revolt of Mother" and "A New England Nun" by Mary Wilkins Freeman and "The White Heron" and selections from *The Country of the Pointed Firs* by Sarah Orne Jewett. Although today's readers are familiar with Louisa May Alcott's *Little Women* and many certainly know Harriet Beecher Stowe's *Uncle Tom's Cabin*, far too often knowledge of and appreciation for Alcott and Stowe end with those popular selections. Thus, despite recent efforts to expand the canon and reexamine American literature, readers often know only the "token" pieces.

The purpose, then, of this collection is to pursue the work of broadening the canon and to focus specifically on women writers from New England in the latter half of the nineteenth century, when they had an audience. In this introduction, I will give a brief overview of the seven authors I include in this collection: Harriet Beecher Stowe, Rose Terry Cooke, Sarah Johnson Prichard, Louisa May Alcott, Harriet Prescott Spofford, Sarah Orne Jewett, and Mary Wilkins Freeman. In addition, I will suggest some of the literary developments over the years that have affected the status and reputations of these writers. I will also summarize some of the cultural and economic changes affecting the New England region during the latter part of the nineteenth century. Finally, I will suggest some of the themes or ideas connecting the thirteen stories by these seven writers. The stories included cover the latter four decades in the nineteenth century beginning with Cooke's "Ann Potter's Lesson" in 1858 and ending with Freeman's "The Revolt of Sophia Lane" in 1903.

The Writers

In a literary career that spanned almost fifty years, Mary Wilkins Freeman wrote fifteen collections of short stories, sixteen novels, a play, and eight volumes of poetry and prose for children. In her best fiction—written before her unsuccessful marriage in 1902 to Dr. Charles Manning Freeman when she was forty-nine years old— Freeman wrote about the rural New England mill towns and villages. Randolph, Massachusetts, a town that she knew well from having lived there in her early years, serves as a model for the village life she captures in her stories. Perry Westbrook, one of Freeman's biographers, regards her as the "most truthful recorder in fiction of New England village life" (*Mary Wilkins Freeman.* [New York: Twayne Publishers, Inc., 1967], p. 15). Located about fourteen miles from Boston, Randolph was in many ways the quintessential nineteenth-century New England community. Here, Freeman experienced the security of a community in which one's neighbors shared ancestral codes of behavior. She knew well the homogeneity of community experiences, but she also knew well the eccentricities and oddities of human character resulting from generations of rural isolation. In her treatment of a New England environment in transition following the Civil War, Freeman focuses on the common and ordinary experiences of typical men and women, women's roles, their relationships with men, their status in society, and their children.

Sarah Orne Jewett published nearly 150 stories over a lifetime career that began with her first published story at age eighteen. Aspiring to be a doctor like her father but never achieving that ambition because of poor health, Jewett wrote about the people, the villages, and the sea she knew so well from having lived in South Berwick, Maine. In accompanying her father as he made calls on patients in the various communities surrounding South Berwick, Jewett developed a lasting and deep appreciation for the people and villages of the Maine seacoast. Throughout her career, she heeded the advice of her father, not to "write about people and things, [but rather] tell them just as they are!" (Sarah Orne Jewett, *Letters.* Ed. Richard Cary. [Waterville: Colby College Press, 1967], p. 19). With an eye for authenticity, Jewett captures the spirit of seacoast communities in decline and neglect because of the dwindling importance of the fishing industry. Reflective of the diminished importance of these villages is the absence of men who have left these communities to seek adventure and fortune elsewhere. In the absence of men, the females in Jewett's fiction are the leaders and sustainers of the communities. In Jewett's fiction, then, we meet the aged spinsters, the herbalists, the deteriorating towns, and often the failed lives of men. Harriet Spofford notes about Jewett that ". . .her intimacy with the deeper things of life, and her understanding of small troubles, was something wonderful" (*A Little Book of Friends.* [Boston: Little Brown, 1917], p. 37). Paula Blanchard, a recent biographer of Jewett, notes her positive emphasis on what could be the application of harsh New England values: "her moral vision and her regionalism are two sides of the same coin, for Jewett's belief that every person shapes his or her life within a certain God-given arena was expressed in her art through the tradition of Maine stoicism" (*Sarah Orne Jewett.* [New York: Addison-Wesley, 1994], p. 244). Through her writing, Jewett depicts the richness of ordinary moments—a conversation, a visit with friends, a garden harvest, the values of close friendships, the significance of the ordinary.

Like Jewett, Harriet Prescott Spofford grew up in Maine. Unlike Jewett, however, Spofford at age fourteen learned the meaning of financial need when her father left the family to seek a fortune in Oregon. Out of necessity, she turned to writing. In fact, in one three-year period which produced over one hundred tales, Spofford wrote with an arm and hand sometimes swollen from writing fifteen hours a day. Growing up with her mother, three sisters, four aunts, her grandmother, and one brother, she wrote, not surprisingly, about that that she knew best—the lives and experiences of women. In her fiction, she challenges the prevalent nineteenth-century stereotype which divides women into good and bad by writing about pairs of contrasting women who discover their sisterhood. In a career spanning sixty years, besides short fiction Spofford wrote poems, novels, novellas, children's books, literary essays, essays and books on domestic issues, travel books, and personal reminiscences. As one might expect from her voluminous output, by the turn of the century she had become one of America's most popular writers. From her position of high regard and popularity early in this century, today she is scarcely noted.

Unlike the diminished reputation today of Harriet Prescott Spofford and the limited access modern day readers have to her works, Harriet Beecher Stowe, another New England writer, still enjoys a wide reading audience. Despite raising six children, keeping house without much money, and being subject to depression and poor health, Harriet Beecher Stowe wrote numerous novels and short fiction. In fact, during 1853 and 1854 she wrote an average of one magazine article every two weeks. As the sister of seven ministers and the daughter of an eighth minister—the distinguished Lyman Beecher—it is not surprising that Harriet Beecher Stowe's writing is marked by a desire to instruct and encourage. *Uncle Tom's Cabin*, her most famous work, catapulted her to international fame after its publication in 1852, and she became one of America's best-paid and most-sought-after writers. When she met Lincoln at the White House in 1862, he is said to have remarked, "So you're the little woman who wrote the book that started this great war!" Although she wrote numerous stories and many novels after the publication of *Uncle Tom's Cabin*, that book which has generated so much controversy in the twentieth century almost single-handedly contributed to her success and fame in the nineteenth century. Her popularity and substantial reputation caused her 70th birthday in 1881 to become a national event. Newspaper editorials were written in her honor and the school children in her hometown of Hartford, Connecticut, were given a holiday in her name. As Judith Fetterley has poignantly observed: "She can be dismissed, she can be trivialized, but she can not be ignored" (*Provisions*. [Bloomington: Indiana University Press, 1985], p. 374.

Like Stowe, Rose Terry Cooke was born and raised in Connecticut. Like Stowe, Cooke, too, reflects a religious influence in her writing, having joined the Congregational Church at age sixteen and remaining a committed Christian throughout her life. Nonetheless, in her fiction at least, she demonstrates an ongoing argument with the church as an institution, as shown in "Squire Paine's Conversion," one of Cooke's stories included in this collection. Cooke's first love was writing poetry, which she began at an early age for the entertainment of herself and friends. In the course of her lifetime, she published two volumes of poetry; however, Rose Terry Cooke's real achievement is in the genre of the short story. Harriet Prescott Spofford recognized Cooke's superior prose: ". . . as story followed story, each better than the other, she kindled the ambition and had the felicitation of every other young woman who turned the pages throughout the country,—for most of us felt as if all girlhood were honored in her who carried her light before men with such proud strength and beauty" (Harriet Prescott Spofford, "Rose Terry Cooke," *Our Famous Women*. [Hartford: Worthington, 1884], p. 175). Although it is not completely clear when Cooke began to write prose, in 1855 she contributed eight stories to *Putnam's Magazine*, and in 1857 *The Atlantic Monthly* magazine invited her to contribute to their inaugural first issue in November of that year. She, too, reflects her New England region in her writing through her use of characters and setting. What is particularly noteworthy of Cooke is that she was the first in a group of writers that followed to make dialect an integral part of American fiction. In addition to her use of dialect, much of her best fiction is characterized by the use of humor.

Unlike so many works by other nineteenth-century New England women writers, or for that matter women writers in general, Louisa May Alcott's *Little Women* has never suffered obscurity. On the other hand, it has never achieved a status of being something other than a children's book, nor has Louisa May Alcott achieved much status as being someone other than a writer for children. Because she grew up in Concord, Massachusetts, during the 1840s, interest in social reform, independence, and self–reliance came easy for her through her exposure to and association with some of the leading social reformers and literary figures of the day: Henry David Thoreau, Ralph Waldo Emerson, Nathaniel Hawthorne, and Margaret Fuller, along with her own father, Amos Bronson Alcott. Interested in numerous social and intellectual experiments, Bronson Alcott was never particularly successful in supporting his family. In fact, his family was constantly on the brink of poverty. His noted grand failure was the debacle in the early 1840s of Fruitlands, one of New England's utopian communities. Because her father came to regard bread winning as inconsistent with the transcendental philosophy of the day, Louisa May Alcott's self–reliance probably resulted more from economic necessity than from intellectual advantage and social privilege. Because debt and deprivation made such an impression on Louisa, she became determined to be self–sufficient and to provide for her mother and sisters. Out of this determination came her literary contributions in the areas of poetry, novels, short stories, and plays. Although recognized primarily as a writer for children, Alcott wrote four novels for adults. Probably because of her exposure to transcendentalism, Concord philosophers, and ideas of utopias, Alcott became a realist of the first order. Stories in this collection that grew out of her experiences as a nurse during the Civil War illustrate both her realism and her "adult" side.

Of the seven New England writers in this collection, the least known today is Sarah Johnson Prichard. Born January 11, 1830, in Waterbury, Connecticut, Prichard was well educated for the time. During her life she published more than a dozen books along with numerous short stories, some of them in *The Atlantic Monthly*. Today she receives neither mention nor footnote in collections of nineteenth–century literature.

Changing Literary Status

Quite obviously, then, these New England women were extensively published and recognized in the nineteenth century. Nathaniel Hawthorne's disparaging reference to his contemporaries as the "damned mob of female scribblers," a remark that has lingered to this day, has undoubtedly contributed to the damaged reputations and diminished recognition of nineteenth–century women writers in this century. Also contributing to their marginalization in the twentieth century has been a critical interpretation of them as "local colorists," a term suggesting a depiction of "local" scenes. Known for their focus upon regional peculiarities and eccentricities, local color writers examined local differences in manners, dialect, clothing, and setting. The focus is on the locale and the qualities of a region together with the people, dialect, and culture that make that locale unique. From a critical perspective, "local color" has come to suggest a pejorative connotation for a literary era marked by emerging realism. Too often denigration of "local color" came at the expense of women writers, while the "realism" movement promoted the male writers such as William Dean Howells, Henry James, Hamlin Garland, and, later, Stephen Crane.

To an even larger degree, the naturalists emerging in the 1890s—Frank Norris, Harold Frederic, Stephen Crane, and Jack London—pushed a gender-based literature that excluded women writers. For the naturalist, "real life" meant the city, not the village. Further, it meant the extraordinary, the grotesque, the bestiality of man in nature, and the loss of individuality. Instead of the rural past which the regional writers examined, the naturalists plunged into the urban present. The rise of naturalism and the fall of regionalism are related as Donna Campbell observes: "The gradual decline of women's local color fiction and the rise of American naturalism at the turn of the nineteenth century thus should not, indeed cannot, be seen as discrete events, contemporaneous occurrences that otherwise have little bearing on each other. The rhetoric employed by the writers of the time suggests not a transition but rather a genteelly pitched battle between the two, a conflict ended by the successful subversion and banishment of local color fiction" (*Resisting Regionalism*. [Athens: Ohio University Press, 1997], p. 12).

Another factor, perhaps, in the marginalization of these women writers may be their use of dialect. For women writers to use slang and dialect was a heretical, insurrectionary gesture. As Ann Douglas notes, to use dialect was a violation of the " . . . ideological cult of true womanhood" because "ladies were known by their correct speech" ("Introduction," *Uncle Tom's Cabin*. [New York: Penguin, 1981], p. 15). Although Cooke may be considered the first woman to make dialect a part of her fiction, many of the other writers in this collection also use dialect, most notably, Spofford and Stowe. Besides use of dialect, the themes of these writers and their tendency to focus on the insular and interior aspects of character and relationships rather than rugged individualism may also be added to the reasons for their marginalization.

In short, one after another, reason can be piled upon reason to somehow explain the marginalization of these writers in the twentieth century. Joan Hedrick's observations in her biography of Harriet Beecher Stowe are applicable as well to the other writers in this collection: " . . . her [Stowe's] decline resulted from the removal of literature from the parlor to institutions to which women had limited access: men's clubs, high-culture journals, and prestigious universities" (*Harriet Beecher Stowe: A Life*. [New York: Oxford University Press, 1994], p. ix). Nonetheless, these female New England regional writers had a voice in their generation, and if the extent of their publications is indicative of their popularity, their voices were welcomed. Today, they deserve to be known for more than just one or two token pieces of fiction; this collection seeks to add to our understanding, appreciation, and contributions of these women writers.

Cultural and Economic Changes

As regional New England writers, their fiction illuminates a New England region in upheaval: a post–Civil War era that left many males maimed or dead, a region with soil unproductive for economic survival, the glitter of western gold that beckoned, the turmoil from industrialization that was sweeping the country. These writers depict the economic instability and cycles of the later nineteenth century. From the once significant and productive seaport and sea-faring communities, they write of a fishing industry that no longer offers lifetime security. As a result, women and children work in factories and mills as their income is needed to supplement the diminishing value of a once significant sea economy. Connected with the shrinking sea economy are the lives of people formerly associated with that economy—namely men. In place of once prosperous, hardy, and independent men, we find shells and relics of a noble past. As within the actual families of these writers and as the father of Spofford illustrates in leaving his family and going to Oregon, frequently the men in the stories are away because they are seeking fortune elsewhere. Or they may be leading lives of dissipation. Or they may have been killed or maimed in the Civil War. In an unsettling era of change and economic instability, the villages in the fiction of this region are populated all too often with childless, middle-aged and older, widowed and single women. Besides the village minister, men are noticeably absent. And even the village minister is under threat as Donna Campbell points out: "Wedded to patriarchal values of idealism and legalism, they [the ministers, within the fiction at least] carry out their official duties unaware that both the changing nature of their communities and the shift from a Calvinist doctrine of faith to a doctrine of works has rendered them virtually superfluous" (*Resisting Regionalism*. [Athens: Ohio University Press, 1997], p. 26). Frequently, those men who do remain are marked by failure or live in a vanished past.

A pervasive quiet, stillness, and seeming emptiness permeates the towns and villages of the stories, a quiet almost eery and deathlike in quality. Judged by today's standards, life in these villages and communities seems dull, boring, and uneventful. Within this economic and cultural shift and upheaval, these women writers examine the universal problems of loneliness, loss, change, and survival. Central to their stories are the lives of ordinary women who deal with change and uncertainty and who survive. The great adventure and expeditions to sea, war, and the frontier, so often charted by Herman Melville, James Fenimore Cooper, Stephen Crane, and other nineteenth-century American male writers, are complemented in this collection by the lives of women who demonstrate ingenuity, tenacity, independence, and heroism throughout the struggles of daily existence. Instead of what came to be the dominant tradition in nineteenth-century American literature of portraying the male individualist (Ahab, Natty Bumppo, Henry Fleming, for example) in flight from society, the women writers, as Joyce Warren points out, portray "characters who were enmeshed in a community of interpersonal relationships" (*The [Other] American Traditions: Nineteenth-Century Women Writers*. [New Brunswick, New Jersey: Rutgers University Press, 1993], p. 11). Instead of the individualism, self-assertion, and insularity that became a hallmark of literature by the male writers, the women writers deal with the bonds and connections between friends, parents and children, and strangers, as well as the pain and hurt that are also an inevitable part of human relationships.

Related Ideas within the Fiction

One idea central to this collection of stories is that of loneliness. Cooke's Ann Potter, central character and story namesake, is totally unlike her mother and sister. Ann, instead, readily admits that she takes after her father who was always "downhearted, never thinkin' things could turn out right, or that he was goin' to have any luck." Even after she wins in marriage the man who she thought sought the hand of her sister, Ann spends her time "worryin' a good deal . . . kinder broodin' over my troubles and never thinkin' about anybody but myself." Her inherited tendency to fixate on the negative is amplified when she and her new husband leave their families to homestead in the frontier territory of Indiana on land purchased by her husband's father. In a strange new land with no neighbors nearby, now she truly feels isolated and profoundly alone. In Freeman's "A Gatherer of Simples," Aurelia, the unmarried central character, handles her isolation and loneliness after her father's suicide and mother's death by becoming an herbalist. Because of her loneliness, she surrounds herself with the environment, and her plants became for her " . . . friends and the healing qualities of sarsaparilla and thoroughwort and the sweetness of thyme and lavender, seemed to have entered into her nature, till she almost could talk with them in that way." Even the rich satisfaction of caring for her plants, however, cannot completely assuage the gnawing hunger of emptiness within. One recognizes both the depth of her loneliness and her tendency to depression as she responds to the opportunity to care for and raise a small child: "I feel as if it wasn't right for me to be so perfectly happy."

The loneliness of Aurelia in "A Gatherer of Simples" is examined in another Freeman story, "Evelina's Garden." Indeed, Aurelia's loneliness is taken to another level in this Freeman story as the emotion is examined at length through the life and character of Evelina. Her sense of "maiden decorum" prevents her from expressing her honest and true feelings for Thomas Merriam, a suitor in her youth. Because of the marked difference in social standing, Thomas Merriam perceives Evelina as unapproachable because of her "maidenly decorum" and marries someone else. Committed to a solitary life, Evelina turns to her garden, and it becomes her "passion" of life. The hedge that grows up over the years and surrounds her garden symbolizes Evelina's ever-increasing isolation and loneliness which slowly consumes and destroys her. Unfortunately, her desperate loneliness seems doomed to repeat itself in the person of her cousin and her potential relationship with Thomas Merriam's own son. Only when cousin Evelina demonstrates courageous independence, takes drastic actions and "kills" the garden—the garden nurtured now for decades by these women—by pouring hot water and salt over the plants is she freed from the isolation and loneliness of past generations.

In "A Lost Lover," a story by Jewett, loneliness is also a factor. Although unmarried, Horatia Dane, the central character, is considered widowed because her lover was lost at sea many years ago. Despite the loneliness and isolation over the years, in other ways Horatia Dane has been energized by her lost love. Although she had numerous suitors in the past, she resisted them and immortalizes instead her youthful romance. Her thoughts of what might have been keep her young and give a bounce to her step. Only in her late years and with the totally unexpected return of her love as a world-wandering dissolute do Horatia's dreams vanish. Almost overnight her neighbors notice "that she began to show her age a great deal; she seemed really like an old woman now; she was not the woman she had been a year ago." Through the character of Horatia Dane's much younger cousin Nelly who comes to visit Horatia, Jewett's story in some ways is strikingly similar to Freeman's "Evelina's Garden." Through Nelly's discovery of Horatia's past, Jewett conveys the folly of Horatia'a inclination to romanticize and live in the past when Horatia suggests that Nelly can escape from making a similar mistake of fantasizing a "what-if" scenario: "You are very young yet, and you must not think of such a thing carelessly. I should be so much grieved if you threw away your happiness."

Jewett examines loneliness from another angle in "Marsh Rosemary," suggesting love as an antidote much as the herb rosemary of the title serves as a stimulant and antidepressant. Ann Floyd, the elderly, single, central character, has, to all appearances for people in the community, had a full and richly satisfying life. In thought and deed, she has constantly been there for her neighbors and helped "lift and carry the burdens of their lives." In a move considered baffling and foolish to her townsmen, she marries a much younger ne'er-do-well, noted in local parlance as someone too lazy even "to tend lobster pots." By portraying Ann Floyd as a "lonely soul" living for so long with "the burden of loneliness and lack of love," Jewett illustrates how love is not something exclusively for the young. Even after Jerry Lane leaves her and she knows that she is much better off to be rid of him, she longs for her husband's totally unenlightening conversation and a voice to fill the silence. Her pathos and profound loneliness are apparent as she realizes that, although lazy, dull, and uninteresting, Jerry Lane was at least a companion.

In Prichard's "Sand Island," the central character Nan Ware is rescued from her life of desperate loneliness and isolation as a mill worker by her marriage to John Ware. In what should be a paradisaical existence in tune with the cycles of nature, John and Nan take up residence on Sand Island. For Nan, however, the existence is anything but paradisaical. She spends her days sentenced to the isolation of a fisherman's wife living on an island populated with only one other family. She attempts to find solace in nature, the wind swept sand, the endless sea, human contact with her only neighbor on the other side of the island, and her white kitten, Comfort. Sentenced to this existence, she longs for "eight dollar days," days few and far between of inclement weather when her husband cannot go to sea. Nan's ultimate sense of desolation occurs early in her marriage when her husband is lost at sea and she is left alone in her cottage with Comfort, her kitten.

Countering the idea of loneliness that these writers explore in a number of the stories is the idea of support and companionship. Elaine Showalter comments on how many of the stories in this period reflect the dominant ideology of women's culture and "intense mother-daughter bonds, and intimate female relationships" (*Tradition and Change in American Women's Writing*. [New York: Oxford University Press, 1991], p. 14). Over and over in these stories and sometimes despite the burdens and obstacles encountered by the characters, one notes the strength and support that come in relationships, most frequently the relationships between women. Alcott in "Scarlet Stockings" examines the friendship between Belle and Kate as well as the friendship between Belle and Kate's brother, Lennox. She depicts the comfortableness of Belle and Kate's relationship as Kate plots to push her rather arrogant and proud brother to a friendship with Belle. Set during the Civil War, Lennox learns humility and compassion in accompanying Belle as she cares for children of a poor family in a typhoid-infected home. Through an experience that enhances Lennox's interest in Belle, he learns much regarding the true character and compassion of Belle, but he also learns much about himself. If he wants Belle's respect, he must surrender his arrogant and supercilious characteristics. Caring for sick children of an impoverished family living in a shack is indeed a humbling experience for Lennox.

Neighbors and friendship are a central part of Freeman's stories. Her story "A Gatherer of Simples" depicts a simpler time when neighbors kept doors unlocked so friends could come and go as they pleased. Besides the satisfaction Aurelia gets from collecting and tending her herbs, she has a support group and plenty of meaningful conversation with her neighbors. Mrs. Atwood, Lavinia, and Mrs. Simonds make up Aurelia's network of friends, and when Mrs. Sears comes to take her granddaughter away from Aurelia and rob her of the love that fills her otherwise lonely existence, Mrs. Simonds speaks for her sisters when she offers support and assurance: "Don't feel bad, 'Relia. I know it's awful hard, when you was taking so much comfort. We all feel for you." In "The Revolt of Sophia Lane," Freeman puts a different spin on friendship by suggesting it's not better to give than to receive unless the person giving acts from the heart with an eye on the receiver. However interfering and managing the actions of Sophia Lane, the namesake of the title, may be interpreted, Sophia only means to show her love and concern for her niece who has been courted for three years but prevented from marriage because of the groom's inadequate resources. When Sophia's second cousin and her two daughters come with "useless" wedding gifts of finger bowls and an afternoon tea kettle two days before the wedding, Sophia's frustration is obvious as she tells her relatives of how the previous Christmas she had returned Christmas gifts to the givers because of the impractical nature of the gifts and the givers' insensitivity toward the recipient. No matter what people might think and how offended they might be, Sophia loves her niece and is simply determined to help her niece get the practical things so she can finally be married and establish a household.

Through humor Spofford demonstrates the rich friendship existing between Miss Moggaridge and Miss Keturah in "Miss Moggaridge's Provider." No two people could be more unlike, and yet their existing differences bring them closer. Having inherited money from her father, Miss Moggaridge's generous spirit seems limitless, and the admonitions from Miss Keturah to be frugal for future needs meets resisting ears and the words that "the Lord will provide." Miss Moggaridge uses her inheritance to locate a brother cut off from the family, to provide for a family whose house was destroyed by fire, to help a nephew through college, and to pay for a neighbor's cataract removal. With each generous act, Miss Keturah admonishes Miss Moggaridge, and the response each time is the same: "the Lord will provide." Only in the end of the story when Miss Moggaridge is destitute because of her generosity do we discover the depth of their friendship. Despite the bantering and apparent surface friction between the two women, there exists between them a deep and genuine love that even their numerous differences cannot break. In the end when Miss Keturah "provides" for Miss Moggaridge, we discover that Miss Keturah is more like Miss Moggaridge than she knows or cares to admit herself.

In addition to the themes of friendship and loneliness in these stories, an idea that seems as basic to New England as seafaring, sand dunes, and salty air is also explored: New England values such as hard work and frugality and strength of character. Despite the nobility of these values, we frequently see the New England women writers examining the perversion of these values. Cooke explores New England values gone awry in "Squire Paine's Conversion." That environment shapes character seems readily apparent in this story as Cooke describes the harsh farmland that Squire Paine grew up on as being of "rugged acres, scant pasturage . . . 'medder land' that reluctantly gave corn." In a reflection of these harsh New England farming conditions, Squire Paine himself is described as a "hard-headed Yankee boy," and the narrator observes that "hard work is the initial lesson," with the addendum: "it is slave or starve in New England." Perhaps because of this background and this environment, Squire Paine not surprisingly exemplifies strength, fierce independence, and grudging frugality. Soon after his parents' death at age twenty, Squire Paine buys the only general store within thirty miles with its adjoining house. Successful as he might be regarded, at this early age a clear pattern of a miserly and begrudging character has emerged: "home—no, it was no home—at his store, strict in every matter of business, merciless to his debtors, close and niggardly even to his best customers, harsh to his clerk; and greedy of every smallest profit." Cooke's harsh portrayal makes it clear that the values of thrift, frugality, and hard work have been perverted in the life of Squire Paine.

Similarly in Freeman's "Evelina's Garden" we also see the perversion of what should be regarded as noble values. After Evelina's "maidenly decorum" prevents her from conveying her genuine feelings for Thomas Merriam, she places all her energies into cultivating an elaborate garden. And what a garden it is: "There had never been in the village such a garden as this of Evelina Adams's." Over the years as the garden flourished and the hedge grew to keep neighbors out, Evelina became increasingly reclusive and isolated: "Summer and winter, spring and fall, Evelina Adams never was seen outside her own domain of old mansion-house and garden, and she had not set her slim lady feet in the public highway for nearly forty years, if the stories were true." In the absence of any other connection with life and fellowship with neighbors, Evelina found through her garden something to do and something to care for. In short, cultivation of her garden becomes her life—her obsession.

Values gone awry may also be noted in Spofford's "Miss Moggaridge's Provider." Spofford characterizes Moggaridge's village as one on the surface that exudes Christian values of love and caring for one's neighbor, values, in fact, preached by Miss Moggaridge's father, the village minister. Indeed, Miss Keturah refers to him as Moggaridge's "sainted Father, a Christian minister for fifty years breaking the bread of life in this parish." What we discover instead is a person less than saintly in the eyes of his own daughter; a man who preaches love and forgiveness, but refuses to forgive even his own flesh and blood when his son runs away to sea: "the stern clergyman, his father, having satisfied his mind on the point that there was no earthly reclamation possible for Jack, had with true old-style rigor commenced and carried on the difficult work of tearing the boy out of his heart" The hypocrisy of the saintly minister typifies in many ways the character of most of the people in the village. Spofford portrays them as nosy, gossipy, and back biting. They are as skeptical and unforgiving of Miss Moggaridge's generosity as Miss Keturah is: "It was no wonder the townsfolk were incensed against her, for her conduct implied a reproof of theirs that was vexatious; why in the world couldn't she have let Master Sullivan's eyes [Miss Moggaridge pays for his cataract operation] alone?"

Perhaps one of the best examples of a writer questioning the values of frugality and hard work occurs in "On Sand Island," the short story by Prichard. Day after day the men in this story toil long hours on potentially dangerous seas. Their incomes from fishing are only meager, at best. Never do they seem to be able to get ahead. Meanwhile their wives, children, and loved ones are left behind alone with the sky and sea and fears about what the storm clouds portend. Almost guiltily Nan longs for the inclement weather which will prevent her husband from fishing. And for all the days, weeks, and months of her husband's hard toil, what does Nan have when her husband is lost at sea on what was to be his last fishing day before winter? Her prayer expresses her desperation: "Who makes dreams? God knows I tried to be thankful; I was thankful, and now to mock me so!" To survive, Nan must return to the only work she knew but hated before her marriage: life as a mill worker. Prichard portrays the harsh, dehumanizing, and obliterating conditions of the industrial world as Nan resumes her place in the factory and her "former ways so thoroughly, that oftentimes, when the motion and the noise about her in the great mill filled her sight and hearing, she tried to think that life on Sand Island was only a dream."

Despite the sobering and critical portrayal of once noble values gone awry, over and over in the fiction of these New England writers one senses the strength and independence of the characters. Roxy Keep, Squire Paine's second cousin in Cooke's story, outplays Squire Paine at his own game of frugality and negotiation when she agrees to do household work after Paine's wife dies: "She required of the squire a written guarantee that her services continue for two years in any case, subject only to her own change of mind, that her salary should be paid quarterly." Interestingly, Cooke uses a woman to "best" Squire Paine at his own game. In addition, however, to the economic savvy of Roxy Keep, Cooke gives us a woman with a heart. As used to power and control as Squire Paine is, even to the point of excessive control and power over his own daughter's life, Roxy Keep in this story represents the voice of reason and level-headedness to challenge and prod Paine's insensitivity: "I don't believe no great in hinderin' young folks's ways, Squire Paine; it's three wheels to a wagon to be young, an' hinderin' don't overset nothin'; it's more apt to set it, a long sight." Only through the strong voice of Roxy does Paine finally come to truly see himself as the person he has become over the years: "You've ben a-buyin' an' a-sellin' an' a-rakin' an' a-scrapin' till your soul—ef you've got any—is nigh about petered out. . . . You've ended by drivin' your only daughteer, your own flesh an' blood, the best thing the Lord ever give ye, out o' house an' home 'cause you was mad after money." In Cooke's "Ann Potter's Lesson," Ann Potter's sister Mary Jane and her mother serve as contrasts to the self-absorbed Ann. They are the typically strong, independent characters who always are there for Ann and give her the strength and support she needs so often. And near the end of the story, when a tornado strikes the Indiana territory and leaves Ann trapped under a barn roof, besides being frightened and alone, she has plenty of time to think. In her solitude and prayer "to be made good," Ann has her conversion and becomes much more like the strong and compassionate models of her mother and sister.

For all the negative qualities that we might associate with Evelina in Freeman's "Evelina's Garden"—isolation, reclusiveness, obsession—Evelina, nonetheless, is a strong and fiercely independent woman. Like the family home that Freeman describes as "one fine old mansion-house, with its white front propped on great Corinthian pillars, overlooking the village like a broad brow of superiority," Evelina over the years stands firm and resolute, truly a pillar of strength. Similarly, in what could be anathema to her survival in a small community, Sophia Lane, a character in Freeman's "The Revolt of Sophia Lane," willingly takes on relatives and friends to set them straight about gift-giving. As Robert Luscher correctly observes, the majority of Freeman's stories "involve women stripped of external support who become engaged in some form of spiritual struggle with either parents, other women, marriage, loneliness or poverty" ("Reviews," *Studies in Short Fiction.* [Summer 1993], p. 424). No matter what we might think of her characters, they are sometimes outspoken, sometimes defiant, sometimes lonely, but always strong and independent. Her women challenge traditional social expectation as well as the patriarchal establishment. Over and over in Freeman's fiction, we note the female protagonists who "actively determine and maintain places of their own choosing, enclosing themselves in situations and choices that reflect personalities and purposes conducive to the affirmation of self" (Janice Daniel, "Redefining Place: Femmes Covert in the Stories of Mary Wilkins Freeman," *Studies in Short Fiction.* [Winter 1996], p. 70).

Like Freeman's characters, Jewett's female protagonists are survivors. Like the independent Evelina and Sophia Lane of Freeman's stories, Ann Floyd, the central protagonist of Jewett's "Marsh Rosemary" is not about to let town gossip affect her desire to marry the much younger Jerry Lane. Whether or not she marries Jerry is "nobody's business." Further, Ann is "ready for warfare with any and all of [the world's] opinions." Her devil-may-care attitude and bold determination are exemplified in the wedding itself when she makes no effort whatsoever to camouflage the age difference between herself and Jerry Lane. That she decides to wear an old bonnet which actually makes her look old enough to be the groom's mother doesn't matter.

Ann does it her way. Beyond her defiant and independent stance, Ann becomes a symbol for older women everywhere by defying the social assumption that, when women reach a certain age, the need for love and companionship disappears or sexual desires are gone. Like a teen, Ann fixates on Jerry's looks, fixes her hair and blushes a bit just thinking about him, fantasizes about pulling one of his "handsome curls" to make it straight so she can see it spring back again, and thinks of his kisses. When her husband later deserts her and she learns he has married someone else, Ann reflects the plant the story is named after: sturdy, inconspicuous, and independent. She keeps her husband's second marriage secret, and like the plant, decides she will stand "in her own place."

In a twist of social expectation and convention, "Tom's Husband," another Jewett story, presents a central female character who defies the role society expects of her and demonstrates her managerial skills by reopening the failed business inherited by her husband, Tom. Conversely, Mary's husband in this role-reversal story becomes the house husband. First published in 1882, Jewett's futuristic story speaks to contemporary readers. Described by Jewett as having "inherited a most uncommon business talent" and a father who said "it was a mistake that she [Mary] was a girl instead of a boy," Mary exemplifies a courageous and independent spirit. In spite of hostility and being laughed at by the community, Mary's long hours and energy spent in learning the business ultimately lead to success: within two years she declares a small dividend, and after three years she has significant profits as well as one of the most successful mills in the area. As unusual, as strong, as role-challenging, and as independent as Mary is, she is successful, but so also is the egalitarian marriage of the story. Jewett portrays a talented, energetic, successful woman with a mind. As confining and restrictive as the communities may be to the central characters in the fiction, these characters withstand the gossip, hostility, and efforts to fit a mold no matter how it might affect their own survival. They exemplify courage, determination, and strong will.

"Miss Moggaridge's Provider" is another case in point. Spofford describes in harsh language the narrow-mindedness of the community where "it had become so much a matter of course for one neighbor to discuss the various bearings of all the incidents in another neighbor's life, and . . . the customary duty of keeping the other neighbor's conscience." No matter what the community might think or say about Miss Moggaridge, she disregards it. Spofford creates a character who refuses to become the victim of small town pettiness and hypocrisy. In the end, we admire Miss Moggaridge as one of the exceptions to community hypocrisy as she stands tall in her convictions.

If ever we see a person reflecting strength of character despite all odds, it must be Nan Ware in Prichard's "On Sand Island." Rescued from mind-deadening mill work through marriage but then "widowed" when her husband is lost at sea before she is twenty years old, Nan Ware knows hardship and adversity. Before her husband is lost at sea, she faces endless days of isolation and loneliness on an island inhabited by only one other family. Without family, Nan is left alone with nature, and Prichard describes nature as being anything but comforting: "she had outwardly the cold, relentless rim of black, seething water"; "the wind was biting cold; the sun had put out from under the clouds a hard, yellow, metallic fact that gleamed coldly into hers"; "between the two houses, in very high storms, the ocean on the north shakes hands with the ocean on the south, gripping the sands in their grinding palms, and giving small promise of letting go while a grain remains to be shaken." This is Nan's environment. To most people, it would be an environment for utter despair and madness. Nan struggles and she suffers, but she endures and she survives. In the hands of Prichard, Nan displays strength of human character of heroic dimensions.

One notes in the fiction of these women writers the capability and strength of the central characters. With the exception of "Tom's Husband," the women and their behavior are anything but radical. And even Mary in "Tom's Husband" goes about the business of running a business in a reasonable fashion. Despite the lack of vociferous calls for change, the women in the stories represent change. In sometimes quiet, but nonetheless firm ways, these women illustrate that they have tenacity, strength, and courage equal to men. We might even say that Sophia Lane and Roxy Keep have chutzpah. They accomplish much. They bring about change. As determined and methodical as they are in their ways, they are not overbearing. Instead, through prodding and with determination and humor, change comes.

In addition to the numerous qualities or characteristics unifying this collection—loneliness, New England values of hard work and frugality, friendship and support, strength and independence—humor is another connecting element. Perhaps as well, humor has contributed to these writers' marginalization in the twentieth century because humorous literature has not typically been considered serious literature. As Karen Kilcup observes, whether "writing traditional fiction, or advice, or poetry, or autobiography, these women [the nineteenth–century American women writers of her anthology] cavorted, somersaulted, jabbed, reveled, and ironized in ways that traditional wisdom says we did (or should) not" (*Nineteenth-Century Women Writers*, p. xlii). Rather than strident demands and harshness, humor in the hands of many of these women writers becomes a gentle weapon for achieving change.

One of the better examples of humor used for this purpose is in Freeman's "The Revolt of Sophia Lane." Sophia Lane sees herself as a determined but also comic character as she loads the sleigh on the bitter cold day right before Christmas to return impractical gifts. Her dramatic action is also partially responsible for her success, since a lone woman on a bitter cold day is disarming in itself. By generating a responsive note of sympathy for travel in wintry weather, Sophia takes the sting from her mission—to return impractical gifts—and successfully fulfills that mission. In some ways Roxy Keep in "Squire Paine's Conversion" may exemplify frugality and thrift gone awry as much as it does for Paine himself, but the harsh and unforgiving side of the Squire is negated immediately with Roxy's arrival and the approach she uses. After hard-nosed negotiations regarding Roxy's pay and working conditions as housekeeper after the Squire's wife has died, we learn that negotiations on Roxy's part were actually pro forma since she had made the decision to stay even before she arrived. In response to the query of how soon Roxy can begin her duties, the Squire is caught off-guard when he learns that Roxy is ready immediately, since before her arrival in Bassett she had sold her house, settled her affairs, and sent her luggage: "Land alive! I should think not!" Roxy's premeditated actions are startling, and funny. From this point, Squire Paine, the man in such absolute mastery and control of his own fate as well as the fate of others, has met his match. Humor is used as a reductive force to humanize Squire Paine. In the process, he becomes a caring and sensitive person.

Likewise, humor is used as a reductive force in "Miss Moggaridge's Provider." When Miss Moggaridge asserts that it is her

"Christian duty" to locate her lost brother, Miss Keturah challenges Moggaridge's word choice. By suggesting that no one other than Moggaridge's father, a minister of more than fifty years, can be a judge of what constitutes "Christian duty," Spofford begins the leveling of the minister's saintliness. Spofford uses Keturah as the voice of the community, but then pokes fun at the community and Keturah through her words and actions. Moggaridge repels the challenge of it being her "Christian duty" to seek her brother and replaces it with it being her "natural duty." As expected, that response raises the ire of the sanctimonious Miss Keturah even more: "And you dare to set a natural duty, a duty of our unregenerate condition, above the duties of such as are set apart from the world." In a response that is devastating yet funny and witty, Miss Moggaridge cuts to the heart of the matter and assaults Keturah's hypocrisy for all to see: "My dear Kitty, . . . I am not sure that we ever are or ever should be set apart from the world; that we are not placed here to work in it and with it till our faith and our example leven it." Through such words as "the Lord will provide" and what are perceived as preposterous but generous deeds of Moggaridge, ever so slowly Keturah herself comes to put off her harsh, sanctimonious, and judgmental side to accept Moggaridge's approach as being honest and more attuned to a genuine Christian spirit. In contrast to Keturah's slow perception of the minister's preaching at odds with true Christian spirit, Spofford, through her narrator, shares her ironic observations of the minister's true character early on with her readers: "[p]oor Miss Moggaridge's father had been that extraordinary phenomenon, a clergyman."

In "Miss Elderkin's Pitcher" by Stowe, humor with realism comes crashing through at a most-unexpected sober moment: the reading of Elderkin's father's will. Of all the members of the family, Miry Elderkin has been there for her father at all times but had never been appreciated by her father while he was alive. In a character that might be perceived as being modeled after Stowe's own father, Miry Elderkin's father, Black Hoss John, is overbearing, domineering, and controlling. He steals Miry's letters, forbids her to see visitors, and orders her around night and day during his illness. In many ways, then, Miry's action during the reading of the will when she smashes in a fit of rage the only thing left her—a cheap pitcher, which she detests—is understandable. As comical as the action is, Miry's feelings are honest and genuine. Appropriately, the solemnity of the occasion is shattered along with the pitcher. Adding to the humor is the irony of the situation as gold coins come flying out of the breaking pitcher. Miry's mean-spirited father wanted her to be left with absolutely nothing. Had Black Hoss John known of the coins hidden within, the pitcher would have been left to someone else.

With one exception, we can examine the stories in this collection and find unifying characteristics of loneliness, the New England character, independence, female relationships, and humor. Alcott's "The Brothers" stands apart. Perceived as a writer for children and connected with the idyllic qualities of Concord, Massachusetts, Alcott breaks that mold with "The Brothers" story. Although not widely known, Alcott served as a nurse in a Washington, D.C., military hospital for six weeks during the Civil War. This story grows out of that experience. Besides the issue of slavery, she deals in the story with the issue of miscegenation as it pertains to the "brothers," one white and the other mulatto. In addition, a physical attraction between the mulatto and the white nurse is suggested. Clearly, "The Brothers" shatters Alcott's *Little Women* stigma.

Throughout this entire collection of short stories, the authors present the lives and actions of ordinary people and their daily existence. In many ways, their lives and actions may seem unremarkable, even dull. These are typical lives and yet in so many ways they are truly remarkable. Characters struggle, they have broken hearts, they are lonely, they are dissolute, they seek love, they experience loss, they are greedy, they seek recognition. In treating these ordinary lives, Freeman, Jewett, Stowe, Spofford, Prichard, Cooke, and Alcott show us their universality. What is more remarkable about these stories is that, in them, we see not just the struggle of the human condition but in most instances the triumph of the human condition. Characters in these stories may be flawed and have botched lives, but they carry on. They survive and endure. What also adds to the remarkable qualities is that characters support each other. Petty, constrictive, and hypocritical as life might be within these communities, these women reach out and help one another. Clearly these writers hold up the significant lives and actions of these women as something to emulate, an idea in sharp contrast with what has come to represent the canon in the twentieth century: individualism and self-assertion of the lone American male. Over and over in these short stories, the central characters are portrayed as capable women who think and act for themselves. By creating stories with women as central characters, the writers show us that women in themselves—their lives, their activities, their actions, their emotions—are both interesting and important. No wonder they had an appreciated voice in the nineteenth century, a voice that still resonates for us today.

Harriet Beecher Stowe

(1811-1896)

Born in Litchfield, Connecticut, on June 14, 1811, the seventh child of Lyman Beecher and his first wife Roxanna Foote, Harriet Beecher spent her early years, and for that matter most of her life, in an environment dominated by ministers and educators. Her father, Lyman Beecher, was a noted Calvinist minister. Of her seven brothers who were ministers, Henry Ward Beecher became the best-known preacher of his day. Besides her father's later involvement with education as president of Lane Theological Seminary in Cincinnati, Ohio, Harriet's older sister pioneered the movement for women's education in this country. Later, after her marriage to Calvin Stowe, Harriet's connections with both religion and education continued as her distinguished preacher-husband was sought out by institutions of higher learning.

As one might imagine, the Beecher household was a stimulating and competitive one. Harriet's first formal schooling began at age five, shortly after her mother died, when she started to attend the district school in Litchfield. At age eight, she enrolled in Sarah Pierce's School for Young Ladies in Litchfield. In 1824, shortly after her sister Catherine started her female seminary in Hartford, Connecticut, Harriet, now thirteen, joined her as a student. Learning Latin, French, and Italian and studying history and moral theology, Harriet studied at her sister's school in Hartford for eight years until 1832, when her father accepted the presidency at Lane Theological Seminary in Ohio and moved his entire family.

Throughout her years of education, Harriet stood out as a writer, having won first prize at the age of twelve for her essay, "Can the Immortality of the Soul Be Proved by the Light of Nature?" When her sister Catherine started the Western Female Institute in Cincinnati after the family moved there, Harriet joined her first as a student and later as a teacher. She continued with her writing, and in 1834 won the fifty-dollar prize for "A New England Sketch" in a contest sponsored by the *Western Monthly* in Cincinnati. At this point, Stowe had found her career but in the years ahead would face challenges pursuing it.

In Cincinnati in 1836, Harriet married Calvin Stowe, minister and professor at Lane Theological Seminary and widower of a friend. Besides giving birth to four children within four years of her marriage, Harriet faced the responsibility of raising the children and running the household, since her husband was away frequently. In addition, Harriet experienced poor health and bouts of depression. Perhaps because of the numerous demands in her life, writing became both an escape and a necessity. In any event, she began writing and contributing essays, articles, and stories to various magazines, contributions that would provide for household expenses.

During this period of time in Cincinnati while she was running the household, raising children, and earning income from writing, she first became acquainted with runaway slaves and the Underground Railroad. She had also crossed the Ohio River and seen slavery and plantation life firsthand. Having been reared in a Christian family and married to a minister, Harriet's commitment to and sense of urgency regarding abolition increased over the next several years. With passage of the Fugitive Slave Law in 1850, Stowe's passion regarding the slavery question only intensified.

In 1850, when Calvin Stowe accepted a position at Bowdoin College in Maine, Harriet, nearing the end of her seventh pregnancy, made the long journey to Brunswick, Maine, by railroad and steamboat. Under extraordinary conditions at Brunswick, Harriet continued her writing—"nothing but deadly determination enables me ever to write; it is rowing against wind and tide" (Annie Fields, *Life and Letters of Harriet Beecher Stowe.* [Boston: Houghton Mifflin, 1897] p. 128). In 1852, Calvin Stowe moved again, this time to join the faculty at Andover Theological Seminary in Andover, Massachusetts. In that same year, *Uncle Tom's Cabin* appeared, and within the first few months of its publication Harriet earned $10,000 and international fame. She now became the major breadwinner in the family. Her success permitted the family to live comfortably in Andover and, later, to build a rambling Victorian mansion in Hartford.

Besides her move to Hartford, Connecticut, in 1863 when her husband retired from Andover, Harriet also spent time in Florida. In Mandarin, Florida, she bought an orange grove and established a school for former slaves. She continued to write novels, sketches, and essays well into the 1870s. She died July 1, 1896, in Hartford, Connecticut. For a woman who wrote dejectedly to her husband when

she was thirty-one years old, "Life is half gone! What have we done? .
. . It is time to prepare to die," Harriet lived on to a ripe old age of
eighty-six years. And certainly she accomplished much. Judith
Fetterley's observations in *Provisions* are to the point regarding
Stowe's significant accomplishments: "Single-handedly Harriet
Beecher Stowe has kept the category of mid-nineteenth-century
American women prose writers from complete oblivion "
(Bloomington: Indiana University Press, 1985, p. 374).

"Mis' Elderkin's Pitcher" first appeared in *The Atlantic
Monthly* in August 1870, and later became part of a collection entitled
Sam Lawson's Oldtown Fireside Stories that Stowe published in 1872.
Central to the collection and to "Mis' Elderkin's Pitcher" is the
framed story; in this case Sam Lawson is the storyteller. Stories in
Oldtown Fireside Stories and *Oldtown Folks,* an earlier collection,
which Stowe published in 1869, chronicle the life of Natick,
Massachusetts, the town where Stowe's husband, Calvin, spent his
early years. In addition, the stories grow out of Calvin's reminiscences
and oral storytelling. Noted for her use of dialect, Stowe in "Mis'
Elderkin's Pitcher" captures the eastern vernacular through Sam
Lawson, a model for the older, lower–class inhabitants of her region.
Black Hoss, Miry Elderkin's father and a figure that may be based on
Stowe's own father, represents the stern, authoritative New England
figure. Lyman Beecher, who took over child rearing responsibilities at
his wife's death when Harriet was five, was not noted as a particularly
nurturing person. Mirroring some of the same negative feelings
between Black Hoss and Miry in the story, Lyman Beecher supposedly
remarked about his daughter Harriet: "Hattie is a genius. I would give
a hundred dollars if she was a boy" (*Nineteenth-Century American
Women Writers*. [Cambridge, Mass.: Blackwell, 1997], p. 132). In
Miry, we find the self-effacing, devoted daughter and also the strong
and defiant woman. Described as having a "snap to her tongue," a
"consid'able stiff will," and one who "gave every fellow as good as he
sent," Miry is devoted to her father but can also stand her ground. Her
defiant and independent streak is best seen in the ironic and humorous
ending. In what may be a strikingly personal tale of New England life,
Stowe gives us a picture of the potentially grim reality of family
relations and discord.

Selected Primary Works

Uncle Tom's Cabin, 1852; *Dred: A Tale of the Dismal Swamp*, 1856; *The Minister's Wooing*, 1859; *The Pearl of Orr's Island*, 1862; *The Chimney Corner*, 1868; *Oldtown Folks*, 1869; *Sam Lawson's Oldtown Fireside Stories*, 1872; *Women in Sacred History*, 1873; *Poganuc People*, 1878; *Our Famous Women*, 1884.

"Mis' Elderkin's Pitcher"

The Atlantic Monthly, August 1870

"Ye see, boys," said Sam Lawson, as we were gathering young wintergreen on a sunny hillside in June,—"ye see, folks don't allers know what their marcies is when they sees 'em. Folks is kind o' blinded, and when a providence comes along, they don't seem to know how to take it, and they growl and grumble about what turns out the best things that ever happened to 'em in their lives. It's like Mis' Elderkin's pitcher."

"What about Mis' Elderkin's pitcher?" said both of us in one breath.

"Didn't I never tell ye now?" said Sam; "why, I wanter know?"

No, we were sure he never had told us, and Sam, as usual, began clearing the ground by a thorough introduction, with statistical expositions.

"Wal, ye see Mis' Elderkin, she lives now over to Sherburne in about the handsomest house in Sherburne,—a high white house with green blinds and white pillars in front,—and she rides out in her own kerridge, and Mr. Elderkin, he's a deacon in the church and a colonel in the malitia, and a s'lectman, and pretty much atop everything there is goin' in Sherburne, and it all come of that are pitcher."

"What pitcher?" we shouted in chorus.

"Lordy massy! That are's jest what I'm a goin' to tell ye about; but ye see a feller's jest got to make a beginnin' to all things.

"Mis' Elderkin she thinks she's a gret lady nowadays, I s'pose, but I 'member when she was Miry Brown over here 'n Oldtown, and I used to be waitin' on her to singing-school.

"Miry and I was putty good friends along in them days,—we was putty consid'able kind o' intimate. Fact is, boys, there was times in them days when I thought whether or no I wouldn't take Miry myself," said Sam, his face growing luminous with the pleasing idea of his former masculine attractions and privileges. "Yis," he continued, "there was a time when folks said I could a had Miry ef I'd asked her, and I putty much think so myself, but I didn't say nothin'; marriage is allers kind o' venturesome; an' Miry had such up-and-down kind o' ways, I was sort o' fraid on 't.

"But Lordy massy, boys, you mustn't never tell Hepsy I said so, 'cause she'd be mad enough to bite shingle-nail in two. Not that she sets so very gret by me neither, but then women's backs is allers up ef they think anybody else could a had you, whether they want you themselves or not.

"Ye see, Miry she was old Black Hoss John Brown's da'ter, and lived up there in that are big brown house by the meetin'-house that hes the red hollyhock in the front yard. Miry was about the handsomest gal that went into the singers' seat a Sunday.

"I tell you she wa'n't none o' your milk-and-sugar gals neither,—she was 'mazin' strong built. She was the strongest gal in her arms that I ever see. Why, I've seen Miry take up a barrel o' flour and lift it right into the kitchen, and it would jest make the pink come into her cheeks like two roses, but she never seemed to mind it a grain. She had a good strong back of her own, and she was straight as a poplar, with snapping black eyes, and I tell you there was a snap to her tongue, too. Nobody never got ahead o' Miry; she'd give every fellow as good as he sent, but for all that she was a gret favorite.

"Miry was one o' your briery, scratchy gals, that seems to catch fellers in thorns. She allers fit and flouted her beaux, and the more she fit and flouted 'em the more they'd be arter her. There wa'n't a gal in all Oldtown that led such a string o' fellers arter her, 'cause you see she'd now and then throw 'em a good word over her shoulder, and then they'd all fight who should get it, and she'd jest laugh to see 'em do it.

"Why, there was Tom Sawin, he was one o' her beaux, and Jim Moss, and Ike Bacon; and there was a Boston boy, Tom Beacon, he come up from Cambridge to rusticate with Parson Lothrop, he thought he must have his say with Miry, but he got pretty well come up with. You see he thought 'cause he was Boston born that he was kind o' aristocracy, and had a right jest to pick and choose 'mong country gals, but the way he got come up with by Miry was too funny for anything."

"Do tell us about it," we said, as Sam made an artful pause, designed to draw forth solicitation.

"Wal, ye see, Tom Beacon he told Ike Bacon about it, and Ike he told me. 'Twas this way. Ye see, there was a quiltin' up to Mis' Cap'n Broad's, and Tom Beacon he was there, and come to goin' home with the gals, Tom he cut Ike out, and got Miry all to himself, and 't was a putty long piece of a walk from Mis' Cap'n Broad's up past the swamp and the stone pastur' clear up to old Black Hoss John's.

"Wal, Tom he was in high feather 'cause Miry took him, so that he didn't reelly know how to behave; and so as they was walkin' along past Parson Lothrop's apple orchard, Tom thought he'd try bein' familiar, and he undertook to put his arm around Miry. Well, if she didn't jest take that little fellow by his two shoulders and whirl him over the fence into the orchard quicker 'n no time. 'Why,' says Tom, 'the fust I knew I was lyin' on my back under the apple trees lookin' up at the stars.' Miry, she jest walked off home and said nothin' to nobody,—it wa'n't her way to talk much about things,—and if it hadn't been for Tom Beacon himself nobody need 'a' known nothin' about it. Tom was a little fellow, you see, and 'mazin' good-natured, and one of the sort that couldn't keep nothin' to himself, and so he let the cat out o' the bag himself. Wal, there didn't nobody think the worse o' Miry. When fellers find a gal won't take saace from no man, they kind o' respect her, and then fellers allers think ef it had been *them*, now, things 'd 'a' been different. That's jest what Jim Moss and Ike Bacon said; they said, why Tom Beacon was a fool not to know better how to get along with Miry,—*they* never had no trouble. The fun of it was that Tom Beacon himself was more crazy after her than he was afore, and they say he made Miry a right up-and-down offer, and Miry she jest wouldn't have him.

"Wal, you see that went agin old Black Hoss John's idees,— old Black Hoss was about as close as a nut and as contrairy as a pipperage-tree. You ought to 'a' seen him. Why his face was all a perfect crisscross o' wrinkles. There wa'n't a spot where you could put a pin down that there wa'n't a wrinkle—and they used to say that he

LIBRARY
COLBY-SAWYER COLLEGE
NEW LONDON, NH 03257

held onto every cent that went through his fingers till he'd pinched it into two. You couldn't say that his god was his belly, for he hadn't none, no more 'n an old file; folks said that he'd starved himself till the moon'd shine through him.

"Old Black Hoss was awfully grouty about Miry's refusin' Tom Beacon, 'cause there was his houses and lots o' land in Boston. A dreffful worldly old crittur Black Hoss John was; he was like the rich fool in the Gospel. Wal, he's dead and gone now, poor crittur, and what good has it all done him? It's as the Scriptur' says, 'He heapeth up riches, and knoweth not who shall gather them.'

"Miry had a pretty hard row to hoe with old Black Hoss John. She was up early and down late, and kep' everything a goin'. She made the cheese and made the butter, and between spells she braided herself handsome straw hats and fixed up her clothes; and somehow she worked it so when she sold her butter and cheese that there was somethin' for ribbins and flowers; you know the Scriptur' says, 'can a maid forget her ornaments?' Wal, Miry didn't. I 'member I used to lead the singin' in them days, and Miry she used to sing counter, so we sot putty near together in the singers' seats; and I used to think Sunday mornin's when she come to meetin' in her white dress and her red cheeks and her bonnet all tipped off with laylock, that 'twas for all the world jest like a June sunrise to have her come into the singers' seats. Them was the days that I didn't improve my privileges, boys," said Sam, sighing deeply. "There was times that ef I'd a spoke, there's no knowin' what mightn't 'a' happened, 'cause you see, boys, I was better lookin' in them days than I be now. Now you mind, boys, when you grow up, ef you get to waitin' on a nice gal, and you're 'most mind to speak up to her, don't you go and put it off, 'cause ef you do, you may live to repent it.

"Wal, you see from the time that Bill Elderkin come and took the academy, I could see plain enough that it was time for me to hang up my fiddle. Bill he used to set in the singers' seats, too, and he would have it that he sung tenor. He no more sung tenor than a skunk blackbird, but he made b'lieve he did, jest to git next to Miry in the singers' seats, and then they used to be a writin' backward and forward to each other till they tore out all the leaves of the hymn-books, and the singin' books besides. Wal, I never thought that the house o' the Lord was jest the place to be courtin' in, and I used to get consid'able shocked at the way things went on atween 'em. Why,

LIBRARY
COLBY-SAWYER COLLEGE
NEW LONDON, NH 03257

they'd be a writin' all sermon-time; and I've seen him a lookin' at her all through the long prayer in a way that wa'n't right, considerin' they was both professors of religion. But then the fact was, old Black Hoss John was to blame for it, 'cause he never let 'em have no chance to home. Ye see old Black Hoss he was sot ag'in Elderkin 'cause he was poor. You see his mother, the old Widdah Elderkin, she was jest about the poorest, peakedest old body over to Sherburne, and went out to days' works, and Bill Elderkin he was all for books and larnin', and old Black Hoss John he thought it was just shiftlessness; but Miry she thought he was a genius, and she got it sot in her mind that he was goin' to be President o' the United States, or some sich.

"Wal, old Black Hoss he wa'n't none too polite to Miry's beaux in gineral, but when Elderkin used to come to see her he was snarlier than a saw; he hadn't a good word for him noways; and he'd rake up the fire right before his face and eyes and rattle about fastening up the windows, and tramp up to bed and call down the chamber-stairs to Miry to go to bed, and was sort o' aggravatin' every way.

"Wal, ef folks wants to get a gal set on havin' a man, that are's the way to go to work. Miry had a consid'able stiff will of her own, and ef she didn't care about Tom Beacon before, she hated him now; and if she liked Bill Elderkin before, she was clean gone over to him now; and so she took to goin' to the Wednesday-evening lecture, and the Friday-evening prayer-meetin', and the singing-school, jest as regular as a clock, and so did he; and afterwards they allers walked home the longest way. Fathers may jest as well let their gals be courted in the house, peaceable, 'cause if they can't be courted there, they'll find places where they can be: it's jest human natur'.

"Wal, come fall Elderkin he went to college up to Brunswick; and then I used to see the letters as regular up to the store every week, comin' in from Brunswick, and old Black Hoss John he see 'em too, and got a way of droppin' 'em in his coat-pocket when he come up to the store, and folks used to say that the letters that went into his coat-pocket didn't get to Miry. Anyhow, Miry she says to me one day, says she, 'Sam, you're up round the post-office a good deal,' says she. 'I wish if you see any letters for me, you'd jest bring 'em along.' I see right into it, and I told her to be sure I would; and so I used to have the carryin' of great thick letters every week. Wal, I was waitin' on Hepsy along about them times, and so Miry and I kind o' sympathized. Hepsy was a pretty gal, and I thought it was all best 't was; any way, I knew I couldn't get Miry, and I could get Hepsy, and that made all the difference in the world.

"Wal, the next winter old Black Hoss was took down with rheumatism, and I tell you if Miry didn't have a time on 't! He w'n't noways sweet tempered when he was well; but come to be crooked up with the rheumatis and kep' awake nights, it seemed as if he was determined there shouldn't nobody have no peace so long as he couldn't.

"He'd get Miry up and down with him night after night a makin' her heat flannels and vinegar, and then he'd jaw and scold so that she was eeny-most beat out. He wouldn't have nobody set up with him, though there was offers made. No, he said Miry was his daughter, and 't was her bisness to take care on him.

"Miry was clear worked down; folks kind o' pitied her. She was a strong gal, but there's things that wears out the strongest. The worst on 't was it hung on so. Old Black Hoss had a most amazin' sight o' constitution. He'd go all down to death's door, and seem hardly to have the breath o' life in him, and then up he'd come ag'in! These 'ere old folks that nobody wants to have live allers hev such a sight o' wear in 'em, they jest last and last; and it really did seem as if he'd wear Miry out and get her into the grave fust, for she got a cough with bein' up so much in the cold, and grew thin as a shadder. 'Member one time I went up there to offer to watch jest in the spring o' the year, when the laylocks was jest a buddin' out, and Miry she come and talked with me over the fence, and the poor gal she fairly broke down and sobbed as if her heart would break a tellin' me her trouble.

"Wal, it reelly affected me more to have Miry give up so than most gals, 'cause she'd allers held her head up, and had sich a sight o' grit and resolution, but she told me all about it.

"It seems old Black Hoss he wa' n't content with worryin' on her, and gettin' her up nights, but he kep' a hectorin' her about Bill Elderkin, and wantin' on her to promise that she wouldn't heve Bill when he was dead and gone, and Miry she wouldn't promise, and then the old man said she shouldn't have a cent from him if she didn't, and so they had it back and forth. Everybody in town was sayin' what a shame 't was that he should sarve her so; for though he hed other children, they was married and gone, and there wa'n't none of them to do for him but jist Miry.

"Wal, he hung on till jest as the pinys in the front yard was beginnin' to blow out, and then he began to feel he was a goin', and he sent for Parson Lothrop to know what was to be done about his soul.

"'Wal,' says Parson Lothrop, 'you must settle up all your worldly affairs; you must be in peace and love with all mankind, and if you've wronged anybody you must make it good to 'em.'

"Old Black Hoss he bounced right over in his bed with his back to the minister.

"'The Devil!' says he, "'twill take all I've got.' And he never spoke another word, though Parson Lothrop he prayed with him, and did what he could for him.

"Wal, that night I sot up with him, and he went off 'tween two and three in the mornin', and I laid him out regular. Of all the racks o' bone I ever see, I never see a human crittur so poor as he was. 'T wa'n't nothin' but his awful will kep' his soul in his body so long as it was.

"We had the funeral in the meetin'–house a Sunday, and Parson Lothrop he preached a sarmon on contentment on the text, We brought nothin' into the world, and it's sartin we can carry nothin' out, and having food and raiment, let us be therewith content. Parson Lothrop he got round the subject about as handsome as he could; he didn't say what a skinflint old Black Hoss was, but he talked in a gineral way about the vanity o' worryin' an' scrapin' to heap up riches. Ye see Parson Lothrop he could say it all putty easy, too, 'cause since he married a rich wife he never had no occasion to worry about temporal matters and folks allers preaches better on the vanity o' riches when they's in tol'able easy circumstances. Ye see when folks is pestered and worried to pay their bills and don't know where the next dollar's to come form, it's a great temptation to be kind o' valooin' riches, and mebbe envyin' those that's got 'em; whereas when one's accounts all pays themselves, and the money comes jest when its wanted regular, a body feels sort o' composed like, and able to take the right view of things, like Parson Lothrop.

"Wal, after sermon the relations all went over to the house to hear the will read, and as I was kind o' friend with the family I jest slipped in along with the rest.

"Squire Jones he had the will, and so when they all got sot round all solemn, he broke the seals and unfolded it, cracklin' it a good while afore he begun, and it was so still you might a heard a pin drop when he begun to read. Fust, there was the farm and stock, he left to his son John Brown over in Sherburne. Then there was the household stuff and all them things, spoons and dishes, and beds and kiver-lids and so on, to his da'ter Polly Blanchard. And then, last of all, he says, he left to his da'ter Miry *the pitcher that was on the top o' the shelf in his bedroom closet.*

"That are was an old cracked pitcher that Miry allers had hated the sight of, and spring and fall she used to beg her father to let her throw it away; but no, he wouldn't let her touch it, and so it stood gatherin' dust.

"Some on 'em run and handed it down, and it seemed jest full o' scourin' sand and nothin' else, and they handed it to Miry.

"Wal, Miry she was wrathy then. She didn't so much mind bein' left out in the will, 'cause she expected that, but to have that are old pitcher poked at her so sort o' scornful was more'n she could bear.

"She took it and gin it a throw across the room with all her might, and it hit ag'in the wall and broke into thousand bits, when out rolled hundreds o' gold pieces; great gold eagles and guineas flew round the kitchen jest as thick as dandelions. I tell you, she scrabbled 'em up pretty quick and we all helped her.

"Come to count 'em over, Miry had the best fortin of the whole, as 't was right and proper she should. Miry she was a sensible gal, and she invested her money well; and so, when Bill Elderkin got through his law studies he found a wife that could make a nice beginning with him. And that's the way, you see, they came to be doin' as well as they be.

"So, boys, you jest mind and remember an' allers see what there is in a providence afore you quarrel with it, 'cause there's a good many things in this world turns out like Mis' Elderkin's pitcher."

Rose Terry Cooke
(1827-1892)

Born on a farm six miles outside Hartford, Connecticut, on February 17, 1827, Rose Terry Cooke was the older daughter of Henry Wadsworth Terry and Anne Wright Hurlburt. Because delicate health and illness marked her early years, Cooke spent much time outside with her landscape–gardener father who gave her an appreciation for nature and a knowledge of gardening. From her mother, she learned discipline and the art of writing by learning a page of the dictionary each day and by recording daily events in a copybook. Later, she would credit her mother for her literary accomplishments. As her friend and fellow writer Harriet Prescott Spofford commented, "love of her mother" was one of the strongest feelings she had (*A Little Book of Friends*. [Boston: Little, Brown, 1997], p. 155).

At an early age she attended the Hartford Female Seminary established by Catherine Beecher. Her formal schooling ended at age sixteen when she graduated from the Seminary. That same year she joined the Congregational Church and remained a lifelong Christian, although at times she would argue with the church as an institution.

In 1843 at age sixteen, she took a teaching position in Burlington, New Jersey, and remained there for four years before returning to Hartford, Connecticut, where she continued to teach until 1848. In 1848 at age twenty-one, Cooke received an inheritance from an uncle that enabled her to give up teaching and devote herself to writing.

Although she published two volumes of poetry during her life and considered herself a poet, Harriet Prescott Spofford and others regarded her particularly for her prose writing. Over the course of her writing career, she produced nearly two hundred stories, over two hundred poems, and two novels. Biographers are uncertain as to exactly when Cooke began writing her fiction; however, a clear record begins in 1855 with her publication of "The Mormon's Wife" in *Putnam's*. In fact, between 1855 and 1857 eight of her stories appeared in *Putnam's*. In 1856, she began contributing to *Harper's*, and in 1857 she was invited to contribute to the first issue of the prestigious *Atlantic Monthly*. "Sally Parsons's Duty" appeared in the *Atlantic*'s first issue.

As a result of poor health and caring for her sister's children, her writing slackened in the decade of the 1860s. At age forty–six in 1873, Rose Terry married Rollin Cooke, and her literary career took another turn. Cooke, a banker, was not particularly successful and worked only sporadically. In addition, Cooke's father-in-law used her money for his own unsuccessful business ventures. Used to economic independence before her marriage, her situation changed significantly after her marriage. As a result, she found herself in a situation where she was forced to write to make money, turning her attention from serious writing to didactic potboilers and children's stories.

In 1887, Cooke followed her husband to Pittsfield, Massachusetts, in his attempt to start a new business. On July 18, 1892, she died in Pittsfield. Unquestionably, her most significant contribution to literature is in the genre of the regional story. Although overshadowed by such other regional writers as Sarah Orne Jewett and Mary Wilkins Freeman, Cooke has made important contributions to American literature. In addition, Cooke was the first among a group of other women writers to use dialect in her fiction. And as Judith Fetterley points out in *Provisions*, her fiction "is grimly realistic and much of it documents the consequences for women of living within a world defined by masculine values and masculine institutions" (*Provisions*. [Bloomington: Indiana University Press, 1985], pp. 345-346).

In the two stories in this collection, "Ann Potter's Lesson," from the September 1858 issue of *The Atlantic Monthly,* and "Squire Paine's Conversion," from the March 1878 issue of *Harper's New Monthly*, Cooke's masterful handling of dialect is evident. Not possessing a positive approach to life like her sister and mother, Ann Potter tends to focus on the negative. However, the courage and strength that her mother demonstrates after her father's death serve as an inspiration to her later. Despite having to sell the West Connecticut farm that had scarcely provided a living in the best of times, Ann's mother exudes strength and confidence that the community will help, and if not, then she and her two daughters will manage quite capably on their own. In an action that is commonplace for New Englanders in the last half of the century, Ann moves to the Indiana frontier with her new husband where she faces significant adversity but has her "lesson." Besides Cook's skilled use of dialect in the story, her realistic treatment of the Indiana frontier illustrates her wide-ranging talent as a writer and reminds us of Caroline Kirkland's earlier realism of the Michigan frontier in *A New Home—Who'll Follow?*

In a story that questions the church as an institution and examines the perversion of the Protestant work ethic, "Squire Paine's Conversion" illustrates another quality of Cooke's gifts as a story teller: her humor. By presenting characters in comic situations and viewing them from comic perspectives, they become models for later writers in the development of regional types. In the story, Squire Paine illustrates New England values gone awry: "Samuel Paine forgot how his childish flesh had wept and cringed under the hardships of his early life; how his childish soul had flamed with rage under the torture and insult of the unjustly applied shingle, and the constant watching of stern and pitiless eyes." In his domination of his wife and daughter, Paine becomes the very adult he despised as a child. Resulting from her unsuccessful marriage, Cooke learned the significance and power of women's voice and the danger of their silence, an idea important in her fiction and evidenced so forcefully in the person of Roxy Keep in "Squire Paine's Conversion." Through Roxy, Paine comes to see himself for the miscreant he has become. With Cooke's masterful handling, characters and actions in the fiction take on a universality that transcends the designation of Cooke as only a regional writer.

Selected Primary Works

Poems, 1861; *Somebody's Neighbors*, 1881; *Root-Bound and Other Sketches*, 1885; *The Sphinx's Children*, 1886; *Happy Dodd*, 1887; *Poems*, 1888; *Huckleberries Gathered from New England Hills*, 1891; *Little Foxes*, 1904.

"Ann Potter's Lesson"

The Atlantic Monthly, September 1858

My sister Mary Jane is older than I,— as much as four years. Father died when we were both small, and didn't leave us much means beside the farm. Mother was rather a weakly woman; she didn't feel as though she could farm it for a living. It's hard work enough for a man to get clothes and victuals off a farm in West Connecticut; it's uphill work always; and then a man can turn to, himself, to ploughin' and mowin';— but a woman a'n't of no use, except to tell folks what to do; and everybody knows it's no way to have a thing done, to send.

Mother talked it over with Deacon Peters, and he counseled her to sell off the farm but the home-lot, which was cut out for an orchard with young apple trees, and had a garden spot to one end of it, close by the house. Mother calculated to raise potatoes and beans and onions enough to last us the year round, and to take in sewin' so's to get what few groceries we was goin' to want. We kept Old Red, the best cow; there was pasture enough for her in the orchard, for the trees wa'n't growed to be bearin' as yet, and we 'lotted a good deal on milk to our house; besides, it saved butcher's meat.

Mother was a real pious woman, and she was a high-couraged woman too. Old Miss Perrit, an old widder-woman that lived down by the bridge, come up to see her the week after father died. I remember all about it, though I wa'n't but ten years old; for when I see Miss Perrit comin' up the road, with her slimpsy old veil hanging off from her bumbazine bonnet, and her doleful look, (what Nancy Perrit used to call "mother's company-face") I kinder thought she was comin' to our house; and she was allers so musical to me, I went to the back-door, and took up a towel I was hemmin', and set down in the corner, all ready to let her in. It don't seem as if I could 'a' been real distressed about father's dyin' when I could do so; but children is just like spring weather, rainin' one hour and shinin' the next, and it's the Lord's great mercy they be; if they begun to feelin' so early, there wouldn't be nothin' left to grow up. So pretty quick Miss Perrit knocked, and I let her in. We hadn't got no spare room in that house; there was the kitchen in front, and mother's bedroom, and the buttery, and the little back-space opened out on't behind. Mother was in the bedroom; so, while I called her, Miss Perrit set down in the splint rockin'-chair that creaked awfully, and went to rockin' back and forth, and sighin' till mother came in.

"Good-day, Miss Langdon!" says she, with a kind of a snuffle, "how dew you dew? I thought I'd come and see how you kep' up under this here affliction. I rec'lect very well how I felt when husband died. It's a dreadful thing to be left a widder in a hard world; — don't you find it out by this?"

I guess mother felt quite as bad as ever Miss Perrit did, for everybody knew old Perrit treated his wife like a dumb brute while he was alive, and died drunk; but she didn't say nothin'. I see her give a kind of a swaller, and then she spoke up bright and strong.

"I don't think it is a hard world, Miss Perrit. I find folks kind and helpful, beyond what I'd any right to look for. I try not to think about my husband, any more than I can help, because I couldn't work, if I did, and I've got to work. It's most helpful to think the Lord made special promises to widows, and when I remember Him I a'n't afeard."

Miss Perrit stopped rockin' a minute, and then she begun to creak the chair and blow her nose again, and she said —

"Well, I'm sure it's a great mercy to see anybody rise above their trouble the way you do; but, law me! Miss Langdon, you a'n't got through the fust pair o' bars on't yet. Folks is allers kinder neighborly at the fust; they feel to help you right off, every way they can,— but it don't stay put, they get tired on't; they blaze right up like a white-birch-stick, an' then they go out all of a heap; there's other folks die, and they don't remember you, and you're just as bad off as though you wa'n't a widder."

Mother kind of smiled,—she couldn't help it; but she spoke up again just as steady.

"I don't expect to depend on people, Miss Perrit, so long as I have my health. I a'n't above takin' friendly help when I need to, but I mean mostly to help myself. I can get work to take in, and when the girls have got their schoolin' they will be big enough to help me. I am not afraid but what I shall live and prosper, if I only keep my health."

"Hem, well!" whined out Miss Perrit. "I allers thought you was a pretty mighty woman, Miss Langdon, and I'm glad to see you're so high minded; but you a'n't sure of your health, never. I used to be real smart to what I am now, when Perrit was alive; but I took on so, when he was brought home friz to death, that it sp'iled my nerves; and then I had to do so many chores out in the shed, I got cold and had the dreadfullest rheumatiz! And when I'd got past the worst spell of that and was quite folksy again, I slipped down on our door-step and kinder wrenched my ankle, and ef't hadn't 'a' been for the neighbors, I don't know but what Nancy and I should 'a' starved."

Mother did laugh this time. Miss Perrit had overshot the mark.

"So the neighbors were helpful, after all!" said she. "And if ever I get sick, I shall be willin' to have help, Miss Perrit. I'm sure I would take what I would give; I think givin' works two ways. I don't feel afraid yet."

Miss Perrit groaned a little, and wiped her eyes, and got up to go away. She hadn't never offered to help mother, and she went off to the sewing-circle and told that Miss Langdon hadn't got no feelings at all, and she b'lieved she'd just as soon beg for a livin' as not. Polly Mariner, the tailoress, come and told mother all she said next day, but mother only smiled, and set Polly to talk about the best way to make over her old cloak. When she was gone, I begun to talk about Miss Perrit, and I was real mad; but mother hushed me right up.

"It a'n't any matter, Ann," said she. "Her sayin' so don't make it so. Miss Perrit's got a miserable disposition, and I'm sorry for her; a mint of money wouldn't make her happy; she's a doleful Christian, she don't take any comfort in anything, and I really do pity her."

And that was just the way mother took everything.

At first we couldn't sell the farm. It was down at the foot of Torringford Hill, two good miles from meetin', and a mile from the school-house; most of it was woodsy, and there wa'n't no great market for wood about there. So for the first year Squire Potter took it on shares, and, as he principally seeded it down to rye, why, we sold the rye and got a little money, but 'twa'n't a great deal,—no more than we wanted for clothes the next winter. Aunt Langdon sent us down a lot of maple sugar from Lee, and when we wanted molasses we made it out of that. We didn't have to buy no great of groceries, for we could spin and knit by firelight, and, part of the land bein' piny woods, we had a good lot of knots that were as bright as lamps for all we wanted. Then we had a dozen chickens, and by pains and care they laid pretty well, and the eggs were as good as gold. So we lived through the first year after father died pretty well.

Anybody that couldn't get along with mother and Major (I always called Mary Jane "Major" when I was real little, and the name kind of stayed by) couldn't get along with anybody. I was as happy as a cricket whilst they were by, though, to speak truth, I wasn't naturally so chirpy as they were; I took after father more, who was a kind of a despondin' man, down-hearted, never thinkin' things could turn out right, or that he was goin' to have any luck. That was my natur', and mother see it, and fought ag'inst it like a real Bunker-Hiller; but natur' is hard to root up, and there was always times when I wanted to sulk away into a corner and think nobody wanted me, and that I was poor and humbly, and had to work for my living.

I remember one time I'd gone up into my room before tea to have one of them dismal fits. Miss Perrit had been in to see mother, and she'd been tellin' over what luck Nancy'd had down to Hartford: how't she had gone into a shop, and a young man had been struck with her good looks, an' he'd turned out to be a master shoe-maker, and Nancy was a-goin' to be married, and so on, a rigmarole as long as the moral law,—windin' up with askin' mother why she didn't send us girls off to try our luck, for Major was as old as Nancy Perrit. I'd waited to hear mother say, in her old bright way, that she couldn't afford it, and she couldn't spare us, if she had the means, and then I flung up into our room, that was a lean-to in the garret, with a winder in the gable end, and there I set down by the winder with my chin on the sill, and begun to wonder why we couldn't have as good luck as the Perrits. After I'd got real miserable, I heard a soft step comin' up stairs, and Major come in an looked at me and then out of the winder.

"What's the matter of you, Anny?" she said.

"Nothing," says I, as sulky as you please.

"Nothing always means something," says Major, as pleasant as pie; and then she scooched down on the floor and pulled my two hands away, and looked me in the face as bright and honest as ever you see a dandelion look out of the grass. "What is it, Anny? Spit it out, as John Potter says; you'll feel better to free your mind."

"Well," says I, "Major, I'm tired of bad luck."

"Why, Anny! I didn't know as we'd had any. I'm sure, it's three years since father died, and we have had enough to live on all that time, and I've got my schooling, and we are all well; and just look at the apple trees,—all as pink as your frock with blossoms; that's good for new cloaks next winter, Anny."

"'Ta'n't that, Major. I was thinkin' abut Nancy Perrit. If we'd had the luck to go to Hartford, maybe you'd have been as well off as she; and then I'd have got work, too. And I wish I was as pretty as she is, Major; it does seem too bad to be poor and humbly too."

I wonder she didn't laugh at me, but she was very feelin' for folks, always. She put her head on the window-sill along of mine, and kinder nestled up to me in her lovin' way, and said, softly,—

"I wouldn't quarrel with the Lord, Anny."

"Why, Major! You scare me! I haven't said nothing against the Lord. What do you mean?" said I,—for I was touchy, real touchy.

"Well, dear, you see we've done all we can to help ourselves; and what's over and above, that we can't help,—that is what the Lord orders, a'n't it? and He made you, didn't He? You can't change your face; and I'm glad of it, for it is Anny's face, and I wouldn't have it changed a mite: there'll always be two people to think it's sightly enough, and maybe more by–and–by; so I wouldn't quarrel with it, if I was you."

Major's happy eyes always helped me. I looked at her and felt better. She wasn't any better lookin' than I; but she always was so chirk, and smart, and neat, and pretty–behaved, that folks thought she was handsome after they knowed her.

Well, after a spell, there was a railroad laid out up the valley, and all the land thereabouts riz in price right away; and Squire Potter he bought our farm on speculation, and give a good price for it; so't we had two thousand dollars in the bank, and the house and lot, and the barn, and the cow. By this time Major was twenty-two and I was eighteen; and Squire Potter he'd left his house up on the hill, and he'd bought out Miss Perrit's house, and added on to't, and moved down not far from us, so's to be near the railroad-depot, for the sake of bein' handy to the woods, for cuttin' and haulin' of them down to the track. "'Twasn't very pleasant at first to see our dear old woods goin' off to be burned that way; but Squire Potter's folks were such good neighbors, we gained as much as we lost, and a sight more, for folks are greatly better'n trees,—at least, clever folks.

There was a whole raft of the Potters, eight children of 'em all, some too young to be mates for Major and me; but Mary Potter, and Reuben, and Russell, they were along about as old as we were; Russell come between Major and me; and the other two was older.

We kinder kept to home always, Major and me, because we hadn't any brothers to go out with us; so we were pretty shy of new friends at first. But you couldn't help bein' friendly with the Potters, they was such outspoken, kindly creatures, from the Squire down to little Hen. And it was very handy for us, because now we could go to singin' schools and quiltin's, and such-like places, of an evenin'; and we had rather moped at home for want of such things,—at least I had, and I should have been more moped only for Major's sweet ways. She was always as contented as a honey-bee on a cloverhead, for the same reason, I guess.

Well, there was a good many good things come to us from the Potters' movin' down; but by-and-by it seemed as though I was goin' to get the bitter of it. I'd kept company pretty steady with Russell. I hadn't give much thought to it, neither; I liked his ways, and he seemed to give in to mine very natural, so't we got along together first rate. It didn't seem as though we'd ever been strangers, and I wasn't one to make believe at stiffness when I didn't feel it. I told Russell pretty much all I had to tell, and he was allers doin' for me and runnin' after me jest as though he'd been my brother. I didn't know how much I did think of him, till, after a while, he seemed to take a sight of notice of Major. I can't say he ever stopped bein' clever to me, for he didn't; but he seemed to have a kind of a hankerin' after Major all the time. He'd take her off to walk with him; he'd dig up roots in the woods for her posy-bed; he'd hold her skeins of yarn as patient as a little dog; he'd get her books to read. Well, he'd done all this for me; but when I see him doin' it for her, it was quite different; and all to once I know'd what was the matter. I'd thought too much of Russell Potter.

Oh, dear! those was dark times! I couldn't blame him; I knew well enough Major was miles and miles better and sweeter and cleverer than I was; I didn't wonder he liked her; but I couldn't feel as if he'd done right by me. So I schooled myself considerable, talking to myself for being jealous of Major. But 'twasn't all that;—the hardest of it all was that I had to mistrust Russell. To be sure, he hadn't said nothin' to me in round words' I couldn't ha' sued him; but he'd looked and acted enough; and now,—dear me, I felt all wrung out and flung away!

By-and-by Major begun to see somethin' was goin' wrong, and so did Russell. She was as good as she could be to me, and had patience with all my little pettish ways, and tried to make me friendly with Russell; but I wouldn't. I took to hard work, and, what with cryin' nights, and hard work all day, I got pretty well overdone. But it all went on for about three months, till one day Russell come up behind me, as I was layin' out some yarn to bleach down at the end of the orchard, and asked me if I'd go down to Meriden with him next day, to a pic-nic frolic, in the woods.

"No!" says I, as short as I could.

Russell looked as though I had slapped him. "Anny," says he, "what have I done?"

I turned round to go away, and I catched my foot in a hank of yarn, and down I come flat on to the ground, havin' sprained my ankle so bad that Russell had to pick me up and carry me into the house like a baby.

There was an end of Meriden for me; and he wouldn't go, either, but come over and sat by me, and read to me, and somehow or other, I don't remember just the words, he gave me to understand that—well—that he wished I'd marry him.

It's about as tirin' to be real pleased with anything as it is to be troubled, at first. I couldn't say anything to Russell; I just cried. Major wasn't there; mother was dryin' apples out in the shed; so Russell he didn't know what to do; he kind of hushed me up, and begged of me not to cry, and said he'd come for his answer next day. So he come, and I didn't say, "No," again. I don't believe I stopped to think whether Major liked him. She would have thought of me, first thing;—I believe she wouldn't have had him, if she'd thought I wanted him. But I a'n't like Major; it come more natural to me to think about myself; and besides, she was pious, and I wasn't. Russell was.

However, it turned out all right, for Major was 'most as pleased as I was; and she told me, finally, that she'd known a long spell that Russell liked me, and the reason he'd been hangin' round her so long was, he'd been tellin' her his plans, and they'd worked out considerable in their heads before she could feel as though he had a good enough lookout to ask me to marry him.

That wasn't so pleasant to me, when I come to think of it; I thought I'd ought to have been counselled with. But it was just like Major; everybody come to her for a word of help or comfort, whether they took her idee or not,—she had such a feelin' for other folks's trouble.

I got over that little nub after a while; and then I was so pleased, everything went smooth again. I was goin' to be married in the spring; and we were goin' straight out to Indiana, onto some wild land Squire Potter owned out there, to clear it and settle it, and what Russell cleared he was to have. So mother took some money out of the bank to fit me out, and Major and I went down to Hartford to buy my things.

I said before, we wasn't either of us any great things to look at; but it come about that one day I heerd somebody tell how we did look, and I thought considerable about it then and afterwards. We was buyin' some cotton to a store in the city, and I was lookin' about at all the pretty things, and wonderin' why I was picked out to be poor when so many folks was rich and had all they wanted, when presently I heerd a lady in a silk gown say to another one, so low she thought I didn't hear her,—"There are two nice looking girls, Mrs. Carr."

"Hem,—yes," said the other one; "they look healthy and strong: the oldest one has a lovely expression, both steady and sweet; the other don't look happy."

I declare, that was a fact. I was sorry, too, for I'd got everything in creation to make anybody happy, and now I was frettin' to be rich. I thought I'd try to be like Major; but I expect it was mostly because of the looks of it, for I forgot to try before long.

Well, in the spring we was married; and when I come to go away, Major put a little red Bible into my trunk for a weddin' present; but I was cryin' too hard to thank her. She swallowed down whatever choked her, and begged of me not to cry so, lest Russell should take it hard that I mourned to go with him. But just then I was thinkin' more of Major and mother than I was of Russell; they'd kept me bright and cheery always, and kept up my heart with their own good ways when I hadn't no strength to do it for myself; and now I was goin' off alone with Russell, and he wasn't very cheerful dispositioned, and somehow my courage give way all to once.

But I had to go; railroads don't wait for nobody; and what with the long journey, and the new ways and things and people, I hadn't no time to get real down once before we got to Indiana. After we left the boat there was a spell of railroad, and then a long stage-ride to Cumberton; and then we had to hire a big wagon and team, so's to get us out to our claim, thirty miles west'ard of Cumberton. I hadn't no time to feel real lonesome now, for all our things hed got to be onpacked, and packed over ag'in in the wagon; some of 'em had to be stored up, so's to come another time. We was two days gettin' to the claim, the roads was so bad,—mostly what they call corduroy, but a good stretch clear mud-holes. By the time we got to the end on't, I was tired out, just fit to cry; and such a house as was waitin' for us!—a real log shanty! I see Russell looked real beat when he see my face; and I tried to brighten up; but I wished to my heart I was back with mother forty times that night, if I did once. Then come the worst of all, clutterin' everything right into that shanty; for our frame-house wouldn't be done for two months, and there wa'n't scarce room for what we'd brought, so't we couldn't think of sendin' for what was stored to Cumberton. I didn't sleep none for two nights, because of the whip-poor-wills that set on a tree close by, and called till mornin' light; but after that I was too tired to lie awake.

Well, it was real lonesome, but it was all new at first, and
Russell was to work near by, so't I could see him, and oftentimes hear
him whistle; and I had the garden to make, round to the new house,
for I knew more about the plantin' of it than he did, 'specially my
posy-bed, and I had a good time gettin' new flowers out of the woods.
And the woods was real splendid,—great tall tulip-trees, as high as a
steeple and round as a quill, without any sort o' branches ever so fur
up, and the whole top full of the yeller tulips an the queer snipped-
lookin' shiny leaves, till they looked like great bow-pots on sticks;
then there's lots of other great trees, only they're all mostly spindled
up in them woods. But the flowers that grow round on the ma'sh edges
and in the clearin's do beat all.

So time passed along pretty glib till the frame-house was
done, and then we had to move in, and to get the things from
Cumberton, and begin to feel as though we were settled for good and
all; and after the newness had gone off, and the clearin' got so fur that
I couldn't see Russell no more, and nobody to look at, if I was never so
lonesome, then come a pretty hard spell. Everything about the house
was real handy, so't I'd get my work cleared away, and set down to
sew early; and them long summer days that was still and hot, I'd set,
and set, never hearin' nothin' but the clock go "tick, tick, tick," (never
"tack," for a change) and every now'n'then a great crash and roar in
the woods where he was chopppin', that I knew was a tree; and I
worked myself up dreadfully when there was a longer spell 'n common
come betwixt the crashes, lest that Russell might 'a' been ketched
under the one that fell. And settin' so, and worryin' a good deal, day
in and day out, kinder broodin' over my troubles, and never thinkin'
about anybody but myself, I got to be of the idee that I was the worst-
off creature goin'. If I'd have stopped to think about Russell, maybe I
should have had some sort of pity for him, for he was jest as lonesome
as I, and I wasn't no kind of comfort to come home to,—'most always
cryin' or jest a-goin' to.

So the summer went along till 'twas nigh on to winter, and I
wa'n't in no better sperrits. And now I wa'n't real well, and pined for
mother, and I pined for Major, and I'd have given all the honey and
buckwheat in Indiana for a loaf of mother's dry rye-bread and a drink
of spring-water. And finally I got so miserable, I wished I wa'n't never
married,—and I'd have wished I was dead, if 'twa'n't for bein'
doubtful where I'd go to, if I was. And worst of all, one day I got so
worked up I told Russell all that. I declare, he turned as white as a

turnip. I see I'd hurt him, and I'd have got over it in a minute and told him so,—only he up with his axe and walked out of the door, and never come home till night, and then I was too stubborn to speak to him.

Well, things got worse, 'n' one day I was sewin' some things and cryin' over 'em, when I heard a team come along by, and, before I could get to the door, Russell come in, all red for joy, and says,—

"Who do you want to see most, Anny?"

Somehow the question kind of upset me;—I got choked, and then I bu'st out a–cryin'.

"Oh, mother and Major!" says I; and I hadn't more'n spoke the word before mother had both her good strong arms round me, and Major's real cheery face was a-lookin' up at me from the little pine cricket, where she'd sot down as nateral as life. Well, I was glad, and so was Russell, and the house seemed as shiny as a hang-bird's nest, and by-and-by the baby came;—but I had mother.

"'Twas 'long about in March when I was sick, and by the end of April I was well, and so's to be stirrin' round again. And mother and Major begun to talk about goin' home; and I declare, my heart was up in my mouth every time they spoke on't, and I begun to be miserable ag'in. One day I was settin' beside of mother; Major was out in the garden, fixin' up things, and settin' out a lot of blows she'd got in the woods, and singin' away, and says I to mother—

"What be I going to do, mother, without you and Major? I 'most died of clear lonesomeness before you come!"

Mother laid down her knittin', and looked straight at me.

"I wish you'd got a little of Major's good cheer, Anny," says she. "You haven't any call to be lonely here; it's a real good country, and you've got a nice house, and the best of husbands, and a dear little baby, and you'd oughter try to give up frettin'. I wish you was pious, Anny; you wouldn't fault the Lord's goodness the way you do."

"Well, Major don't have nothin' to trouble her, mother," says I. "She's all safe and pleasant to home; she a'n't homesick."

Mother spoke up pretty resolute—

"There a'n't nobody in the world, Anny, but what has troubles. I didn't calculate to tell you about Major's; but sence you lay her lively ways to luck, maybe you'd better know 'em. She's been engaged this six months to Reuben Potter, and he's goin' off in a slow consumption; he won't never live to marry her, and she knows it."

"And she come away to see me, mother?"

"Yes, she did. I can't say I thought she need to, but Russell wrote you was pinin' for both of us, and I didn't think you could get along without me, but I told her to stay with Reuben, and I'd come on alone. And says she, 'No, mother, you a'n't young and spry enough to go alone so fur, and the Lord made you my mother and Anny my sister before I picked out Reuben for myself. I can't never have any kin but you, and I might have had somebody beside Reuben, though it don't seem likely now; but he's got four sisters to take care of him, and he thinks and I think it's what I ought to do; so I'm goin' with you.' So she come, Anny; and you see how lively she keeps, just because she don't want to dishearten you none. I don't know as you can blame her for kinder hankerin' to get home."

I hadn't nothin' to say; I was beat. So mother went on—

"Fact is, Anny, Major's always thinkin' about other folks; it comes kind of nateral to her, and then bein' pious helps it. I guess, dear, when you get to thinkin' more abut Russell an' the baby, you'll forget some of your troubles. I hope the Lord won't have to give you no harder lesson than lovin', to teach you Major's ways."

So, after that, I couldn't say no more to mother about stayin'; but when they went away, I like to have cried myself sick,—only baby had to be looked after, and I couldn't dodge her.

Bym-by we had letters from home; they got there all safe, and Reuben wa'n't no worse, Major said;—ef't had been me wrote the letter, I should have said he wa'n't no better!—And I fell back into the old lonesome days, for baby slept mostly; and the summer come on extreme hot; and in July, Russell, bein' forced to go to Cumberton on some land business, left me to home with baby and the hired man, calculatin' to be gone three days and two nights.

The first day he was away was dreadful sultry; the sun went down away over the woods in a kind of a red-hot fog, and it seemed as though the stars were dull and coppery at night; even the whip-poor-wills was too hot to sing; nothin' but a doleful screech-owl quavered away, a half a mile off, a good hour, steady. When it got to be mornin', it didn't seem no cooler; there wa'n't a breath of wind, and the locusts in the woods chattered as though they was fryin'. Our hired man was an old Scotchman, by name Simon Grant; and when he'd got his breakfast, he said he'd go down the clearin' and bring up a load of brush for me to burn. So he drove off with the team, and, havin' cleared up the dishes, I put baby to sleep, and took my pail to the barn to milk the cow,—for we kept her in a kind of a home-lot like, a part that had been cleared afore we come, lest she should stray away in the woods, if we turned her loose; she was put in the barn, too, nights, for fear some stray wildcat or bear might come along and do her a harm. So I let her into the yard, and was jest a-goin' to milk her when she begun to snort and shake, and finally giv' the pail a kick, and set off, full swing, for the fence to the lot. I looked round to see what was a-comin', and there, about a quarter of a mile off, I see the most curus thing I ever see before or since,—a cloud as black as ink in the sky, and hangin' down from it a long spout like, something like an elephant's trunk, and the whole world under it looked to be all beat to dust. Before I could get my eyes off on't, or stir to run, I see it was comin' as fast as a locomotive; I heerd a great roar and rush,—first a hot wind, and then a cold one, and then a crash,—an' 'twas all as dark as death all round, and the roar appeared to be a-passin' off.

I didn't know for quite a spell where I was. I was flat on my face, and when I come to a little, I felt the grass against my cheek, and I smelt the earth; but I couldn't move, no way; I couldn't turn over, nor raise my head more'n two inches, nor draw myself up one. I was comfortable so long as I laid still; but if I went to move, I couldn't. It wasn't no use to wriggle; and when I'd settled that, I jest went to work to figger out where I was and how I got there, and the best I could make out was that the barn roof had blowed off and lighted right over me, jest so as not to hurt me, but so't I couldn't move.

Well, there I lay. I knew baby was asleep in the trundle-bed, and there wa'n't no fire in the house; but how did I know the house wa'n't blowed down? I thought that as quick as a flash of lightnin'; it kinder struck me; I couldn't even see, so as to be certain! I wasn't naterally fond of children, but somehow one's own is different, and baby was just gettin' big enough to be pretty; and there I lay, feelin' about as bad as I could, but hangin' on to one hope,—that old Simon, seein' the tornado, would come pretty soon to see where we was.

I lay still quite a spell, listenin'. Presently I heerd a low, whimperin', pantin' noise, comin' nearer and nearer, and I knew it was old Lu, a yeller hound of Simon's, that he'd set great store by, because he brought him from the Old Country. I heerd the dog come pretty near to where I was, and then stop, and give a long howl. I tried to call him, but I was all choked up with dust, and for a while I couldn't make no sound! Finally, I called, "Lu! Lu! Here, Sir!" and if ever you heerd a dumb creature laugh, he barked a real laugh, and come springin' along over towards me. I called ag'in, and he begun to scratch and tear and pull,—at boards, I guessed, for it sounded like that; but it wa'n't no use, he couldn't get at me, and he give up at length and set down right over my head and give another howl, so long and so dismal I thought I'd as lieves hear the bell a-tollin' my age.

Pretty soon, I heerd another sound,—the baby cryin'; and with that Lu jumped off whatever 'twas that buried me up, and run. "At any rate," thinks I, "baby's alive." And then I bethought myself if 'twa'n't a painter, after all; they scream jest like a baby, and there's a lot of them, or there was then, right round in our woods; and Lu was dreadful fond to hunt 'em; and he never took no notice of baby;—and I couldn't stir to see!

Oh, dear! The sweat stood all over me! And there I lay, and Simon didn't come, nor I didn't hear a mouse stir; the air was as still as death, and I got nigh distracted. Seemed as if all my life riz right up there in the dark and looked at me. Here I was, all helpless, maybe never to get out alive; for Simon didn't come and Russell was gone away. I'd had a good home, and a kind husband, and all I could ask; but I hadn't had a contented mind; I'd quarreled with Providence, 'cause I hadn't got everything,—and now I hadn't got nothing. I see just as clear as daylight how I'd nussed up every little trouble till it growed to a big one,—how I'd sp'ilt Russell's life, and made him

wretched,—how I'd been cross to him a great many times when I had
ought to have been a comfort; and now it was like enough I shouldn't
never see him again,—nor baby, nor mother, nor Major. And how
could I look the Lord in the face, if I did die? That took all my strength
out. I lay shakin' and chokin' with the idee, I don't know how long; it
kind of got hold of me and ground me down; it was worse than all. I
wished to gracious I didn't believe in hell; but then it come to mind,
What should I do in heaven, ef I was there? I didn't love nothin' that
folks in heaven love, except the baby; I hadn't been suited with the
Lord's will on earth, and 'twa'n't likely I was goin' to like it any
better in heaven; and I should be ashamed to show my face where I
didn't belong, neither by right nor by want. So I lay. Presently I heerd
in my mind this verse, that I'd learned years back in Sabbath School—

"Wherefore He is able also to save them to the uttermost"—

there it stopped, but it was a plenty for me. I see at once there wasn't
no help anywhere else, and for once in my life I did pray, real earnest,
and—queer enough—not to get out, but to be made good. I kind of
forgot where I was, I see so complete what I was; but after a while I
did pray to live in the flesh; I wanted to make some amends to Russell
for pesterin' on him so.

It seemed to me as though I'd laid there for two days. A rain
finally come on, with a good even-down pour, that washed in a little,
and cooled my hot head; and after it passed by I heerd one whip-poor-
will singin', so't I knew it was night. And pretty soon I heerd the
tramp of a horse's feet;—it come up; it stopped; I heerd Russell say out
loud, "O Lord!" and give a groan, and then I called to him. I declare,
he jumped!

So I got him to go look for baby first, because I could wait;
and lo! She was all safe in the trundle-bed, with Lu beside of her, both
on 'em stretched out together, one of her little hands on his nose; and
when Russell looked in to the door she stirred a bit, and Lu licked her
hand to keep her quiet. It tells in the Bible about children's angels
always seein' the face of God, so's to know quick what to do for 'em, I
suppose; and I'm sure her'n got to her afore the tornado; for though
the house-roof had blowed off, and the chimbley tumbled down, there
wa'n't a splinter nor a brick on her bed, only close by the head on't a

great hunk of stone had fell down, and steadied up the clothes-press from tumblin' right on top of her.

So then Russell rode over, six miles, to a neighbor's, and got two men, and betwixt 'em all they pried up the beams of the barn, that had blowed on to the roof and pinned it down over me, and then lifted up the boards and got me out; and I wa'n't hurt, except a few bruises: but after that day I begun to get gray hairs.

Well, Russell was pretty thankful, I b'lieve,—more so'n he need to be for such a wife. We fixed up some kind of shelter, but Lu howled so all night we couldn't sleep. It seems Russell had seen the tornado to Cumberton, and, judgin' from its course 'twould come past the clearin', he didn't wait a minute, but saddled up and come off; but it had crossed the road once or twice, so it was nigh about eleven o'clock afore he got home; but it was broad moonlight. So I hadn't been under the roof only about fifteen hours; but it seemed more.

In the mornin' Russell set out to find Simon, and I was so trembly I couldn't bear to stay alone, and I went with him, he carryin' baby, and Lu goin' before, as tickled as he could be. We went a long spell through the woods, keepin' on the edge of the tornado's road; for't had made a clean track about a quarter of a mile wide, and felled the trees flat,—great tulips cut off as sharp as pipe-stems, oaks twisted like dandelion-stems, and hickories curled right up in a heap. Presently Lu give a bark, and then such a howl! And there was Simon, dead enough; a big oak had blowed down, with the trunk right acrost his legs above the knees, and smashed them almost off. 'Twas plain it hadn't killed him to once, for the ground all about his head was tore up as though he'd fought with it, and Russell said his teeth and hands was full of grass and grit where he'd bit and tore, a-dyin' so hard. I declare, I shan't never forget that sight! Seems as if my body was full of little ice-spickles every time I think on't.

Well, Russell couldn't do nothin; we had no chance to lift the tree, so we went back to the house, and he rode away after neighbors; and while he was gone, I had a long spell of thinkin'. Mother said she hoped I wouldn't have no hard lesson to teach me Major's ways; but I had got it, and I know I needed it, 'cause it did come so hard. I b'lieve I was a better woman after that. I got to think more of other folks's comfort than I did afore, and whenever I got goin' to be dismal ag'in I used to try 'n' find somebody to help; it was a sure cure.

When the neighbors come, Russell and they blasted and chopped the tree off Simon, and buried him under a big pine that we calculated not to fell. Lu pined, and howled, and moaned for his master, till I got him to look after baby now and then, when I was hanging out clothes or makin' garden, and he got to like her in the end on't near as well as Simon.

After a while there come more settlers out our way, and we got a church to go to; and the minister, Mr. Jones, he come to know if I was a member, and when I said I wa'n't, he put in to know if I wasn't a pious woman.

"Well," says I, "I don't know, Sir." So I up and told him all about it, and how I had had a hard lesson; and he smiled once or twice, and says, he,—

"Your husband thinks you are Christian, Sister Potter, don't he?"

"Yes, I do," says Russell, a–comin' in behind me to the door,—for he'd just stepped out to get the minister a basket of plums. "I hadn't a doubt on't, Mr. Jones."

The minister looked at him, and I see he was kinder pleased.

"Well," says he, "I don't think there's much doubt a woman's bein' pious when she's pious to home; and I don't want no better testimony'n yours, Mr. Potter. I shall admit you to full fellowship, sister, when we have a church meetin' next; for it's my belief you experienced religion under that blowed–down barn."

And I guess I did.

"Squire Paine's Conversion"

Harper's New Monthly, March 1878

Samuel Paine was a heard–headed, "hard-featured" Yankee boy who grew up in the old homestead without brothers or sisters.

Had any of those means of grace shared his joys and sorrows, perhaps his nature would have been modified; but he was sole heir of the few rugged acres, scant pasturage for the old red cow, and the bit of "medder land" that reluctantly gave corn and rye and potatoes enough for the household, and barely hay sufficient to winter the cow and the venerable horse that belonged to old Dibble Paine, Samuel's father. Now in such a case it is slave or starve in New England. Hard work is the initial lesson. Samuel's youth of labor began early. At three years old, in brief garments of yellow flannel, and a flaxen thatch of hair for head–covering, he toddled in and out of the kitchen with chips in a basket; he fed the chickens, he rode the hay wagon, and was, moreover, ruled already with a rod of iron, or rather a stout shingle, which hung, ready to hand, by the chimney-piece. At seven, the Assembly's Catechism was drilled into him, and he trudged daily a mile and back to the red school–house, doing "chores" at every odd interval; getting up by daylight in summer, and long before in winter, to fetch and carry for the poor pale woman who was wife and mother in that meager household; going to meeting Sundays as faithfully as Parson Wires himself; and in the course of years growing up to be a goodly youth, saving, industrious, correct; perfectly self-satisfied, and conscious of his own merits and other people's demerits.

But the course of years takes as well as gives. When Samuel was twenty he was fatherless and motherless. The old farm was let on shares, and behind the counter of a country store in Bassett he dealt out, with strict justice—to his employer!—scant yards of calico, even measures of grass seed, small pounds of groceries, weakly rum, sugar not too sweet, and many other necessities of life in the same proportion. Old S. Jones never had so thrifty a clerk, never made so much money in the same time, and never had so few loungers about. In due time Samuel experienced religion—or said he did; was duly examined, glibly reeled off his inward exercises to the admiring deacons, and at the proper season was propounded and admitted to the church in Bassett. He had always been a strictly moral young man and a sober one—not in the sense of temperance, but sober in habit and manner.

Samuel Paine never indulged in those youthful gayeties that so many boys rejoice in. He did not waste his hard–earned substance in riotous picnics, husking frolics, boat rides, or sleighing parties; he never used tobacco in any form, never drank cider, or "waited" on any girl in Bassett, though there was the usual feminine surplus of a New England village in this one. In the evening he read law diligently in Squire Larkin's office, because he thought it might be useful to him hereafter. He sat in the singers' seat in the meeting house, his straight long face, cold gray eyes, sleek light hair, and immaculate linen looking respectable enough for a whole congregation. He had a class in Sunday-school—a class of big girls, all of whom hated him thoroughly, but never dared own it. Armed with *Barnes's Notes* and *Cruden's Concordance*, he did his duty to his class in explaining and expounding the doctrine of the lesson; but while he impressed the letter on their minds, the sweet and living spirit never lit his cool eye or warmed his accurate speech. Whatever else those young girls learned of Samuel Paine, they never learned to love the Lord or His words, for he knew not how to teach them. His soul had never yet found its level, had never had the lesson that comes to us all some time in our lives, whether we accept it or not, and he went on in his own narrow way without let or hindrance.

Before Samuel was twenty–five, Si Jones retired from business in Bassett, being persuaded by his wife to remove into Vermont where his friends lived. He had made a good deal of money, and being childless and well under his wife's thumb, she had induced him to sell out and go back to her old home. Now came the time Samuel Paine had long looked for. He had saved, spared, pinched, to this end. He bought out the store and the small frame house that contained it—a house with two rooms up stairs and a kitchen in the little wing. Part of the money he paid down in cash; part borrowed on a mortgage; the rest he was forced to give notes for.

"Well," said 'Bijah Jones, a far-off cousin of Si's, and the village loafer and joker, "guess folks'll hev to keep their eyes peeled now. I tell ye, Samwell Paine beats the Dutch to drive a bargain. Ye won't know where ye be, fust ye know any thing; he'll sell ye a pair o' store pants in five minnits when ye don't want 'em no more'n a toad wants a pocket."

"Dew tell!" sputtered old Grandsir Baker, who had just come over from the townhouse with a hank of yarn to trade off for some molasses. "Well! Well! Well! Hows–ever, he can't sell me nothin', cos I hain't got no money; ye can't get blood outen a stun, nohow. He! He! He!"

"Blessed be nothin'!" dryly put in 'Bijah.

And all this while Samuel was announcing his principles in the store to a knot of farmers and village worthies come in for their weekly supplies for the first time since S. Paine's name had been seen above the door.

"Yes, Sir! yes, Sir! I've cleaned up considerable; I hope to clear up more. I 'xpect to conduct this business on a line, gentlemen— a straight line, so to speak, seemin'ly, as it were. There ain't no rewl better for all things than the golden rewl; that contains the sperrit and principle of the hull thing. Do's you'd like ter be done by; that's my idee in short partikelar metre."

A dry rattling laugh emphasized this conclusion, and a sort of unwilling "Haw! Haw!" chorused it from the audience. 'Bijah Jones had drawn near enough to the open door to hear part of the sentence, and grinned widely.

"Come along, grandsir," shouted he to the hobbling old fellow from the poor-house. "Strike while th' iron's hot. He's talking Scripter with all fury; naow's your time to swap that air yarn. Bet you'll git a hull cask o' 'lasses!"

Grandsir Baker did not quicken his halting pace for this advice, and it is not on record that he got any more molasses than he expected to; but when he got back to the poor–house he told Mrs. Wells that molasses had riz and yarn hadn't; Samwell Paine told him so.

A village store—*the* store—is not a matter of hazard, but a vital necessity. There is no competition to be dreaded in a place like Bassett. Nobody else had capital or experience to set up an opposition shop; there was no better place to trade within twenty miles, and it was by the very doors of Bassett people; if they did not quite like the way things were conducted, they must still abide by it, for there was no help. And in many things the business was mightily improved since Si Jones's time: the shop itself was clean and orderly; cod-fish did not lurk in a dusty corner behind patent ploughs, and tea leaves did not fall into the open flour barrel; if sand was suspected in the sugar, there were certainly no chips of tobacco in its grainy mass; and calico and candy did not live on the same shelf, or raisins, bar soap, and blacking occupy a drawer together; the floor was swept, washed, and sanded, the counters scoured off, the cobwebs banished, the steps repaired, the windows kept bright and clear, the scales shining. If S. Paine's clerk had hard work for a lad of eighteen, his employer could quote Scripture with tremendous fluency and fitness when the boy's old mother remonstrated.

"Well, Miss Bliss, I don't deny John has to work. So do I; so do I. It is good for a man to bear the yoke in his youth, Scripter says. There ain't nothin' better for no man than work. 'By the sweat o' thy brow,' ye know. The sperrit an' principle of the golden rewl is my sperrit an' principle: do's you'd be done by. Yes, yes; ef I was a boy again, I'd want ter be fetched up jest as I was fetched up—on hard work an' poor livin.' That rouses the grit, I tell ye. I'm a–doin' by John jest as I was done by, so don't ye resent it. It's fur his best int'rest, soul an' body." With which chopped straw poor Mrs. Bliss's motherly heart was forced to content itself, for there was no other refreshment.

Perhaps in this application of the "golden rewl" Samuel Paine forgot how his childish flesh had wept and cringed under the hardships of his early life; how his childish soul had flamed with rage under the torture and insult of the unjustly applied shingle, and the constant watching of stern and pitiless eyes. He may not have remembered how his growing bones ached under heavy burdens, and his spare flesh craved enough even of such diet as pork, cabbage, and rye bread to allay the pangs of childish hunger and the demands of daily growth. But if he did not, is that excuse? Is not the command explicit to "remember all the way the Lord thy God led thee;" and is forgetfulness without sin?

But the man kept on in his respectable career, buying and selling—buying at the lowest rates and selling at the highest; faithful externally to all his duties; ever present in church, never late at his Sunday school class, never missing a prayer-meeting; a zealous exhorter, "a master-hand at prayin'," as Widow Bliss allowed; deeply interested in the work of missions, and a stated contributor to the Bible Society; but at home—no, it was no home—at his store, strict in every matter of business, merciless to his debtors, close and niggardly even to his best customers, harsh to his clerk, and greedy of every smallest profit. Nobody ever went to him for friendly offices; nobody asked him to be neighborly; no subscription list for a poor man with a broken leg or a burned-down barn ever crossed the door-sill of the store. When all other young men went to quiltings and sociables, he staid at the desk, amusing himself with his ledger, or a ponderous law-book borrowed from Squire Larkin. So he lived—or existed—till he was thirty years old; and one fine day Squire Larkin died, and left behind him an only daughter, a goodly sum of money, and a vacant office of postmaster. Now was Samuel's time again. He attended the funeral, and appeared to be deeply affected by the loss of an old acquaintance. He called on Miss Lucy as early as was proper, and made an offer for the Squire's law books. They were useless to Lucy now, and she had not thought of selling them; the nearest city was full thirty miles away, and she had not even a friend in its busy sphere; nobody in Bassett wanted law books, so Samuel Paine bought them for a quarter of their value, and Lucy never found it out. His next step was to petition for the post office; here again nobody interfered. It would be very convenient to all concerned that the post office should be in the store: that was its natural and fit situation. When Squire Larkin took it into his hands, his old law office stood close by Si Jones's place of business; but that tiny tenement had been burned this long time, and the mails carried to Mr. Larkin's house and distributed in the south parlor, where also his books and his few clients found a place. Now if S. Paine got the office, it wold be "everlastin' handy," everybody said; so everybody signed the petition, and Postmaster Paine was sworn in.

Lucy Larkin was no longer young; she was twenty-eight at least—a gentle, faded, pretty woman, with mild blue eyes, and thin soft hair of dull brown, and soft trembling lips. She was not forcible or energetic; she pottered about the house a good deal, and had headaches, and went punctually to sewing circles. Her literary tastes were not violent; she was fond of Tupper and the *Lady's Book*, and every day she read a chapter of the Bible, and tried with all her simple heart to be good. But she had not much vitality in body or soul; and after her father, who had always been her tender companion and guide, left her to herself, Lucy was dreadfully lonely. The squire left her money well tied up, but she had all the income, and the principal was also well invested. Here was another opening for S. Paine.

"It really seems providential," he said to himself, as he carefully sanded the last barrel of sugar, having first filled his own jar; for since he had taken the store he had lived in the two rooms above it, taken care of his own wants himself, and hired Widow Bliss one day in the week to do his washing, ironing, and mending, all of which must be achieved within those twelve hours, or her dollar (according to agreement) was forfeited. "Yes, it does seem to be a leadin'. She can't sell that house; there ain't nobody in Bassett wants to buy a house, an' it's really handy to the store. I can put Widder Bliss up stairs, an' then John won't lose no time a-comin' an' a-goin' to his meals; he'll be real handy to his work, an' I can stop the rent out o' his wages, so's to be sure on't. Guess I won't move them law books yet. Things seems to be gittin' inter shape somehow. I'll fetch round there tomorrow night if I'm spared, an' visit with her a little." And covering up the sugar carefully; Samuel Paine took himself off to bed.

Poor Lucy was lonely, and Mr. Paine made himself agreeable. He condoled with her in good set terms—quoted Scripture, and threw in verses of Dr. Watts in an appropriate manner; blew his nose sonorously when Lucy cried a little, and thereby produced in her innocent mind the impression that he was crying too. And after he had cheered her up a little with tender exhortations not to give way too much to her feelings, to remember that man was made to mourn, that every body must die some time or other, and that no doubt Squire Larkin (or rather "our dear departed friend") enjoyed the "hallelooyers" of heaven much better than his daughter's society and keeping post-office, with other appropriate remarks of the same kind, he bade her goodnight, tenderly squeezing her hand as he left, and causing the poor little woman to feel lonely, and to wish he would come back.

Ah! why do we try to comfort those whom death has bereft? Why do we go over these vain conventionalisms which we know are futile? Can words like these bring back the smile, the voice, the touch, for which we hunger with maddening eagerness? Can it help us in our hopeless longing to know that others suffer the same vital anguish? That to die is the sure fate of all we love, sooner or later? Or that we must submit to these solitudes and cryings and strong tears because we can not help ourselves? No! Ten thousand times no! There is but one consolation of real virtue, and that is the closer clinging of the soul to Him who can not die. The rings that clasped these broken supports must close on higher branches, even on the Tree of Life; and if human love takes us in its tender arms and silently kisses away our tears, it may bring us still nearer to the Divine; for if we so love one another, shall not God, who made us, love us eternally and infinitely? But Lucy Larkin was one of the bending sort of women who never break under any blow. She went her placid way about the world she knew, did all her tranquil duties, and prayed hard to be resigned. It made resignation easier to have Mr. Paine come in once or twice a week; and when, after a decent interval, he proposed to fill the vacant place in her heart, the little smitten plant rose up meekly and accepted the pallid sunshine with gentle surprise and content. She was so glad not to be lonely any more, and so astonished that such a smart, pious man as Samuel Paine should have thought to make her an offer—"she that wasn't talented, nor good-lookin', nor real young."

Unworldly little soul! her twenty thousand dollars were more to this "smart" man than the beauty of Helen, the gifts of Sappho, or the divine sparkle and freshness of ideal girlhood; but she never guessed it. So, they were married just a year after her father's death. Mrs. Bliss was installed into the tenement over the store, and Squire Larkin's handsome old house being freshened up with paint and set in thorough order, though without any expense of new furnishings, seemed to renew its youth. Perhaps when Mrs. Paine learned to know her husband better, she did not experience all that superhuman bliss which poets and romancers depict as the result of matrimony; but then who does? Most of us learn to be content if we can rub along easily with our life partners, and cultivate a judicious blindness and deafness, in the wise spirit of good old Bishop Ken's well-known hymn:

> "O that mine eyes might closed be
> To what becomes me not to see;
> That deafness might possess mine ear
> To what becomes me not to hear!"

Lucy was not consciously so wise as this; but she had the greatest respect for her husband's piety and smartness, and if she could not understand certain of his manners and customs, she still thought a man could not err who made such long and fervent prayers at family devotions, and who always had the golden rule on his lips as a professed rule of life. She was not naturally demonstrative; few New England women are. If they were as afraid of being angry, or cross, or peevish before people as they are of being affectionate and tender, life would be mightily sweetened to many of us; but when our sour but sublime old Puritan fathers made it a legal offense for a man to kiss his wife on Sunday, what wonder that their descendants' teeth should be set on edge?

But if Mrs. Paine was not caressing and affectionate in manner, Mr. Paine was still less so; if he had any heart beside the muscular organ of that name, he had it yet to discover; certainly Lucy had not awakened it any more than his last investment in groceries. Things went on very calmly with the pair for a year or two; the only disturbance being a sudden and unreasonable crying fit of Lucy's, in which Mr. Paine detected her, coming home on an errand quite unexpectedly.

"I ca-ca-can't help it!" she sobbed, hysterically, when he sternly demanded,

"What on airth's the matter with ye, Loocy? Stop, now, right off—stop, I tell ye, an' speak up."

"Oh, o-h, o-h, husband! Miss Nancy Tuttle's been here; she's been a-talkin' awful. She said she considered 'twas her dooty to come an' deal with me, becoz—becoz—oh, o-h, o-h!"

"Stop it, now, thunderin' quick, Loocy! I can't stan' here all day."

"O-h! She said she heard a lot of talk against you, husband, an' she thought I'd ought to know it, so's't I could use my influence with you, an' kinder persuade you to do different."

A grim smile twisted S. Paine's stiff lips: Lucy's influence with him, indeed!

"Well, well," said he, "go ahead; let's hear what I've been a-doin'."

"Oh, oh dear! She said you sanded the sugar down to the store, an' put water into the sperrits, an' asked folks two prices for butter. Oh dear! I never was so beat in all my days."

"H-m," growled Mr. Paine. "I'll settle with her myself, Loocy!"

"Oh, you can't, you can't noways. She's gone off in the stage to York State to live. She said she felt as though she must free her mind before she went, so she jest stepped in."

"Darn her!"

Luckily for Lucy, she was sobbing so hard she did not hear this expletive, which had all the force of a stronger oath, coming from those decorous lips, yet was not quite open profanity.

"Look a-here, Loocy," Mr. Paine began. "Jest you shut your head about that scandalous old maid's talk. Hain't I told ye time an' agin that the sperrit an' principle o' the golden rewl was my sperrit an' principle? What's the harm ef I sell poor folks butter a leetle mite cheaper'n I sell it to folks with means? An' ef I put a pint o' water inter 'Bijah Jones's rum jug, I do't out o' consideration for his family; he can't afford to buy clear sperrit. As for shoogar, it's sanded afore it comes to me, you better believe! Now don't ye go a-tellin' every body all these lies; they grow every time they're sot out in fresh ground. There ain't nothin' so good for a fool's talk nor a liar's as a hull-some lettin' alone." With which piece of verbal wisdom Samuel Paine went his way, and Lucy subsided to her customary and domestic meekness.

But the current of their lives was mightily disturbed some months after this conversation by the advent into the quiet household of a big obstreperous baby. Lucy was blessed for once in her life to the very overflowing of her torpid heart. Mr. Paine would have been better pleased with a boy, to take the store and the post-office after him; but still he was pleased. An odd stir of feeling astonished him when he saw the helpless little creature, and with natural forecast he reflected that there might be a boy yet, and so forgave her for being only a girl. However, when years slipped by and no boy came, the sturdy, bright, merry little girl made her way boldly into her father's good graces and almost reconciled him to her sex. Miss Louise ruled her mother, of course—that was in the nature of things; but all the village looked on in wonder to see the mastery she achieved over Samuel Paine, or, as he was now called—partly because of the legal information he had acquired, and on a pinch dispensed, from his father-in-law's library, and partly because he had well stepped into that gentleman's shoes otherwise—Squire Paine.

Louise was an unaccountable offshoot from the parental tree, certainly. Her vivid complexion, waving dark hair, brilliant brown eyes, and well-made figure were not more at variance with the aspects of her father and mother than her merry, honest, and fearless nature was with their dispositions. Neither of them tried to govern her, after a few futile attempts. Her mother did not see any need of it. To her the child was perfect—a gift from God, held in fear and trembling lest He should recall it from mortal idolatry, but being such a gift, to be entertained as an angel. Squire Paine never held any such nonsensical idea as this; but if he undertook to scold or reprove mademoiselle, she instantly sprang into his arms, wound her fat hands in his coat collar, and snuggled her curly head against his lips with a laugh like a bobolink's, and, utterly routed, the squire would lift her to his shoulder and march her off to the store, to range among raisin boxes, sugar barrels, and candy jars to her heart's content, feeling all the while half ashamed of the unwonted warmth in his breast, the difficulty of speech, the soft cowardice that carried him away captive, bound to the chariot of this small conqueror, who was gracious enough not to triumph only because she conquered unconsciously.

So matters went on year after year. In spite of sweets and spoiling, Louise grew up strong and healthy, thanks to the open air in which it was her royal pleasure to live and move and have her being. A city mother would have wept over the brown complexion, in which living crimson burned with a warm splendor unknown to milk and roses, and any boarding-school phalanx would have shuddered at the well-tanned slender hands that were so deft at nutting, fishing, picking berries, and digging roots. But Bassett people were not fine. They only laughed and nodded, as Louise tore down the wide street on the squire's ancient horse, lashed to a horrid gallop by an old trunk strap whanged about his sides, and the thumps of stout country boots when he dared relax this spirited pace.

By-and-by Lucy, quite ashamed of herself in all these years of mild motherly bliss to think she had never given her husband a son, began to fade and fail a little, and at last declined into her grave as gently as a late spring snow-drift melts into the brown grasses. Louise was fifteen now, and knew no more about housekeeping than a deer in the forest, though successive seasons at the academy had given her a fair education for a country girl who did not need or intend to teach for her living. She mourned for her dear patient little mother far more than she missed her, for Lucy was too inert, too characterless, to leave a wide vacancy in her home. There are some people whose departure takes the sunshine of our days, the salt of our food, the flavor of our pleasures, yea, the breath of our lives, away with them; whose loss is a wound never to be healed, always bleeding, smarting, burning into our very souls, till time shall be no more. And there are others whose death, after the first natural burst of feeling, fails to impress itself deeply even on their nearest and dearest; the selfish, the exacting, the tasteless, timid natures that were scarce more than vegetable in their humanity—these are lightly mourned; and of these last was Lucy Paine.

It became necessary, it is true, to pay a housekeeper in her place, for the "hired girl" whom Squire Paine had unwillingly consented to install in the kitchen when his wife's strength began to fail could not be trusted to manage the household; so Mr. Paine bethought himself a second cousin living in a small village up the country, of whom he had now and then heard incidentally, and happened to know was still unmarried and pursuing her trade of tailoress about Hermon and the vicinity. So he wrote to Miss Roxy Keep to come down at once to Bassett and see him, as Hermon was too far for him to go, taking time from his business, and her answer was as business-like as could be desired. She could not, she said, afford a journey to Bassett unless it resulted in some purpose of good; if Squire Paine wanted to see her enough to pay her fare one way, she was willing to "risk" the other half. This curt and thrifty note rather pleased the squire, for though he did not want to risk his money any more than Miss Roxy, still he thought her proposition showed her to be of his own frugal and forehanded sort, and he at once closed with those terms.

It might be a curious matter of investigation to note the influence different occupations have upon those who pursue them. Why is it that a tailoress was always incisive, practical, full of resource, acute, fearless, and even snappy? Did any body ever see a meek woman useful with cloth and shears? Do the masculine habiliments which she fashions impart a virile vigor, and the implements of her trade a man-like strength, to the mind which plans and the hand which wields them? But we have no time for inductive science here. When Squire Paine met Roxy Keep at the door, he was at once struck by her compact aspect and entire self-possession. Her gown of dark homemade gingham and thick plaid shawl were simply the most useful garments that could be. Beauty did not excuse their being, much less that of the severe Leghorn bonnet, without flower or feather, tied down under her chin with a sturdy greenish ribbon that must have been her grandmother's. But over all these the sensible face, the keen dark eyes, firm mouth, and dominant nose forbade any idea of ridicule or contempt to be associated with Miss Roxy, whatever she chose to wear. The squire was as urbane as he knew how to be.

"Set down, Cousin Roxy, set down. I'll take ye over to the house in a minnit. I've had to put in a new clerk, ye see. John Bliss he tho't he could do better in the city, so he up an' left me sudden—too sudden, re'lly, considerin' him an' me hed ben together so long; an' now 'Lisha Squires has took his place. 'Lisha's a likely young man, for what I know—well eddicated; father's a minister o' the Gospel; got run down a-preachin'; his wife had means—not much, not much, but 'nough to buy a farm; so they traded with me for th' old humstead, an' he's a-farmin' on't, an' 'Lisha he's gi'n up goin' to college, an' took John Bliss's place here. He's ruther high-strung, to be sure, but he's smart, real smart, an' I don't know as I could ha' did better. He's a-onheadin' some barr'ls now. A-h! there he is."

And a handsome young fellow, grave and sad beyond his years, came up from the cellar with a hatchet in his hand. Miss Roxy's keen eyes read that open face at once. She felt the purest pity for the misplaced boy, whose education was wasted and his nature disgusted by the repellent character of his duties as well as his employer. Elisha was indeed misplaced; but he was, in his daily way, a hero, and to be heroic in the petty drudgery of a distasteful life is a thousand times harder than to win splendid battles. He had given up everything to help his feeble father and his six sisters; so had his mother; and neither of them looked upon their sacrifices as more than a matter of course, which, perhaps, was the one touch superior even to heroism.

But Miss Roxy, used to that sort of intercourse with many, perhaps most, of the families in her neighborhood which is attributed to the proverbial *valet de chambre*, was yet so much more perceptive than that stupid French man-servant that she knew a hero even in a country store; and she turned away with the squire carrying in her heart a fund of admiration and good-will that was to stand Elisha in stead at a future time of need.

In the library of Squire Larkin's time the next hour was spent by Samuel Paine and Roxy Keep in a passage of arms. He was determined to secure Roxy to manage his establishment on his own terms; and she was willing to be secured, but it must be on her terms, and being a tailoress, she carried the day. In consideration of the little home she left in Hermon and the lucrative trade she left, she required of the squire a written guarantee that her services should continue for two years in any case, subject only to her own change of mind, that her salary should be paid quarterly, under pain of her immediate departure if it failed to come to hand, and that the aforesaid salary should be a sufficient equivalent for the trade she gave up. After much conversation the squire yielded all these points, though with no good grace.

"Well, now I've gi'n up to ye," said he, "I'd like to know how soon ye can come, Roxy. Things is a-goin' every which way here. Lowisy's a good girl—she's a good enough girl, but she ain't nothing but a girl, an' she ain't no more fit to run a house 'n she is to preach a sermon; so I'd like ye to come back's quick as ye can."

"I dono's I need to go," curtly and promptly answered Miss Roxy. "I reckoned I should stay when I come, so I sold out my house to Deacon Treadwell's widder, an' I fetched my trunks along; they're over to Reading depot, and the stage-driver he'll take the checks to-morrer and fetch 'em back. I don't never let no grass grow under *my* feet, Squire Paine."

"Land alive! I should think not!" ejaculated the astonished squire. So Miss Roxy staid, and the house was stirred up from beneath to meet her. Bridget gave notice just in time not to have it given to her, and brush in hand, the fiercest of bandana handkerchiefs tied over her crisp black hair, Miss Roxy began that awful "setting to rights" which is at once the privilege and the necessity of strenuous souls like hers. At first Louise was half inclined to rebel: the slipshod family rule—or misrule—had just suited her youthful carelessness; but Miss Roxy's keen humor, pleasant common-sense, and comfortable efficiency soon enlisted Louise on her side, and the girl could not help enjoying the bright order, the speckless comfort, the savory meals, the thrift that was not meanness, and the frugality that could be discreetly generous which followed Miss Roxy's reign, and at the end of two years the squire was glad enough to renew the guarantee which this foreseeing woman still demanded of him. Well for her, well for all of them, was it that he did so sign!

In the mean time Squire Paine had gone his way, buying and selling and talking much about the "golden rewl," and many small tiffs had ensued between him and Miss Roxy on points of domestic economy; but the squire knew, if he had never read, that discretion is the better part of valor, and considering just in time that housekeeping was not his forte, and was Miss Roxy's, he always beat a retreat after these battles, and not always with flying colors. But now, toward the beginning of this third year, there began to be trouble in the camp. Elisha Squires, in common with various other youths of Bassett, had found out that Louise Paine was charming above all other girls of the vicinity, and the squire's house became a sort of besieged castle, greatly to his disgust and indignation.

"I won't hev it! I won't hev it!" stormed he, one fine night, when the last of seven callers had gone from the front-door, and Louise judiciously slipped off to bed.

"Won't hev what?" calmly inquired Roxy, who sat by the "keeping room" table, toeing off a stocking.

"Why, I won't hev so many fellers a-comin' here the hull eternal time. There ain't no use on't, an' I tell ye I won't hev it. I won't, as sure's ye live."

"What be you goin' to do about it?" was Roxy's cool rejoinder.

"I'll lock the doors."

"Then they'll come into the back winder," smiled the exasperating spinster. "Look here, Squire Paine," and she laid down her knitting, and confronted him as one who

"Drinks delight of battle with his peers,"

"you're a master-hand to talk about the golden rewl; how'd you ha' liked it ef Squire Larkin had locked the door to this house on you?"

"He hadn't no call to; he was dead."

"Now don't jump no fences that way; s'pose he'd ben alive?"

"I dono's I'm called to tell ye. I'm a professor in good an' reg'lar standin', an' the golden rewl hes allers ben my standard o' livin', an' the sperrit an' principle o' the golden rewl is to do to others as you'd wish to be done by; an' ef I was a gal I should be glad to hev the doors locked on a passel o' fellers that come foolin' around nights."

"You're life-everlastin' sure o' that, be ye?" was the dry rejoinder.

"Well, ef she ain't, she'd orter be; an' I'm free to conclude that Lowisy doos what she'd outer, bein' my child—an' her ma's."

"I don't believe no great in hinderin' young folks's ways, Squire Paine; it's three wheels to a wagon to be young, an' hinderin' don't overset nothin'; it's more apt to set it, a long sight. Don't you never expect Lowisy to git married?"

"I dono's I do, an' I dono as I don't. Married life is an onsartin state. Mebbe Lowisy'd be better off to stay to hum with me. Anyway, there ain't no sech hurry; 'tain't the best goods go off the fust; an' I tell ye what, Roxy, I do expect she'll hark to me about who she marries, and not go an' git tied up to some poor Jack."

"Then I tell *you* what, Samwell Paine, you expect nothin' an' you'll sup sorrow! Girls will pick out their own husbands to the day after never, for all you! I always hold that there's two things a woman had oughter pick out for herself, spite o' fate, and them two is her husband an' her carpets."

"An' I expect to pick 'em both out for Lowisy," answered the undaunted squire, as he marched off to bed, holding his tallow candle askew, and dropping hot tears—of tallow—as he went.

But as fate, or Louise, would have it, Squire Paine was not to pick out either of these essentials for his daughter; she was fast drifting into that obstinate blessedness which is reserved for youth and love, which laughs at parents and guardians, defies time and circumstance, and too often blinds the brightest eyes, and brings the most fastidious hands to

"Wreathe thy fair large ears, my gentle joy,"

and finds out too late it is Botton, the weaver.

In Louise's case, however, there was no danger of such waking: she had good reason for her preference. Elisha Squires, her father's clerk, was a handsome, well-educated, energetic young fellow—a gentleman by nature and breeding both. Louise had pitied him ten thousand times for his unfit position in her father's employment before he perceived that she was interested the least in him or his occupation, and when it dawned on the busy and weary soul that one bright blossom looked over the paling into his desert life, what was the natural impulse that followed? It is not a young man who "loves the wild rose and leaves it on its stalk," literally or figuratively, and these juvenile idiots fell fathoms deep in love with each other, entirely unconscious of the melancholy fact that one was the richest girl in Bassett, and the other working for daily bread. Arcadia could not have shown more divine simplicity; but Bassett was not Arcadia, and when sundry jealous and disappointed swains discovered the "Lowisy Paine" would go home from prayer meetings with 'Lisha Squires, had actually been seen lingering with him at her father's front gate in the starry May darkness even after the nine-o'clock bell had rung, and was sure to welcome him on a Sunday night, though she might snap and snarl at them, then Louise's troubles began. Prayer meetings must be attended, but the squire went to and from with her himself, and Elisha could not be spared from the store to attend them at all. Squire Paine hated to lose his clerk, but he would not lose his daughter, so, with the obtuse perception of the heavy father from time immemorial, he rushed into the *milee*, like some floundering elephant into a flower bed.

"Lowisy," said he, one Sunday night, after the row of adorers were dispersed, Elisha Squires among them, "hear to me now! I ain't a-goin' to hev you courted the hull time by these here fellers. You've got to stop it. 'Specially I won't have ye careerin' around with 'Lisha; he's poorer 'n poverty, an' as stuck up as though he was mighty Caesar. I've fetched ye up an' gi'n ye a good eddication, an' you ain't a-goin' to throw yourself away on no sech trash."

The hot color rushed up to Louise's forehead, her red lip curled, and unspeakable disdain expressed itself, as she looked straight into her father's face; but she did not say a word; she left the room with perfect composure, stopping to pick a dry leaf from her pet geranium, and walked up the stairs with a slow precision that ought to have spoken volumes to her father's ear, as it did to Roxy's.

"Well, you've done it now," remarked that respectable woman.

"Yes, I guess I hev," was the squire's complacent answer, quite misapprehending the sense in which he had done it. "I guess I've put a spoke inter that wheel, an' sideways too."

Roxy gave one of the silent chuckles which meant deep amusement, and took herself off to bed. She was not a woman to interfere with the course of true love between Louise and Elisha, both of whom had become special favorites of hers since their first acquaintance; but, as she said to herself, she would not "make nor meddle" in this matter, having full confidence in Louise's power of managing her own affairs, and far too much reverence and delicacy in her own nature to be a match-maker. But the squire went on from bad to worse, and, in his blind zeal to have his own way, brought things to a swift conclusion; for having given Elisha notice that he should need him no longer, he was more than surprised one fine July morning to find that Louise had left him too—that the pair had gone together. The squire was black with rage when the fact was announced to him by Miss Roxy, and a brief and defiant note from Louise put into his hand. He raved, raged, even swore, in his first wild fury, and paced up and down the kitchen like a wild animal.

Miss Roxy eyed him with a peculiar expression. She felt that her hour had come. As she afterward said, "I'd ben a-hankerin' to give it to him quite a spell, but I held my tongue for Lowisy's sake. But thinks, sez I, now's your time, Roxanny Keep; pitch in an' do your dooty, an' I tell ye it whistled of itself. Seemed as though 'twa'n't me, r'ally, but somethin' makin' a tin horn out o' my lips to rouse him up to judgment." And certainly Miss Roxy was roused herself; she confronted the squire like a Yankee lioness.

"Look a-here, Samwell Paine: it's time somebody took ye to do. You've ben a-buyin' an' a-sellin' an' a-rakin' an' a-scrapin' till your soul—ef you've got any—is nigh about petered out. You call yourself a Christian an' a professor, an' a follerer of the golden rewl, do ye? An' here you be, cussin' an' swearin' like a Hivite an' a Jeboosite an' all the rest on 'em, because things ain't jest as you would have 'em to be. You hain't had no bowels of compassion for Lowisy no more'n ef you was her jailer instead of her pa. What's the matter with 'Lisha Squires? He's a honest, good-disposed, reliable feller as ever was; good enough for any body's girl; a Christian too—not one o' the sugar-sandin', rum-waterin', light-weight kind, but a real one. He don't read the golden rewl t'other side up, as you do, I tell ye. You make it doin' to other folks just what you want to do, an' lettin' them go hang. I tell ye the hypocrite's hope shall perish; an' you're one on 'em as sure as the world. 'Tain't sayin' Lord! Lord! That Makes folks pious; it's doin' the will o' God—justice an' mercy an' loving-kindness."

Here Roxy paused for breath, and the astounded squire ejaculated, "Roxanny Keep!"

"Yes, that's my name; I ain't afeard to own it, nor to set it square to what I've said. I hain't lived here goin' on three year an' seen your ways for nothin'. I've had eyes to behold your pinchin' an' sparin' an' crawlin'; grindin' poor folks's faces an' lickin' rich folks's platters; actin' as though your own daughter was nothin' but a bill of expense to ye, an' a block to show off your pride an' vanity, not a livin', lovin' soul to show the way to heaven to. An' now she's quit. She's got a good, lovin', true-hearted feller to help her along where you didn't know the way, an' didn't want to, neither, an' you're ravin' mad 'cause he hain't got no money, when you've got more'n enough for all on ye. Samwell Paine, you ain't no Christian, not 'cordin' to Gospel truth, ef you have been a professor nigh on to forty year. You no need to think you was converted, for you never was. Folks ain't converted to meanness an' greediness an' self-seekin' an' wrath an' malice: the Lord don't turn 'em into the error of their ways; He turns 'em out on't. Ef you was a minister in the pulpit or a deacon handin' the plate, you ain't no Christian 'thout you act like one, an' that's the etarnal fact on't. You've ben a livin' lie all these years, an' you've ended by drivin' your only daughter, your own flesh an' blood, the best thing the Lord ever give ye, out o' house an' home 'cause you was mad after money. An' it'll happen unto ye accordin' to the Word o' the Lord about sech folks: you'll be drownded in destruction an' perdition, an' pierce yourself through with many sorrers, ef you don't flee for your life from sech things, and foller after righteousness, godliness, an' the rest on 'em. You'd oughter go down on your poor old knees an' pray to be converted at the 'leventh hour. There! I've freed my mind, thank the Lord, an' there won't be none o' your blood found on my skirts ef the last day comes in tomorrer mornin'!" With which the exhausted lecturer heaved a long breath, and began to mop her heated face vigorously with her inseparable bandana handkerchief, which might have symbolized to the audience, had there been any, a homely victorious banner.

The squire stood amazed and afraid. In all the long course of his life nobody had ever before gainsaid him; outward respect and consideration had been his portion; now the ground cracked under his feet, and he found himself in a new land. He did not go to the store that day; he stumbled out of Roxy's sight, and shut himself up in the unused parlor, where alternate storms of rage, conviction, despair, and scorn assailed him for many hours. It was, indeed, a dreadful battle that he fought in the musty silence of that darkened room, pacing up and down like a caged tiger. Roxy had spoken awful words, but they were milk and honey compared to the echo which his late-awakened conscience gave them; still he fought with a certain savage courage against the truths that were toppling over to crush him, and justified himself to his own accusing soul with a persistent hardihood that had better served a better cause. It was reserved for God's own strike to bring sweet waters out of this rock; Moses and the rod had smitten it in vain. Just as his courage seemed to aid him, and he had resolved to send Roxy back to Hermon and her tailoring, and brave out the judgment of his fellow-men and the desertion of Louisa—nay, more, to revenge himself for that desertion by refusing her aid or comfort, or even recognition of any kind—just then, as he had settled down into his self-complacency and willful disregard for God's own words, pelted at him as they had been by Roxy, he heard an outer door open, invading steps, voices of low tumult, a sort of whispering horror and stifled grief drawing nearer to his retreat, and the door opened very slowly, disclosing the stern features of Parson Peters, the village minister. Not altogether stern now was that long and meager visage: a sort of terror mingled with pity softened its rigid lines.

"My brother," he said, lifting one hand, as he was wont to do when praying over a coffin, and facing the troubled and inflamed countenance of Squire Paine—"my brother, the hand of the Lord is upon you this day. Your child has been taken; there has been a terrible accident to the train by which they left Reading station, and news has come that both are—gone."

Like a forest tree into which the wood-man sets his last stroke, the squire tottered, paused for one instant of time, and fell forward prostrate.

Roxy was behind Parson Peters as the old man fell, and pushing that eminent divine out of her way like a spider, she was at once on her knees by his side, promptly administering the proper remedies. It was only a fainting fit, but, when the squire recovered, he was weak, humble, and gentle as a little child. He lay on the sofa in the parlor all day; the unused windows were opened, and the sweet summer air flowed in and out with scents of late roses and new hay on its delicate wings, but Squire Paine did not notice it. He took the broth Roxy brought him without a complaint, and actually thanked her for it. She herself guarded the outside door like a dragon, and even refused admittance to Parson Peters.

"No," said she; "it's good to let him be today. I tell ye the Lord's a-dealin' with the poor old creter, an' we hadn't ought to meddle. Human nater is everlastin' queer, an' there is some folks nobody can tune so well as Him that made 'em. He'll take up his bed an' walk as soon as the meracle works, an' we can't hurry it up any, but I've faith to believe it's a-workin.'"

And it was according to Roxy's faith. As soon as the sun went down the squire rose up, ate what was set before him, put his disordered dress to rights, and walked feebly over to the weekly prayer meeting—for these things happened of a Thursday.

The lights in the little school-house were dim and few, for the night's warm atmosphere made even the heat of the two necessary lamps oppressive, but Squire Paine took no advantage of this darkness, though the room was unusually full. He walked to the very front bench, and seated himself before the deacon who conducted the meeting and as soon as the opening hymn was sung, he waved the good man who was about to follow with a prayer aside with a certain rugged dignity, and rose, facing the assembly, and beginning with broken voice to speak.

"Brethring," he said, "I come here tonight to make a confession. I've lived amongst you for sixty odd year, man an' boy, an' the last forty on 'em I've ben a livin' lie. Brethring, I hev ben a professor in this here church all that time, an' I wa'n't never converted. I was a real stiddy-goin' hypocrite, an' I hain't but jest found it out. The merciful Lord has kinder spared me for a day of repentance, an' it's come—I tell ye, it's come! There was one that dealt with me mightily, an' shook me some; one I may say, that drilled the hole, an' put in the powder of the Word, an' tamped it down with pretty stiff facts; but it didn't do no good. I was jest like a rock bored an' charged, but pooty rugged an' hard yet; but brethring, THE LORD HAS FIRED THE BLAST HIMSELF, an' the nateral man is broken to pieces. I give up right here. The Lord is good. God be merciful to me a sinner! Brethring, can't you pray?"

There was but one answer to the pathetic agony of that appeal. Deacon Adkins rose and prayed as if his lips had been touched with a coal from the altar, and there were sympathetic tears in the hardest eyes there before he finished, while Squire Paine's low sobs were heard at intervals as if they were the very convulsions of a breaking heart.

"Let us sing

"Praise God, from whom all blessings flow,"

said the deacon, after his prayer was over; and when the last line of that noble doxology floated away into the rafters, they all gathered round to shake hands and express their deep sympathy with the repentant and bereaved father. It was almost too much for Squire Paine; the breaking up of the great deep within had worn upon him exceedingly; humbled, sad, yet wonderfully peaceful as his spirit felt, still the flesh trembled and was weak. He was glad when Roxy came up and, taking hold of his arm, led him homeward.

Was he glad or death-smitten, or, as he thought, suddenly in the heavenly places, when his own door opened before his hand touched the latch, and Louise, darting forward, threw her arms about his neck?

"Land o' liberty!" shrieked Roxy. "Do you want to kill your pa outright? An' how came ye here anyway? We heered you an' him was both stun-dead?"

Roxy's curt and curious interposition seemed to restore the equilibrium suddenly. Squire Paine did not faint, and Louise actually laughed. Here was something natural and homely to shelter in after the dream-like agitation of the day.

"No," said Louise's clear voice, "we wa'n't hurt, not much— only stunned and scared a bit. But there was two in the next seat who—well, *they* won't come home to their folks, Aunt Roxy. We thought maybe you would be anxious, and then somebody said, right before us, that we were both killed, and they'd sent the news over to Bassett; so we thought the best thing to do was to come back and show ourselves. Here's 'Lisha."

Squire Paine must have been converted, for he shook his son- in-law's hand with all goodwill, and kissed his daughter heartily. His voice was somewhat weak and husky, but he managed to say, so as to be heard, "An' now ye've got home re'lly, you've got to stay home. I sha'n't hev no more sech risks run. And, 'Lisha, we'll open the store real early tomorrer. I dono when it's ben shut twenty-four hours before."

This was all he said: for the New England man, saint or sinner, has few words when feeling strongest; but the squire's actions spoke for him. He never referred to the past, but strove with his might to live a new and righteous life. Not all at once the granite gave place to gold; there were roots of bitterness and strivings of the old Adam, many and often, but none who had once known him doubted that Squire Paine was a changed man. At his own earnest request he was allowed to make a new profession of religion; and after relating his experiences in due form to the assembled deacons, he wound up the recital in this fashion: "It was the Lord's hand done it fin'lly, brethring; but, next to Him, I owe this here real conversion to Roxanny Keep."

"Halleloojah!" exclaimed Aunt Roxy, when Mrs. Deacon Adkins betrayed her good husband's confidence far enough to tell her this. "I tell ye, Miss Adkins, I took my life in my hand that mornin', but I felt a call to do it. Ye know, David killed Goliath with a pebble, nothin' more; an' I allers could sling straight."

Sarah Johnson Prichard

(1830–1909)

Truly, Sarah Johnson Prichard is one of the nineteenth–century New England writers that has been lost to twentieth–century readers. Other than what can be gleaned from biographical dictionaries, scant information is available. However, information that is available portrays an accomplished woman.

Born January 11, 1830, in Waterbury, Connecticut, to Elizur Edwin and Betsey Jeanette Cooper Prichard, her descendants can be traced back eight generations. Like many of the women writers in this collection, Prichard was well educated for her time. At an early age, she became a student at the Waterbury Academy. From 1846 to 1847 she attended Dwight Place Seminary in New Haven, Connecticut. In 1849, she graduated from Mrs. Emma Willard's Seminary in Troy, New York.

Following her graduation at age nineteen, she devoted herself to writing and historical research. She began writing and publishing in the 1850s and continued until the last decade of the nineteenth century. Over the course of fifty years, she wrote numerous articles and stories for magazines as well as more than a dozen books. Her titles include: *Martha's Hooks and Eyes* (1858), *Kate Morgan and Her Soldiers* (1862), *Rose Marbury* (1870), *Aunt Sadie's Cow* (1872), and *The Only Woman in the Town, and Other Tales of the American Revolution* (1898). Prichard died in 1909.

"On Sand Island," Prichard's story included in this collection, was originally published in the May 1877 issue of *The Atlantic Monthly*. Prichard knew well her New England area and writes realistically of the sea, the lonely lives of women, and the changing economic times. Her portrayal of the two worlds—the life and activity of the men whose livelihood is connected with the sea and the lonely world of those loved ones back home—reminds one of Harriet Beecher Stowe's *The Pearl of Orr's Island* published in 1862.

Selected Primary Works

Martha's Hooks and Eyes, 1858; *Hugh's Fire on the Mountain,* 1861; *The Old Stone Chimney,* 1865; *Margie's Matches,* 1866; *Faye Mar of Stone Cliff,* 1868; *Rose Marbury,* 1870; *Aunt Sadie's Cow,* 1872; *The Only Woman in the Town, and Other Tales of the American Revolution,* 1898.

"On Sand Island"

The Atlantic Monthly, May 1877

The island itself is only one mile long, while in width it is always more or less, the ocean giving it new measure storm by storm and tide by tide.

On the island are two houses, the one with its face to the southwest, the other looking toward the east, and occupying positions as far, the one from the other, as the limits of sand permit. A ridge of rocks rises from the sea near either house, suggesting the possibility of the building site having been chosen with reference to something firm. All else on the island is sand and its belongings. Between the two houses, in very high storms, the ocean on the north shakes hands with the ocean on the south, gripping the sands in their grinding palms, and giving small promise of letting go while a grain remains to be shaken.

In one of the two houses lived, sixteen months ago, John Ware and his wife Nancy. In the other house lived Dick Dixon, his wife, and their children.

A little more than sixteen months ago, one afternoon in May, John Ware and his wife left the mainland in a small rowboat to go and look at the house on the southwest of the island.

"We'll live here this summer," said John, after they had looked at the one-roomed dwelling, "because it will be so handy to run my boat in at night; and then by the fall we'll have money enough to go and live like folks."

"I wonder why the windows are only on one side of the house," said Nancy. "To see the land, one must go outdoors."

"I s'pose it was a queer old fellow that built it; like as not he didn't want to see the land, nohow," said John; and he said no more.

The next week, early in June, they moved. The day after the moving, John Ware sailed his boat, the Silver Thistle, up and down the coast after the fishing yacht Menhaden, in search of bony fish. In the afternoon sixty thousand fish were caught in the seine and put into the carry-away, which was John's boat.

It was near evening when, with a small lad to give him aid, he turned the Silver Thistle toward the mainland. On a point that stretched down oceanward a full mile stood a mill for the making of fish oil. When near the place, John gave signal from a horn to announce his approach. The fish were hoisted from the boat into a car, and drawn up the bit of wooden railway into the dark entrance to the great mill, where millions of fish disappeared, and from whence came thousands of gallons of oil.

John Ware's share of that sixty thousand fish was eight dollars. He went home with the good news. Nancy was waiting for him on the sands. "Eight dollars a day!" he said, boyishly. "Why, Nan, we'll be able to live quite like folks by fall, at this rate."

"I'm so glad," she said; "but there will be rainy days, and days when it blows too hard for you to go fishing, and my eight dollar days will come then."

"Lonely a'ready, hey?" with a gentle commiseration in his voice.

"It makes a long day with not a soul to speak to. Now that you have come, don't let's talk about it," she said.

"I'm going to the main after I've had my supper, Nan; but the twilight is long, and I'll be back afore it's gone."

"I'll go in the boat with you."

He hesitated in speaking, as he answered, "I'm sorry, Nan, but I'm going in the dingey tonight, and I've something to fetch back; there won't be room for you."

She was silent and grieved, and let him depart without going down the sand to see him off; but after he had gone she watched the boat as long as she could see its dim outline, as long as she could discern a dark speck in the distance.

The twilight lingered long that night, but it had been gone two hours when Nan heard a low cry. She listened a moment, then opened the door, and a white kitten rubbed itself in and purred about her feet.

Had it been a wild Indian, it would not have surprised her more. Outside, the wind was moving the ocean in an uncertain, desultory way; now a whiff from the south, then a puff from the west, and then a "dying away," to be followed by a brisk bit of air out of the north.

Nan took the kitten in her arms; she stroked it as she sat listening and wondering how the cat came to be there. Then she arose and went outside to keep her watch. The heavens above seemed very near to the low roof as she went, thinking, "It will be a rough sea soon, and John ought to be here before the wind blows much harder."

From what seemed to be a cloud, lying to the north and west, rays of flashing light went up toward the zenith. They lit up the troubled sea with a weird light, and made the very sands of the island instinct with strange life.

"I'm glad there's northern lights; it will help him home," she thought, and went down near the shore, the kitten in her arms. As she went, she saw something that made her draw breath quickly. It was her husband, and he was rolling up the sands a barrel of flour.

Laughing half at the momentary fear that held her, as she knew who it was, and half at the relief she felt in learning why he had not taken her with him in the boat, she dropped the kitten and ran to help him.

"I thought I'd fetch something home for you to speak to when I'm away," he said, "and even a kitten is better than nothing."

"A whole barrel of flour!" said Nan in surprise.

"Yes, why not? You set me a-thinking tonight about storms and so on, and I just made up my mind to have it on hand while the weather was just right. It isn't every night I'd feel willing to row over with a barrel of flour in that mite of a boat."

"I wish you had told me, John, what you were going for," she said, stooping to aid in rolling the barrel up the sands.

"I wanted to surprise you, Nan," was all that he said.

And that little "difference" was the only cloud that came into the fair sky of John and his wife that summer.

Every morning John Ware went to his work on the ocean; every day Nan worked and waited, and now and then, walked across the island to visit her neighbors, taking care to choose a time for her visiting when the tide should be low, for the sands were wet at high water.

Pleasure parties went sailing past her, sometimes, as she sat alone in her doorway, but there was nothing to tempt any one of them to land on the island. There was only sun and sand and a bit of a weather-brown house.

Nan gave the white kitten a name. She called it Comfort. It did comfort her, for it winked and mewed and purred in reply to the words and the fish she gave it.

John Ware worked hard, was happy, and did prosper amazingly. "A good load today, and I'll have my two hundred clear to keep us this winter," he said one morning, as he stepped into his small boat and pushed off to the Silver Thistle. He ran up the sail, looking at his wife as he made it fast. Nan had Comfort in her arms.

A breeze, with September in its every breath, blew down from the mainland. Mad little white caps chased each other far out to sea. The Silver Thistle danced on the short waves while the sail filled, and then the boat shot steadily away before the wind.

The fishing season was nearly over in that region, which was exposed to the full force of ocean waves, and the small boats were not built to weather heavy storms. Nan shivered as she turned away. "It's cold, Comfort," she said, "and we love warmth, don't we?"

Comfort purred, and lay still in her arms as she went in toward the house.

It was Monday. Nan began to wash, wishing that she had a larger pile of clothes than lay in the corner; the day would be so long and the September twilight would come so early. When she went outside to fasten up the clothesline, she saw the Silver Thistle, a distant speck of white, following the yacht Menhaden down the coast.

The wind was blowing harder and faster; the sand began to flutter in little rows across the island, and Nan's clothes whipped so on the line that she took them down shortly after she put them up. "If it was only from the other way the wind blew, I'd get one of my eight dollar days," she thought, "for 't would send the boats scudding in."

As the day deepened into noon, the wind suddenly veered. Presently the short seas changed to a long roll, then quickened and grew into breakers that boomed along the sands. Nan got down the spy-glass and looked across the ocean. Once she saw, or thought she saw, the Silver Thistle in the distance. "It's him," she said, "coming in at last! I see the patch that I put in, after the Menhaden's boom ran through the sail." Then she hastened to get all signs of suds and tubs out of sight, to make the one-roomed house look tidy for its master's coming.

Nan had been a mill girl from her very early childhood. She knew nothing of home until she had part and lot in this one. She was very grateful for it; gratitude, in her nature, arose to a height that love could not reach. Every moment the wind increased and the breakers grew. Nan made biscuit for tea, thinking, as she took the flour from the barrel, of the night when it came home, and how she had laughed at John the next morning for supposing they two would stay on the island long enough to eat a barrel of flour. "Why, it's two thirds gone a'ready, but the sea makes hungry," was the thought with which she opened the door of the oven in the stove and quickly thrust her pan of biscuit in.

"Now, I'll take another look out," she said. Comfort lay in John's easy-chair and blinked lazily as her mistress spoke. Nan put her eye to the glass, but, seeing nothing, rubbed the glass with her apron and looked again. A ship was sailing away on the distant horizon; only one! She scanned every mile that lay within sight. Then she thought that she must have been much longer than usual making the biscuit, and that the Silver Thistle had sailed round to the upper side of the island. She laughed softly as she remembered how simple she had been to suppose that John could anchor his boat on that side in such a blow. Nan was sorry and a good deal out of patience that the house had been built with all its windows (there were but two) on one side. She wanted to watch for her husband to come across the eddying sands, and it blew too hard to go out and wait. An hour went by. The biscuit had baked and browned and been taken from the oven. Supper was ready, but John was not come. Clouds had gathered. It was growing near to night.

Nan had run round the corner a dozen times within that hour, but had seen only the ridges of sand shifting and blowing and rising behind the house to a height that prevented sight of the coastline on the north.

"I must go up where I can see," she said, at last; never doubting for an instant but that, her battle through, the wind would yield to her vision the Silver Thistle at anchor, and her husband, somewhere.

Her feet sank in the sands; the wind swept her on with a force that bent her strong young figure. Two or three times she fell, tangled in the dense undergrowth that the sea had swept in. Half blinded by the blowing of her hair in her face, she reached the crest of the island and looked across the wide space that lay between it and the mainland. She could discern masts rocking in the distant harbor, but no trace of any boat, or sail, or man, nearer than the town up the coast.

"He's gone in, for fear of his boat," she thought, "and I must stay alone tonight. I'll hurry home before it gets dark;" and she faced the wind. It took away her breath and made her gasp and turn again to catch it. Boom! Boom! Boom! The breakers ran up the sands as she reached her door.

Comfort got up and yawned, and turning around three times lay down again as Nan went in.

"Pussy, pussy, my little comfort you are, tonight! Let me sit down!" she said, gathering up the furry creature and taking its place in the chair. The supper was cold when she ate of it, and she thought how lonely John would be, for he had grown to be a home-man that summer.

All the September night the waves tore in upon the sands of the island. Once or twice Nan, lying in her bed, felt a qualm like seasickness, as the poor little dwelling trembled with the force of the wind. "God bless the poor fellows on the sea tonight," murmured the woman, repeating the words over and over again with a vague feeling that men must be upon the ocean somewhere that night, and that they would need divine aid and friendliness. She quite forgot to pray for herself or for her husband, safe upon the firm mainland. Toward morning the wind lessened and the ocean lost its highest waves. As soon as the day dawned, the staunchest boat in the harbor up the coast put out to sea.

John Ware had, just before the wind changed on the previous day, taken into the Silver Thistle twenty thousand white fish. The lad who usually went with him was suffering from toothache. John was a good seaman; his load was light, and everything seemed fair for a good run to the factory; therefore the boy was left in the cabin of the Menhaden, and he started for the shore alone.

Darkness had fallen, and yet the fish had not been landed at the mill, and the Silver Thistle was not in the harbor. The men of the fishing gang to which John Ware belonged were in that staunch boat on their way to look for him.

"It's no use to look there," one said, with a nod of the head as they passed by the island.

"No, poor thing! She will know soon enough! Let her sleep while she may," said another. But Nan was on the rocks when the day came. She had gone up the few feet of sand to the height of the island and seen the boat put out. Knowing that it would pass the point of rocks, she was waiting there to hail it as the men went by.

Either they did not see her, or seeing her did not respond to the signal she gave. So she learned nothing of the Silver Thistle that morning.

At noonday Nan grew very restless; a vague feeling that something was wrong crept over her, holding every motive to life in check.

The sea could not answer her question. The Menhaden had not gone out as usual; for it she had kept steadfast watch. In her desire to speak to some one of the fear that bound her, she left her home and toiled through the sand to the house on the eastern end of the island. She found no one at home except two of the younger children. Their father and mother had "gone to the main," they said, "before it got so rough the day before, and they two had been alone all night." The children were so happy to see her, and were evidently so reluctant to stay alone, that Nan took them with her when she went back. As she drew near, the boat that had gone out at day break was sailing in toward the island.

The inevitable had come. With words that could not be misunderstood, the rough fishermen told the woman that her husband was lost. Nan could not receive the meaning of this thing that had come to her. She put forth all the resistance of a strong nature against a fact that could not be proved.

"Have you found the Silver Thistle?" she cried. "Till you find that *empty*, I will not believe you."

Poor soul! She seemed to feel that these men were active in forcing sorrow upon her, a sorrow that she could only drink in slowly. Nan was like the earth when it has been drying many days under the strong light and heat of the sun, and a sharp rain-fall descends with violence upon it. Her spirit shook off sorrow as the parched earth shakes off the rain.

"Well for her! Well for her that she will not believe all at once," said the fishermen, as they turned away from the island and went landward.

In a few days the place of the Silver Thistle was occupied by another boat, and at the end of September boats and men went southward, whither the fish had gone.

When Mrs. Ware went to the mill owner for money, she was told that her husband had, the day before he was lost, received all the money due to him. Nan doubted the statement, because John had always told her every particular relating to his money affairs, running to her as gleefully as a boy after a day of good luck on the sea, to tell her all about it.

With her sorrow and her doubt of the truth of the mill owner's statement and her poverty, Nan still stayed in the place that had been her home. She was waiting for something to happen,—for some proof that her husband was lost. For such indication she watched through all the bright October. With every tide that rose by day she walked up and down on the sands, gathering driftwood for her fire, but always looking for fragments of wreck from the farther shore.

Dick Dixon and his wife were kind to Nan in their way, but their way was for her to leave the house and go somewhere on the land; back to the cotton-mill; perhaps, where Nan had earned her bread before she came to her home. They urged this vehemently; they warned her that it would be in winter, and was even already, unsafe to remain there alone.

Nan listened to them with quiet patience, and thanked them, but remained in her one-roomed house at night, haunting the shore by day, until November came. The flour in the barrel was getting low; that with the fish she caught from the ledge of rock was the only food she had for Comfort and herself.

It was growing cold. The winds cut fiercely at times, as poor Nan gathered driftwood, scanning with breathless interest each fragment; she was so certain that she should know if anything came in from the Silver Thistle or the small boat.

One day in November, Mrs. Dixon appeared at Mrs. Ware's cottage just as the latter was at her dinner; that dinner consisted of bread and salt-fish.

"Next week Thursday will be Thanksgiving," said Mrs. Dixon (after having spent at least half an hour in urging Nan to leave the island), "and I should like to have you come over and spend it with us."

Nan promised to go if the weather were clear. When the Thursday came, it was clear with a high wind, after the usual style of that day in November; and Nan went, Comfort following her and shivering in the sharp blast that sent the sands into the air.

"It's wicked!" said Nan, as the fisherman and his family were gathered about the dinner table.

"What is it that's so wicked?" asked Mr. Dixon, as Mrs. Ware stood hesitatingly beside her chair, after all were seated.

"For me to sit down, when it isn't Thanksgiving with me. I'm not thankful. Tell me what I've got to be thankful for!"

"For this dinner. Come! I know you are hungry," said Mr. Dixon.

"For this dinner I am thankful," said the poor woman.

Nan did not tell them that she was living on the smallest allowance of bread, and had been for a week, that she might watch for some token from the sea as many days as possible. She did not betray her hunger, although it was excessive, but she did eat with gratitude. She ate and rose up to go to her own place. In vain they urged her to stay over night.

"Something might wash up, and I not be there," said Nan. "No! I must go!"

Comfort crept out to follow her home, but Nan, with a catch in her breath, put her back; she shut the kitten in and went onward. This woman had shared her bread with the kitten. Soon one or the other must go without food. Secretly, it was more for Comfort's sake than her own that Nan had accepted the invitation to that dinner.

Dick Dixon, following with his eyes the bleak figure toiling in the wind up the sands, said to his wife, "She'll die of cold and starvation."

And she said, in reply, "You must go tomorrow, Dick, to the town, and see about it."

"It shall not be my fault, if she stays there another week," he promised, "for I will report the case tomorrow."

While they talked, Nan was going farther and farther over the sands, until at last her figure crossed the height and went down out of sight on the other side. Nan was thinking as she went. She knew as well as they could know that she must go away somewhere before the snow should fall and the breakers come in edged with ice.

The wind was biting cold; the sun had put out from under the clouds a hard, yellow, metallic face that gleamed coldly into hers as she drew near her home. Suddenly Nan threw out her arms from her shawl (she had walked with them tightly folded in it); she lifted them up above her head, exclaiming, "I will! I will be thankful. I will keep Thanksgiving, if only thou wilt send to me some sure thing to tell me he is gone." Nan turned her eyes from the sky above to the ocean that was spread out southward and eastward as far as human sight could reach. "Cold, awful, cruel sea! Terrible sea!" she cried, her full lips trembling with emotion and the chill quivering in the air.

She went into her little house. It was more lonely than ever. She missed Comfort with her accustomed furry rub against her feet; but she tried to think only of the warmth and food the kitten was certain to have in the other house. She made haste to light the fire, that she might go on her daily quest to the shore. The sun was sinking below the far-away sea line when Nan went out, hurrying, as fast as she could go, up the sands and down again. She gathered much drift and threw it back, as she caught it up, where the tide would not sweep it out again, for she felt a coming storm in all the air, and knew that she might need the wood sorely. Now and then a bit of plank or broken spar was driven deep into the sand, and she pulled many times before getting it free. Her lonely round was over at last, and it was time to go to yonder solitary dwelling. She had ceased to watch ocean or shore. Neither the one nor the other gave answer to her faithful seeking; and yet she did so long, with all her heart, to keep Thanksgiving that night.

When near home she stooped to gather up an armful of wood to keep her little blaze in life awhile longer. When her arm was nearly filled, her hand, outstretched to reach another stick, touched something that was not wood, nor yet was it rock or earth.

Presently she had drawn from under the sand a large piece of old sail-cloth. She dropped her store of firewood and dragged the portion she had found houseward to examine it more closely by the light of the fire. Was it by this that she should gain her Thanksgiving? At last the trophy was drawn in and the door shut against the wind, and the two candles (all she had) were lighted.

With almost reverent hands, Nan unfolded the sail and spread it upon the floor. Near the corner, by the boom, there was a patch. Nan shrieked when she saw it; it was so like the one she had put into the sail of the Silver Thistle. She examined it almost stitch by stitch and thread by thread, and found the very place where she had put in black linen because the white was used up.

At last she cried out, "It is! It is! I do believe that John Ware is drowned. Now I will go and—and"—but Nan's future was very dark. The blackness of it shut down before her like a pall. She knew then how much easier it had been to wait and not believe, than it would be to believe and go—whither? And yet, had she not promised to keep Thanksgiving? Heaven, by its agents, had already prepared the answer to her prayer and guided her hand to its finding; should she not keep her promise?

She kneeled down before John's easy-chair to speak the words that came so slowly back, in responding to emotions from her heart. Burying her face in the cushion, she began to think out her prayer.

Nan was conscientious. She feared to speak words she did not mean, and so she must think about it all.

At last she prayed, "Help me to be thankful! I am, and I am not. Oh, help me!"

The driftwood kindled and shot a ruddy glow out through the chinks in the stove, and the lines of rosy light flickered across the woman's face as she turned it on the cushion; for she had let the candles burn only while she examined the piece of sail-cloth.

It had grown quite dark out-of-doors when, suddenly, Nan felt that she was not alone. John Ware, her husband, stood in the cabin door, and she rushed up to give him welcome, crying out, "I was trying to keep Thanksgiving, John, because I thought you dead. 'Twas a bitter thanksgiving."

And he, with his clear, strong voice, told her how the Silver Thistle had all in a moment capsized and gone down, almost before he could loose the small boat and spring clear of the larger one. He told her of his toil in the buffeting waves before he could get into the little boat.

"I did it for love of you, Nan," he said; "and then I floated without an oar until a ship, outward bound, saw me and saved me, and for those two months I've been going from and getting back to you."

And then, Nan remembered it all: the sight of the Silver Thistle coming in, how it was gone when she looked again, and the ship on the far horizon sailing down the distance. She remembered, too, as one remembers in a dream, her prayers that night for some one on the sea.

"I didn't know, John dear, that I was praying for *you*," she said. "I'm so glad I waited here for you to come. They wanted me to go away somewhere,"—plaintively—"when there isn't *anywhere* without you, for me."

Just as he was answering her, there came from the wood in the stove a loud snapping sound. Nan jumped up from her kneeling position; startled by the noise. Her thanksgiving was over! She was alone in the one-roomed house, even as she had been when she fell asleep and dreamed the dream that gave her husband to her.

The sharpness of her agony knew no bounds. She wrung her hands and cried. "Cruel! Cruel! Who makes dreams? God knows I tried to be thankful; I was thankful, and now to mock me so." She gathered up the sail, and holding it with all the power of crushing that she had, she ran, in the darkness, to the point of rocks and thrust it down into the black boiling sea.

All night poor Nan lay writhing with her agony, for she loved her husband as one may learn to love, having only one object on which to lavish that love. This man, rough fisherman as he had been, to this woman had been all gentleness. He had been to her the very manifestation of divine tenderness and care. And now, what had she to look forward to?

She had outwardly the cold, relentless rim of black, seething waters, four rude walls, a pound or two of flour, a little fire, and a few articles of furniture. She had in her spiritual nature a blank, dead wall, against which her whole being threw itself with blind fury.

Nan, poor Nan, at last fell into sleep. Another morning dawned. Its brightness aroused her. A healthy hunger urged its power. She prepared the flour, piling the driftwood into the stove with lavish hand, and ate her breakfast, careless of the future. Then she put her little house in order, made up a bundle of clothing, went out, and shut the door.

Nan had turned her face away from the spot that had been so cruel to her. She went to her only neighbor. "Will you put me on shore?" she asked; "I'm going back to the mill."

"That's right, woman," said Dick Dixon, and he drew his boat along the icy sands until it floated in clear water. Then he rowed across, with Nan in the boat, to the mainland.

She wrung his hand for thanks, and, with her bundle in her arms, went up into the land, turning only once to glance at the island lying bound in ice in the midst of the sea.

She went to the railroad station. Nan had no money, neither did she owe any man money. Walking up to the ticket office, with a cold, fixed face she drew off her wedding-ring. "Will you," she said, "give me a ticket for this—I have no money."

"For a brass ring?" the man questioned, thoughtlessly.

"For my wedding–ring!" said Nan, proudly. "But—I don't need it anymore; my husband is dead."

The station master looked at Nan a moment. He motioned back the ring almost rudely, and thrusting forward the ticket she needed turned away.

She hesitated. Then she snatched the ring and the ticket, thinking in her heart, "I'll travel back here and pay for this ticket with the first money I earn."

With the outward train went Nan; back into the stir of the town she went. It was night when she reached L—; the mill, where she had toiled before John Ware came into her life, was not far from the station, and she went to it, for the light streaming forth into the November night from its many windows told the story of labor going on within. How well Nan knew the way! It seemed to her, as she opened the office door and went in, bearing her bundle, as though she had never been away.

She trembled as she put the question, "Is loom No. ___ running?" (Loom No. ___ was Nan's old working home.) A sudden affection for the loom grew in Nan's heart. She was skilled in the work of weaving cotton.

"No," was the answer.

"Will you give it to me?" she demanded, hunger helping her eagerness, for Nan had eaten nothing since her breakfast on Sand Island.

"You?" with a questioning look at her parcel. "Do you understand weaving?"

"It is my old loom," she answered.

"And your name is"—

She gave it, forgetting for a moment that it was no longer her name.

The loom was promised to Nan. She went forth to seek lodgings at her old boarding-house, and fell into the same place and the former ways so thoroughly, that oftentimes, when the motion and the noise about her in the great mill filled her sight and hearing, she tried to think that life on Sand Island was only a dream.

While the winds were high and the snows fell and the ice grew, Nan worked patiently and steadfastly from morning until night, six days in the week, weaving cotton.

When the spring, with the warmth of its own rejoicing, made the earth forget its ache of cold, Nan longed to see Sand Island again.

It was midsummer when she went to the town on the coast and made her offering of money and thanks to that station-master who, in November, gave her a passenger ticket for L—. The man looked at her with surprise, for of all the people to whom he had given tickets, this was the first that had returned to give thanks.

At the town wharf Nan found a boatman. He had just come up from the harbor bar, where he had stayed clamming as long as the rising tide would let him.

"Never mind the clams," said Nan, gathering in her dress from contact with them as she stepped into his boat. "It will take too long to get them out, and the wind may rise."

"True! The wind rises now with the tide, mostly. I hope you're not afraid."

"No," said Nan, looking out toward the ocean with unspoken fear in her eyes, while at her heart she had no fear. "Why should I be?" she thought, as the oars touched the water and the boat moved on. "Sand Island and the ocean have done their worst for me."

And yet the place powerfully attracted and repelled her, as she drew near it. Three times she caused the boatman to cease from rowing, thinking in her heart as she did so that she would not land. The fishing boats were within sight. Soon they would be coming in. It was the desire to learn something of the fishing interests that her husband had once had part and lot in that caused her after the third delay to say resolutely, "I will go on."

The boatman crossed his oars and laid them at rest; the boat floated, turning on the tide. Doubtful and perplexed he said, "It isn't my business to know who you are, nor why you're bound for yonder island, but if it's drowning yourself that you're thinking of, don't go there to do it."

"Did any one, ever?" eagerly questioned Nan, smiling softly to herself at the thought, and wondering how any one could have courage to go forward to meet Death.

The boatman made no answer. He was watching her narrowly, and wishing that he had her safely on shore.

"Death isn't so pleasant to me that I should hasten to meet it," she said. "I am Nancy Ware, wife of John Ware." Even then the poor soul could not bring herself to say widow of John Ware.

Nan's story was known in all that region, although her face was not. The boatman looked at her with curiosity and interest as he rowed on toward the island. Presently, he remarked, "You've heard the news, then?"

"What news?" gasped Nan. "I've heard no news," she said, speaking still louder; "What is it?"

"They'll tell you at the house, yonder, all about it," he replied, rowing with vigor, for he saw, fluttering against the blue of the sky, a far-away ruffle of sea, and knew that the wind was moving on the waters and that he had no time to lose in getting back to the mainland. Faster and faster he rowed, nearer and nearer came Sand Island. As the boat touched the shore the man sprang into the tide and hauled it up. "Come," he said, "don't keep me. I've not a moment to spare."

Nan was trembling. She could not walk a boat's length without aid. He lifted her to the ground, and giving his boat a thrust forward, springing into it at the same moment, he was beyond recall when she remembered that she had given him no money. Trying bravely to steady her quivering body and make it do service for her will by taking her to the small brown house on the rocks above, she went forward. With her white face and her asking eyes, she appeared to Mrs. Dixon in the cottage.

"I've been looking for you near a week," said the fisherman's wife. "I knew you was a-coming, but tonight I did n't see any boat crossing over. I'm heartily glad to see you, Nancy Ware."

"Did you send for me? Tell me everything," gasped the excited woman.

"Send for you? No. Where could I send? But I knew you'd have to come; you who looked so long up and down for something."

"Tell me everything," repeated Nan, wondering how this woman could have news for her and not speak it out at once.

For answer Mrs. Dixon went into the adjoining room and fetched from thence an "oil-skin" jacket, which she laid across Nan's lap. "There!" she said. "'Twas found just eight days ago. What do you think of that?"

Nan was turning it over and over in vain search of something that she did not find.

"Oh, there isn't any mistake, not a mite, but what it's your husband's jacket. Every man of the crew identified it, even without the contents."

"Contents!" echoed Nan, her large gray eyes grasping in their sight every possible content that a coat, meant for living man, could hold.

"Poor soul!" cried Mrs. Dixon, reading the thought that grew into expression in her face. "Not that that you think; but I will show you." She went again into the room whence she had brought the jacket, and returned with a small parcel wrapped in paper.

"This was in the breast pocket, buttoned in tight," she said, laying it on the coat. Nan's fingers fell to work taking off the paper wrapping. When it was removed, there lay revealed a shrunken, shriveled, water-worn pocket-book. It was ready to fall into fragments at a touch. On any shore, Nan would have recognized it. It was her gift to John Ware before he became her husband.

A dark, faded blur lay across it. It was the mark of the ocean over the name that Nan had written there with a flush of "dainty shame" that she should dare to write it at all—a name that meant for her, at that time, all the future on earth and much of heaven beside. The well-known characters had faded from sight, but she could read them in the deeper lines graven on her heart. She looked at it with tearless eyes.

Mrs. Dixon ventured to say, "I'd open it, if I was you."

Mechanically Nan fumbled at the rusty clasp. "There is nothing in it, I know," she said. "I remember it was empty the day before he went." While she was speaking, the clasp gave way, and a dry, pulpy mass of paper lay disclosed.

"You mustn't touch it; but it's money, that is!" said the fisherman's wife, eagerly. "It'll all fall to pieces if you try to open it. It's got to go to the bank, or somewhere, afore it's picked out, and then you can get new money for it, so they say."

"Then they did pay John, after all; and I've been thinking wrong, hard thoughts against the mill owner all this time," said Nan, slowly.

"But you are glad to get the money, Nancy Ware, aren't you, now?"

Without giving expression to any feeling of pleasure, she simply asked where it had been found.

Little Dick, who had entered, said that he knew, for he had found it; and at once Nan arose to go to the place with the lad.

As they were going, little Dick said: "It was a tough old storm that did it, Mrs. Ware. The boat was pounded into the sand fit to grown into it, and all covered up, deep down as my arm up to the elbow. We struck it with a stick, and it sounded just like rock; so Mame and me dug down and found the dingey bottom side up. There it is now! The men got it out; and nailed fast to it was the old oiler."

Nan went to the spot. One glance convinced her that it was the small boat in which John used to come on shore at night after anchoring the Silver Thistle. She knelt down on the sand beside it, stroking it softly; coaxing it, the boy said, when he told the story at home, to tell her where it had been and what it had done with John.

On going back to the cottage, she learned the news of the sea, the fishermen, and the boats. When she asked of her home, she was told that it remained as she had left it.

"I don't think," said Mr. Dixon, who had returned from his day of toil, "that a soul has spent a night in the place since you went away."

The southwest wind blowing over the ocean made Nan restless. She knew with what a cool moan the sea was heaving on the sands upon the farther side. When the moon was up, she arose from her chair, and said, "I am going over to spend the night in the old place."

"You're not expecting anything more from the sea, are you?" asked Mr. Dixon, aroused and unwilling to have her go.

"No," she said, "I am not." Nan had never heard of poetic justice, yet she could not help saying it, "The sea took my all from me; why should it not give me back as well?"

In spite of protest, Nan went forth alone. Dick Dixon sat in his house door as she went, and said to his wife: "It's safe enough, but it is the queerest freak. Most women would be frightened to death at the thought."

"Nancy Ware isn't like other women," replied his wife. "She never showed the least mite of pleasure at finding that money. I do believe she cared a great deal more about the old boat that had carried her husband so many times, and the jacket that had kept him dry, than she did for the money that will serve her many a good turn yet."

Meanwhile Nan went up the slope and passed out of sight over the crest of the island, and so came to the one-roomed building that had been to her a home. At the instant she reached the door, a gold-white meteor shot across and down the sky, brighter in its light, for the time, than the moon itself.

"If I were God," said Nan, "and could do things like that, I would do other things, as well. O God," she cried, in anguish of spirit. "Why not? Why not?" After a time, she loosed the rude fastening of the door and went in, the moonlight slanting in after her. The place was still, lonely, weird, and yet it seemed scarcely touched by human hands since the morning she went away from it. With true neighborly instinct Mrs. Dixon had, in November, removed to her own house all the articles liable to be carried off by a chance visitor. The bed was there, and the stove, and the chairs. Nan had no use for them; nevertheless there came to her at the instant a feeling of satisfaction in the knowledge of their possession. Mrs. Dixon had provided Nan with a candle and matches. She closed the door, lit the candle, and looked around the place. Spiders had taken up their unmolested abode in it. She opened the door, the wind extinguishing the flame of the candle in her hand. She knew that when it was full sea the wind would drop away and leave the ocean phosphorescent, as it rocked softly into calm. Drawing John's easy-chair into the moonlight, she moved to and fro in it until the old, uneven boards of the floor creaked.

For the first time since her sorrow came, Nancy Ware thought of her future; thought of it not merely as a life at work weaving cotton today and perhaps tomorrow, but as a period of time, as a series of years to be endured, to be gotten over somehow, as the best that she could do. She was not yet twenty years old. Childhood she scarcely remembered; girlhood she had not had; hard work for bread and shelter had shut that happy lot away from her. The uncared-for, uncanny air of the house oppressed her after a time. A swallow darted past her face and flew out through a broken window pane nearby.

Meanwhile, in the house at the farther end of the island, Dick Dixon and his wife had talked together about Nan's spending the night alone, and had decided that "it would not do at all," and that they must go over and persuade her to return with them. About half-way between the two houses they met, Nan returning of her own wish.

"It is musty over there, shut away from the fresh air," said Nan, simply.

"Nothing like finding out things for one's own self, is there?" said Dick Dixon. "If we'd 'a'told you so, you wouldn't have let it make the least mite of difference with your going."

"You might have waited a night or two and had the place cleaned up a little before you went," said Mrs. Dixon, "but I'm glad you met us part way. I'm tired and sleepy; the days are so long, now." She yawned wearily and struggled through the sand heavily.

"I'm sorry I made you so much trouble," replied Nan; "but I believe I was startled by a swallow in the house. I never liked swallows; they look at you so, and never wink or blink a bit."

The following morning, Nan startled the fisherman's household by the announcement that she was going to take a vacation from the mill work and spend it in the little house. She made the statement with a rising blush that puzzled Dick Dixon, especially as Nan spoke with cheerful tones running through the words she uttered.

"Nancy Ware!" exclaimed Mrs. Dixon.

"Well?"

"Don't you know that you can't stay there all alone?"

"I don't mean to. Here is little Dick. Will you let him stay with me until someone else comes? There is a poor soul in the mill working her very life out without a day of rest, year in and year out. I am going to send for her to come and stay with me. It will do us both good, and the money in the pocket-book will be a blessing to her as well as to me."

"I wish you wouldn't do it," said Mrs. Dixon. "It is right enough for a woman to stay with her husband anywhere; but two women just alone, so far off and so lonely and everything"—

Nan smiled but made no answer, and an hour later she was on her way to the house with a scrubbing pail and soap, accompanied by little Dick with his small hand wagon laden with needful articles.

The weather was perfect. The cool southwest wind met them on the crest of the island and blew in their faces, cooling the air that fell around them as they went down to the little house. Nan's face shone with a nameless happiness. She ran like a child up and down the shore with the boy, gathering driftwood to light a fire. She told no one the secret of her new joy. It had come to her partly by thinking the matter of John's loss over before going to sleep the night before, and coming to the conclusion that, after all, she had not proof enough of John's loss to dare to marry again (not that Nan had any intention of or wish for such an event, only the thought came to her through the suggestion of the possibility of such a thing as marriage); and partly by the repetition of the very dream, in all its minuteness, that she had dreamed on Thanksgiving night. It had seemed so real and so plausible to Nan, and yet she knew too well that no one, certainly not the fisherman or his wife, would feel the hope or see the reasonableness of it all; therefore she went her way alone, and said nothing of her new hope or of the dream.

There were four young swallows in the nest on the ledge over the window near the door. It went hard with Nan to dislodge them. With little Dick's help she carefully removed the nest, built of swamp mud and bits of last year's sedge from the land shore, and, with the parent birds flapping in her face with dives and darts that threatened everything in the way of vengeance, she placed it securely on a projection in the porch at the door.

Nan watched the sea as she worked. It grew dear to her with its old endearing ways of rise and fall and change of hue. At noon, which she knew by the sun, little Dick came in and ate his dinner with her from the basket of provisions that they had brought. In the afternoon, when the room was cleaned, they went back to the cottage together. The next day Dick Dixon went to the town with Nan to get the provisions she needed for her little venture.

He laughed at her about her summer cottage by the sea as they went, but Nan sat by, unmoved and content. She sent off, that afternoon, a letter to the poor, hard-working woman in the mill at L—, inviting her to spend a month on Sand Island, and asking her to report her absence to the superintendent at the mill, also to bring with her Nan's trunk.

The day following this trip to the town on the coast, Nan and little Dick moved in the cottage, and Comfort went with them. A week later came the woman from the mill. Her thankfulness had so much heart-break in it that Nan cried with pity at finding that there was one soul that had had less joy than she had.

The first week, her guest could do little but look at the ocean and lament that she had lived so long and never seen it until so late. The second week, both women began to look for employment; their lives had been too busy to sit long in idleness. The third week they were busy at all odd hours stitching shoes, which Dick Dixon obtained for them. Little Dick, with true fisherman's instinct and luck, caught fish at each day's rise of the tide, from the ledge of rocks. The two cottages grew very neighborly, their inmates interchanging visits nearly every day.

On the sands John's boat still lay; it was beyond repair and would lie there until time or seas should destroy it. Nan shyly visited it when she could do so unobserved. She clung to it simply because it had been near to John since she had.

"My month is over," said Nan's companion, one day; "my month is over tomorrow."

Nan started visibly. "Don't you like it here?" she asked.

"Like it! I would live here forever if I could," she said; " but I must go back to my work."

"Wait with me until the fall winds begin to blow. I'll go then," said Nan, feeling that every day on Sand Island was so much gained,—for what, or by what, she did not stop to ask. "Beside," she added, "we can earn enough to live, even here."

And so it was then and there decided that the two women should stay on until autumn. Pleasure parties, much to Nan's annoyance, began to land at the island and peer curiously into her little cabin as they sauntered by. Nan's story was popular in the village, and strangers were eager to see the woman who had stayed through cold and semi-starvation, waiting for a piece of patched sail-cloth to wash up.

The summer was stealing by. Nan made a little notch with everyday on the window ledge, a tiny stroke with a pin, to tell how fast the days were growing into the last weeks and the final month of her stay. She stitched shoes faster than ever, now, feeling a pride that John's money had not yet been touched to supply her needs. She would like to keep it intact as long as possible.

Once in the week Dick Dixon went to the post-office in the town on the coast; usually that once was on Saturday, in the afternoon. The little errands that were given him to do occupied several hours, so that when he returned the sun was nearly always past its setting. Sometimes on his return he rowed around to Nan's cabin. Sometimes she waited at his cottage to take home the parcels he fetched for her.

The last Saturday in August came. Nan and the woman had an unusual number of shoes to return. Little Dick took the parcel across to his father before dinner on that day. They had worked at them during the morning to the neglect of household duties. As soon as the parcel was ready, Nan began her Saturday's baking, intending to finish it and go across to the cottage in time to fetch back the bundles of new work with little Dick. It was too late to make bread and have it rise in time to bake, and Nan made biscuit. Oddly enough she had not made biscuit since the day John was expected home. As she kneaded the flour before the open window, she said to the woman who sat in the door paring apples for pies: "The fishing boats are coming in early today." She saw the Menhaden, followed by her seine-boats, sailing toward the harbor, and the lighters, fish-laden to the sea's edge, going before a fair wind to the mill.

Dick Dixon at that moment started for the mainland, wishing as he rowed on that the Menhaden would throw him a line and tow him in; but the sloop sailed past and was at the harbor's mouth before he had rowed out half the distance. Before he was at the pier, he saw a group of men on it gesticulating in an excited manner, and at the moment his boat touched the dock a long, loud hurrah went up from a score of fishermen. He laughed. "They've had a good catch today," he thought, as he made his boat fast to the dock and climbed up to learn the news. The instant his head appeared above the timbers, another shout rang out. The men were wringing some one by the hand, and laughing like boys over a snow man.

"Hello!" he called. "What's up? Got a mermaid ashore?"

"There's Dixon! See if he knows him," said the Menhaden's captain; but there was no chance for the test to be put. The man was at Dick Dixon's side.

"How is she, Dick?" were the first words that were spoken.

"Well and hearty, my lad," said Dick Dixon, and then he made feint of clinging a moment to John Ware's hand before dropping down on a timber of the dock. "Who'd ha' thought anything would have struck me so?" he thought, but no one paid attention to Dick Dixon.

"All aboard!" shouted some one.

"For what?" shouted Dick, in return.

"We're going to take him over," said one of the men.

"Not without me in the boat," he said, clinging to a young lad of the crew and following on. The seine-boat had already a dozen men in it.

John Ware was pleased with his reception; it gave him joy to meet so hearty a welcome to his old life; but he would have preferred his own little dingey and a pair of oars to take himself over to Sand Island. The men, eager and curious to learn his story, plied him with many questions, when he longed to keep still. They learned that which Nan had dreamed. The Silver Thistle capsized and went down. John Ware sprang clear of the sinking boat and battled for life, reaching the small boat, from whence, greatly exhausted, he was picked up by one of the boats of the very ship Nan had seen that day sailing down the horizon.

In the hope of meeting some inward-bound sail, by which he could return, he went with the ship on her voyage to the far East. When, months later, it reached its port, he sought out another ship in which he could return as a seaman. That ship met with storms that disabled it so that time was lost in repairs at a foreign port.

"In fact," said John, "I've had a pretty tough time of it from first to last. I'd rather catch bony fish in sight of a home shore all the year round."

To save further questioning, he insisted on taking a turn at the oars, but a dozen hands prevented. Then they fell to wondering how Mrs. Ware would take the sudden news, and they talked over, man-fashion, the best way of telling her what had happened.

"You'd better leave that to the women," spoke Dick Dixon. "They'll manage that."

Nan, on the island, went on with the baking for Sunday. The biscuit were out and the pies were in the oven, when in came little Dick with eyes distended to the utmost.

"Oh, Mrs. Ware!" he cried. "Something's happened, I know! There's lots of men coming over the island, and father's along with 'em, and ma too, 'thout anything on her head."

Nan's first thought was, "What could happen to me?" Her second thought made the blood flash like heat lightning in her face.

"There, now! See the heads coming up over the sand!" cried the boy, running to the corner of the house. Both women had gone out and were at the corner. The group of men had hesitated and were standing still. Mrs. Dixon was coming heavily through the sand, with one hand pressed over her heart and the other holding the corner of her apron over her head.

Nan ran lightly to meet her. "What has happened? Is anything the matter?" she asked.

"No! No! Nothing's the matter," she gasped; then the two meeting, she let go the apron and her heart at the same instant, and clasped Nan in her fat, motherly arms and kissed her. Nan never knew whether the words, "He's come!" or the kiss came first.

"Who's come?"

The coolness of the woman threw Mrs. Dixon off her guard. "Your husband's come!" she said.

"Keep those men away!" said Nan; for Mrs. Dixon had given the signal for approach.

Nan felt that her feet were sinking deeper and deeper in the sand. Then John seemed to come and take hold of her before she went down out of sight.

Louisa May Alcott

(1832-1888)

Known to and popular with audiences in both the nineteenth and the twentieth centuries for her children's books, Louisa May Alcott's reputation today is increasingly transcending the "children's writer" designation. Born to Amos Bronson and Abigail May Alcott on November 29, 1832, in Germantown, Pennsylvania, she moved with her family at an early age to Concord, Massachusetts.

Although never formally educated, Louisa's parents tutored her and her sisters at home. Despite Bronson Alcott's failure in two of his endeavors in the 1840s, the Temple School in Boston and his utopian Fruitlands experiment, he remained interested in education and philosophy, and Louisa appreciated his unconventional teaching methods. Louisa's parents required their daughters to keep journals, which their parents read and critiqued. Louisa particularly appreciated her mother's comments. Beyond the tutoring from her parents in Concord, while Louisa tutored Ralph Waldo Emerson's daughter, Ellen, she studied the classics in philosophy and literature through the unlimited access she had to Emerson's library.

Because of her father's limited success as breadwinner, the financial responsibility to support the family fell increasingly on Louisa, her sisters, and her mother. At an early age Louisa helped support the family with money she earned from jobs that included reading to the elderly, doing laundry for others, sewing, and acting as a companion. In 1850, she began work as a teacher. At the same time, she also discovered that she could earn money by writing sentimental and thriller stories for adult magazines.

Alcott published her first poem, "Sunlight," in 1852, and at the age of twenty-three in 1855 published her first book, *Flower Fables*. After nursing her sister Elizabeth through a lengthy illness that ended with her death in 1858, it's not surprising that Louisa volunteered to work in a Union hospital in the District of Columbia when the Civil War broke out. A combination of poor diet, inadequate ventilation, and the shock of the injured and suffering soldiers in the hospital resulted in Alcott's weakened resistance to disease. As a result, within six weeks she contracted typhoid fever and was forced to return to Concord. Nonetheless, her nursing experiences resulted in the publication of *Hospital Sketches* in 1863 and earned her commercial and critical success. The reception of *Hospital Sketches* convinced her that success lay in realism rather than in flights of fancy. Disappointed with the reception of *Moods*, a book she published in 1865, Louisa traveled to Europe as a companion for an invalid. On her return in 1866, she continued contributing to magazines. In 1867 she became editor of a children's monthly magazine, *Merry's Museum*, and in 1868 *Little Women*, a book completed in six weeks, became an instant success. During the final two decades of her life she wrote a series of novels that are often grouped with *Little Women*. In addition to her well-known works, the transcendental influence is apparent in her writing on prison reform, suffrage, temperance, and child labor. On March 6, 1888, she died, just two days after her father's death. Along with such distinguished neighbors and friends as Ralph Waldo Emerson, Henry David Thoreau, and Nathaniel Hawthorne, she is buried in Concord's Sleepy Hollow Cemetery.

Alcott's two stories included in this collection come from her nursing experiences during the Civil War. Published in the November 1863 issue of *The Atlantic Monthly*, "The Brothers" deals with the conflict between the mulatto Robert, who could pass for white, and his white brother, who raped Robert's wife, Lucy. In its treatment of miscegenation, "passing," and the issue of slavery, the story anticipates Mark Twain's later novel *Pudd'nhead Wilson* and Alice Dunbar-Nelson's story "The Stones of the Village." Alcott's other story included in this collection, "Scarlet Stockings," was published in the July 1869 issue of *Putnam's* magazine. The Civil War setting, complications of the romance between Lennox and Belle, and the reticence of Lennox to enlist all remind us of William Dean Howells's short story on the same subject, "Editha." Although Twain had very limited Civil War experience and Howells had none, recognition of their novel and stories in the twentieth century further illustrates the marginalization of women writers. Alcott's experience in a Civil War hospital is not widely known, nor are her stories that grew out of that involvement. These stories illustrate the mature voice of Alcott and defy her being labeled as only a children's writer.

Selected Primary Works

Flower Fables, 1855; *Hospital Sketches*, 1863; *Moods*, 1865; *Little Women*, 1868; *An Old Fashioned Girl*, 1870; *Little Men*, 1871; *Work:*

A Story of Experience, 1873; *Transcendental Wild Oats*, 1873; *A Modern Mephistopheles*, 1877; *Jo's Boys*, 1886; *Recollections of My Childhood's Days*, 1890; *Behind a Mask: The Unknown Thrillers of Louisa May Alcott* (ed. M. Stern), 1975.

"The Brothers"

The Atlantic Monthly, November 1863

Doctor Franck came in as I sat sewing up the rents in an old shirt, that Tom might go tidily to his grave. New shirts were needed for the living, and there was not wife or mother to "dress him handsome when he went to meet the Lord," as one woman said, describing the fine funeral she had pinched herself to give her son.

"Miss Dane, I'm in a quandary," began the Doctor, with that expression of countenance which says as plainly as words, "I want to ask a favor, but I wish you'd save me the trouble."

"Can I help you out of it?"

"Faith! I don't like to propose it, but you certainly can, if you please."

"Then give it a name, I beg."

"You see a Reb has just been brought in crazy with typhoid; a bad case every way; a drunken, rascally little captain somebody took the trouble to capture, but whom nobody wants to take the trouble to cure. The wards are full, the ladies worked to death, and willing to be for our own boys, but rather slow to risk their lives for a Reb. Now you've had the fever, you like queer patients, your mate will see to your ward for a while, and I will find you a good attendant. The fellow won't last long, I fancy; but he can't die without some sort of care, you know. I've put him in the fourth story of the west wing, away from the rest. It is airy, quiet, and comfortable there. I'm on that ward, and will do my best for you in every way. Now, then, will you go?"

"Of course I will, out of perversity, if not common charity; for some of these people think that because I'm an abolitionist I am also a heathen, and I should rather like to show them, that, though I cannot quite love my enemies, I am willing to take care of them."

"Very good; I thought you'd go; and speaking of abolition reminds me that you can have a contraband for a servant, if you like. It is that fine mulatto fellow who was found burying his Rebel master after the fight, and, being badly cut over the head, our boys brought him along. Will you have him?"

"By all means,—for I'll stand to my guns on that point, as on the other; these black boys are far more faithful and handy than some of the white scamps given me to serve, instead of being served by. But is this man well enough?"

"Yes, for that sort of work, and I think you'll like him. He must have been a handsome fellow before he got his face slashed; not much darker than myself; his master's son, I dare say, and the white blood makes him rather high and haughty about some things. He was in a bad way when he came in, but vowed he'd die in the street rather than turn in with the black fellows below; so I put him up in the west wing, to be out of the way, and he's seen to the captain all the morning. When can you go up?"

"As soon as Tom is laid out, Skinner moved, Haywood washed, Marble dressed, Charley rubbed, Downs taken up, Upham laid down, and the whole forty fed."

We both laughed, though the Doctor was on his way to the dead-house and I held a shroud on my lap. But in a hospital one learns that cheerfulness is one's salvation; for, in an atmosphere of suffering and death, heaviness of heart would soon paralyze usefulness of hand, if the blessed gift of smiles had been denied us.

In an hour I took possession of my new charge, finding a dissipated-looking boy of nineteen or twenty raving in the solitary little room, with no one near him but the contraband in the room adjoining. Feeling decidedly more interest in the black man than in the white, yet remembering the Doctor's hint of his being "high and haughty," I glanced furtively at him as I scattered chloride of lime about the room to purify the air, and settled matters to suit myself. I had seen many contrabands, but never one so attractive as this. All colored men are called "boys," even if their heads are white; this boy was five-and-twenty at least, strong-limbed and manly, and had the look of one who never had been cowed by abuse or worn with oppressive labor. He sat on his bed doing nothing; no book, no pipe, no pen or paper anywhere appeared, yet anything less indolent or listless than his attitude and expression I never saw. Erect he sat, with a hand on either knee, and eyes fixed on the bare wall opposite, so rapt in some absorbing thought as to be unconscious of my presence, though the door stood wide open and my movements were by no means noiseless. His face was half averted, but I instantly approved the Doctor's taste, for the profile which I saw possessed all the attributes of comeliness belonging to his mixed race. He was more quadroon than mulatto, with Saxon features, Spanish complexion, darkened by exposure, color in lips and cheek, waving hair, and an eye full of the passionate melancholy which in such men always seems to utter a mute protest against the broken law that doomed them at their birth. What could he be thinking of? The sick boy cursed and raved, I rustled to and fro, steps passed the door, bells rang, and the steady rumble of army-wagons came up from the street, still he never stirred. I had seen colored people in what they call "the black sulks," when for days, they neither smiled nor spoke, and scarcely ate. But this was something more than that; for the man was not dully brooding over some small grievance; he seemed to see an all-absorbing fact or fancy recorded on the wall, which was a blank to me. I wondered if it were some deep wrong or sorrow, kept alive by memory and impotent regret; if he mourned for the dead master to whom he had been faithful to the end; or if the liberty now his were robbed of half its sweetness by the knowledge that someone near and dear to him still languished in the hell from which he had escaped. My heart warmed to him at that idea; I wanted to know and comfort him; and, following the impulse of the moment, I went in and touched him on the shoulder.

In an instant the man vanished and the slave appeared. Freedom was too new a boon to have wrought its blessed changes yet, and as he started up, with his hand at his temple and an obsequious "Yes Ma'am," any romance that had gathered round him fled away, leaving the saddest of all sad facts in living guise before me. Not only did the manhood seem to die out of him, but the comeliness that first attracted me; for as he turned, I saw the ghastly wound that had laid open cheek and forehead. Being partly healed, it was no longer bandaged, but held together with strips of that transparent plaster which I never see without a shiver and swift recollections of the scenes with which it is associated in my mind. Part of his black hair had been shorn away, and one eye was nearly closed; pain so distorted, and the cruel sabre-cut so marred that portion of his face, that, when I saw it, I felt as if a fine medal had been suddenly reversed, showing me a far more striking type of human suffering and wrong than Michel Angelo's bronze prisoner. By one of those inexplicable processes that often teach us how little we understand ourselves, my purpose was suddenly changed, and though I went in to offer comfort as a friend, I merely gave an order as a mistress.

"Will you open these windows? This man needs more air."

He obeyed at once, and, as he slowly urged up the unruly sash, the handsome profile was again turned toward me, and again I was possessed by my first impression so strongly that I involuntarily said,—

"Thank you, Sir."

Perhaps it was fancy, but I thought that in the look of mingled surprise and something like reproach which he gave me there was also a trace of grateful pleasure. But he said, in that tone of spiritless humility these poor souls learn so soon,—

"I a'n't a white man, Ma'am, I'm a contraband."

"Yes, I know it; but a contraband is a free man, and I heartily congratulate you."

He liked that; his face shone, he squared his shoulders, lifted his head, and looked me full in the eye with a brisk,—

"Thank ye, Ma'am; anything more to do fer yer?"

"Doctor Franck thought you would help me with this man, as there are many patients and few nurses or attendants. Have you had the fever?"

"No, Ma'am."

"They should have thought of that when they put him here; wounds and fevers should not be together. I'll try to get you moved."

He laughed a sudden laugh,—if he had been a white man, I should have called it scornful; as he was a few shades darker than myself, I suppose it must be considered an insolent, or at least an unmannerly one.

"It don't matter, Ma'am. I'd rather be up here with the fever than down with those niggers; and there a'n't no other place fer me."

Poor fellow! That was true. No ward in all the hospital would take him in to lie side by side with the most miserable white wreck there. Like a bat in Aesop's fable, he belonged to neither race; and the pride of one, the helplessness of the other, kept him hovering alone in the twilight a great sin has brought to overshadow the whole land.

"You shall stay, then; for I would far rather have you than my lazy Jack. But are you well and strong enough?"

"I guess I'll do, Ma'am."

He spoke with a passive sort of acquiescence,—as if it did not much matter, if he were not able, and no one would particularly rejoice, if he were.

"Yes, I think you will. By what name shall I call you?"

"Bob, Ma'am."

Every woman has her pet whim; one of mine was to teach the men self-respect by treating them respectfully. Tom, Dick and Harry would pass, when lads rejoiced in those familiar abbreviations; but to address men often old enough to be my father in that style did not suit my old-fashioned ideas of propriety. This "Bob" would never do; I should have found it as easy to call the chaplain "Gus" as my tragical-looking contraband by a title so strongly associated with the tail of a kite.

"What is your other name?" I asked. "I like to call my attendants by their last names rather than by their first."

"I've got no other, Ma'am; we have our master's names, or do without. Mine's dead, and I won't have anything of his about me."

"Well, I'll call you Robert, then, and you may fill this pitcher for me, if you will be so kind."

He went; but, through all the tame obedience years of servitude had taught him, I could see the proud spirit his father gave him was not yet subdued, for the look and gesture with which he repudiated his master's name were a more effective declaration of independence than any Fourth-of-July orator could have prepared.

We spent a curious week together. Robert seldom left his room, except upon my errands; and I was a prisoner all day, often all night, by the bedside of the Rebel. The fever burned itself rapidly away, for there seemed little vitality to feed it in the feeble frame of this old young man, whose life had been none of the most righteous, judging from the revelations made by his unconscious lips; since more than once Robert authoritatively silenced him, when my gentler hushings were of no avail, and blasphemous wanderings or ribald camp-songs made my cheeks burn and Robert's face assume an aspect of disgust. The captain was a gentleman in the world's eye, but the contraband was the gentleman of mine;—I was a fanatic, and that accounts for such depravity of taste, I hope. I never asked Robert of himself, feeling that somewhere there was a spot still too sore to bear the lightest touch; but, from his language, manner, and intelligence, I inferred that his color had procured for him the few advantages within the reach of a quick-witted, kindly treated slave. Silent, grave, and thoughtful, but most serviceable, was my contraband; glad of the books I brought him, faithful in the performance of the duties I assigned to him, grateful for the friendliness I could not but feel and show toward him. Often I longed to ask what purpose was so visibly altering his aspect with such daily deepening gloom. But I never dared, and no one else had either time or desire to pry into the past of this specimen of one branch of the chivalrous "F.F.Vs."

On the seventh night, Dr. Franck suggested that it would be well for some one, besides the general watchman of the ward, to be with the captain, as it might be his last. Although the greater part of the two preceding nights had been spent there, of course I offered to remain,—for there is a strange fascination in these scenes, which renders one careless of fatigue and unconscious of fear until the crisis is passed.

"Give him water as long as he can drink, and if he drops into a natural sleep, it may save him. I'll look in at midnight, when some change will probably take place. Nothing but sleep or a miracle will keep him now. Good night."

Away went the Doctor; and, devouring a whole mouthful of grapes, I lowered the lamp, wet the captain's head, and sat down on a hard stool to begin my watch. The captain lay with his hot, haggard face turned toward me, filling the air with his poisonous breath, and feebly muttering, with lips and tongue so parched that the sanest speech would have been difficult to understand. Robert was stretched on his bed in the inner room, the door of which stood ajar, that a fresh draught from his open window might carry the fever-fumes away through mine. I could just see a long, dark figure, with the lighter outline of a face, and, having little else to do just then I fell to thinking of this curious contraband, who evidently prized his freedom highly, yet seemed in no haste to enjoy it. Doctor Franck had offered to send him on to safer quarters but he had said, "No, thank yer, Sir, not yet," and then had gone away to fall into one of those black moods of his, which began to disturb me, because I had no power to lighten them. As I sat listening to the clocks from the steeples all about us, I amused myself with planning Robert's future, as I often did my own, and had dealt out to him a generous hand of trumps wherewith to play this game of life which hitherto had gone so cruelly against him, when harsh, choked voice called,—

"Lucy!"

It was the captain, and some new terror seemed to have gifted him with momentary strength.

"Yes, here's Lucy," I answered, hoping that by the following fancy I might quiet him,—for his face was damp with the clammy moisture, and his frame shaken with the nervous tremor that so often precedes death. His dull eye fixed upon me, dilating with a bewildered look of incredulity and wrath, till he broke out fiercely,—

"That's a lie! She's dead,—and so's Bob, damn him!"

Finding speech a failure, I began to sing the quiet tune that had often soothed delirium like this; but hardly had a line,

"See gentle patience smile on pain," passed my lips, when he clutched me by the wrist, whispering like one in mortal fear,—

"Hush! She used to sing that way to Bob, but she never would to me. I swore I'd whip the Devil out of her, and I did; but you know before she cut her throat she said she'd haunt me, and there she is!"

He pointed behind me with an aspect of such pale dismay, that I involuntarily glanced over my shoulder and started as if I had seen a veritable ghost; for, peering from the gloom of that inner room, I saw a shadowy face, with dark hair all about it, and a glimpse of scarlet at the throat. An instant showed me that it was only Robert leaning from his bed's-foot, wrapped in a gray army-blanket, with his red shirt just visible above it, and his long hair disordered by sleep. But what a strange expression was on his face! The unmarred side was toward me, fixed and motionless as when I first observed it,—less absorbed now, but more intent. His eye glittered, his lips were apart like one who listened with every sense, and his whole aspect reminded me of a hound to which some wind had brought the scent of unsuspected prey.

"Do you know him, Robert? Does he mean you?"

"Lord, no, Ma'am; they all own half a dozen Bobs: but hearin' my name woke me; that's all."

He spoke quite naturally, and lay down again, while I returned to my charge, thinking that this paroxysm was probably his last. But by another hour I perceived a hopeful change, for the tremor had subsided, the cold dew was gone, his breathing was more regular, and Sleep, the healer, had descended to save or take him gently away. Doctor Franck looked in at midnight, bade me keep all cool and quiet, and not fail to administer a certain draught as soon as the captain woke. Very much relieved, I laid my head on my arms, uncomfortably folded on the little table, and fancied I was about to perform one of the feats which practice renders possible,—"sleeping with one eye open," as we say: a half-and-half doze, for all senses sleep but that of hearing; the faintest murmur, sigh, or motion will break it, and give one back one's wits much brightened by the brief permission to "stand at ease." On this night, the experiment was a failure, for previous vigils, confinement, and much care had rendered naps a dangerous indulgence. Having roused half a dozen times in an hour to find all quiet, I dropped my heavy head on my arms, and, drowsily resolving to look up again in fifteen minutes, fell fast asleep.

The striking of a deep-voiced clock woke me with a start. "That is one," thought I, but, to my dismay, two more strokes followed; and in remorseful haste I sprang up to see what harm my long oblivion had done. A strong hand put me back into my seat, and held me there. It was Robert. The instant my eye met his my heart began to beat, and all along my nerves tingled that electric flash which foretells a danger that we cannot see. He was very pale, his mouth grim, and both eyes full of sombre fire,—for even the wounded one was open now, all the more sinister for the deep scar above and below. But his touch was steady, his voice quiet, as he said,—

"Sit still, Ma'am; I won't hurt yer, now even scare yer, if I can help it, but yer waked too soon."

"Let me go, Robert,—the captain is stirring,—I must give him something."

"No, Ma'am, yer can't stir an inch. Look here!"

Holding me with one hand, with the other he took up the glass in which I had left the draught, and showed me it was empty.

"Has he taken it?" I asked, more and more bewildered.

"I flung it out o'winder, Ma'am; he'll have to do without."

"But why, Robert? Why did you do it?"

"Because I hate him!"

Impossible to doubt the truth of that; his whole face showed it, as he spoke through his set teeth, and launched a fiery glance at the unconscious captain. I could only hold my breath and stare blankly at him, wondering what mad act was coming next. I suppose I shook and turned white, as women have a foolish habit of doing when sudden danger daunts them; for Robert released my arm, sat down upon the bedside just in front of me, and said, with the ominous quietude that made me cold to see and hear,—

"Don't yer be frightened, Ma'am; don't try to run away, fer the door's locked an' the key in my pocket; don't yer cry out, fer yer'd have to scream a long while, with my hand on yer mouth, before yer was heard. Be still, an' I'll tell yer what I'm goin' to do."

"Lord help us! He has taken the fever in some sudden, violent way, and is out of his head. I must humor him till someone comes"; in pursuance of which swift determination, I tried to say, quite composedly,—

"I will be still and hear you; but open the window. Why did you shut it?"

"I'm sorry I can't do it, Ma'am, but yer'd jump out, or call, if I did, an' I'm not ready yet. I shut it to make yer sleep, an' heat would do it quicker 'n anything else I could do."

The captain moved, and feebly muttered, "Water!" Instinctively I rose to give it to him, but the heavy hand came down upon my shoulder, and in the same decided tone Robert said,—

"The water went with the physic; let him call."

"Do let me go to him! He'll die without care!"

"I mean he shall;—don't yer interfere, if yer please, Ma'am."

In spite of his quiet tone and respectful manner, I saw murder in his eyes, and turned faint with fear; yet the fear excited me, and, hardly knowing what I did, I seized the hands that had seized me, crying,—

"No, no, you shall not kill him! It is base to hurt a helpless man. Why do you hate him? He is not your master?"

"He's my brother."

I felt the answer from head to foot, and seemed to fathom what was coming, with a prescience vague, but unmistakable. One appeal was left to me, and I made it.

"Robert, tell me what it means? Do not commit a crime and make me accessory to it. There is a better way of righting wrong than by violence;—let me help you find it."

My voice trembled as I spoke, and I heard the frightened flutter of my heart; so did he, and if any little act of mine had ever won affection or respect from him, the memory of it served me then. He looked down, and seemed to put some question to himself; whatever it was, the answer was in my favor, for when his eyes rose again, they were gloomy, but not desperate.

"I will tell you, Ma'am; but mind, this makes no difference; the boy is mine. I'll give the Lord a chance to take him fust; if He don't, I shall."

"Oh, no! Remember, he is your brother!"

An unwise speech; I felt it as it passed my lips, for a black frown gathered on Robert's face, and his strong hands closed with an ugly sort of grip. But he did not touch the poor soul gasping there behind him, and seemed content to let the slow suffocation of that stifling room end his frail life.

"I'm not like to forget that, Ma'am, when I've been thinkin' of it all this week. I knew him when they fetched him in, an' would 'a' done it long 'fore this, but I wanted to ask where Lucy was; he knows,—he told tonight,—an' now he's done for."

"Who is Lucy" I asked hurriedly, intent on keeping his mind busy with any thought but murder.

With one of the swift transitions of a mixed temperament like this, at my question Robert's deep eyes filled, the clenched hands were spread before his face, and all I heard were the broken words,—

"My wife,—he took her"—-

In that instant every thought of fear was swallowed up in burning indignation for the wrong, and a perfect passion of pity for the desperate man so tempted to avenge an injury for which there seemed no redress but this. He was no longer slave or contraband, no drop of black blood marred him in my sight, but an infinite compassion yearned to save, to help, to comfort him. Words seemed so powerless I offered none, only put my hand on his poor head, wounded, homeless, bowed down with grief for which I had no cure, and softly smoothed the long neglected hair pitifully wondering the while where was the wife who must have loved this tender-hearted man so well.

The captain moaned again, and faintly whispered, "Air!" but I never stirred. God forgive me! Just then I hated him as only a woman thinking of a sister woman's wrong could hate. Robert looked up; his eyes were dry again, his mouth grim. I saw that, said, "Tell me more," and he did,—for sympathy is a gift the poorest may give, the proudest stoop to receive.

"Yer see, Ma'am, his father,—I might say ours, if I warn't ashamed of both of 'em,—his father died two years ago, an' left us all to Marster Ned,—that's him here, eighteen then. He always hated me, I looked so like old Marster: he don't,—only the light skin an' hair. Old Marster was kind to all of us, me 'specially, an' bought Lucy off the next plantation down there in South Car'lina, when he found I liked her. I married her, all I could, Ma'am; it warn't much, but we was true to one another till Marster Ned come home a year after an' made hell fer both of us. He sent my old mother to be used up in his rice-swamp in Georgy; he found me with my pretty Lucy, an' though young Miss cried, an I prayed to him on my knees, an' Lucy run away, he wouldn't have no mercy; he brought her back, an'—took her, Ma'am."

"Oh, what did you do?" I cried, hot with helpless pain and passion.

How the man's outraged heart sent the blood flaming up into his face and deepened the tones of his impetuous voice, as he stretched his arm across the bed, saying with a terribly expressive gesture,—

"I half murdered him, an' tonight I'll finish."

"Yes, yes,—but go on now; what came next?"

He gave me a look that showed no white man could have felt a deeper degradation in remembering and confessing these last acts of brotherly oppression.

"They whipped me till I couldn't stand, an' then they sold me further South. Yer thought I was a white man once;—look here!"

With a sudden wrench he tore the shirt from neck to waist, and on his strong brown shoulders showed me furrows deeply ploughed, wounds which, though healed, were ghastlier to me than any in that house. I could not speak to him, and, with the pathetic dignity a great grief lends the humblest sufferer, he ended his brief tragedy by simply saying—

"That's all, Ma'am. I've never seen him since, an' now I never shall in this world,—maybe not in t'other."

"But, Robert, why think her dead? The captain was wandering when he said those sad things; perhaps he will retract them when he is sane. Don't despair; don't give up yet."

"No, Ma'am, I guess he's right; she was too proud to bear that long. It's like her to kill herself. I told her to, if there was no other way; an' she always minded me, Lucy did. My poor girl! Oh, it warn't right! No, by God, it warn't!"

As the memory of this bitter wrong, this double bereavement, burned in his sore heart, the devil that lurks in every strong man's blood leaped up; he put his hand upon his brother's throat, and, watching the white face before him, muttered low between his teeth,—

"I'm lettin' him go too easy; there's no pain in this; we a'n't even yet. I wish he knew me. Marster Ned! It's Bob; where's Lucy?"

From the captain's lips there came a long faint sigh, and nothing but a flutter of the eyelids showed that he still lived. A strange stillness filled the room as the elder brother held the younger's life suspended in his hand, while wavering between a dim hope and a deadly hate.

In the whirl of thoughts that went on in my brain, only one was clear enough to act upon. I must prevent murder, if I could,—but how? What could I do up there alone, locked in with a dying man and a lunatic?—for any mind yielded utterly to any unrighteous impulse is mad while the impulse rules it. Strength I had not, nor much courage, neither time nor wit for stratagem, and chance only could bring me help before it was too late. But one weapon I possessed,—a tongue,— often a woman's best defense; and sympathy, stronger than fear, gave me power to use it. What I said Heaven only knows, but surely Heaven helped me; words burned on my lips, tears streamed from my eyes, and some good angel prompted me to use the one name that had power to my hearer's hand and touch his heart. For at that moment I heartily believed that Lucy lived, and this earnest faith roused in him a like belief.

He listened with the lowering look of one in whom brute instinct was sovereign for the time,—a look that makes the noblest countenance base. He was but a man,—a poor, untaught, outcast, outraged man. Life had few joys for him; the world offered him no honors, no success, no home, no love. What future would this crime mar? and why should he deny himself that sweet, yet bitter morsel called revenge? How many white men, with all New England's freedom, culture, Christianity, would not have felt as he felt then? Should I have reproached him for a human anguish, a human longing for redress, all now left him from the ruin of his few poor hopes? Who had taught him that self-control, self-sacrifice, are attributes that make men masters of the earth and lift them nearer to heaven? Should I have urged the beauty of forgiveness, the duty of devout submission? He had no religion, for he was no saintly "Uncle Tom," and Slavery's black shadow seemed to darken all the world to him and shut out God. Should I have warned him of penalties, of judgments, and the potency of law? What did he know of justice, or the mercy that should temper that stern virtue, when every law, human and divine, had been broken on his hearthstone? Should I have tried to touch him by appeals to filial duty, to brotherly love? How had his appeals been answered? What memories had father and brother stored up in his heart to plead for either now? No,—all these influences, these associations, would have proved worse than useless, had I been calm enough to try them. I was not; but instinct, subtler than reason, showed me the one safe clue by which to lead this troubled soul from the labyrinth in which it groped and nearly fell. When I paused, breathless, Robert turned to me, asking, as if human assurances would strengthen his faith in Divine Omnipotence,—

"Do you believe, if I let Marster Ned live, the Lord will give me back my Lucy?"

"As surely as there is a Lord, you will find her here or in the beautiful hereafter, where there is no black or white, no master and no slave."

He took his hand from his brother's throat, lifted his eyes from my face to the wintry sky beyond, as if searching for that blessed country, happier even than the happy North. Alas, it was the darkest hour before the dawn!—there was no star above, no light below but the pale glimmer of the lamp that showed the brother who had made him desolate. Like a blind man who believes there is a sun, yet cannot see it, he shook his head, let his arms drop nervelessly upon his knees, and sat there dumbly asking that question which many a soul whose faith is firmer fixed than his had asked in hours less dark than this,— "Where is God?" I saw the tide had turned, and strenuously tried to keep this rudderless life-boat from slipping back into the whirlpool wherein it had been so nearly lost.

"I have listened to you, Robert; now hear me, and heed what I say, because my heart is full of pity for you, full of hope for your future, and a desire to help you now. I want you to go away from here, from the temptation of this place, and the sad thoughts that haunt it. You have conquered yourself once, and I honor you for it, because the harder the battle, the more glorious the victory; but it is safer to put a greater distance between you and this man. I will write you letters, give you money, and send you to good old Massachusetts to begin your new life a freeman,—yes, and a happy man; for when the captain is himself again, I will learn where Lucy is, and move heaven and earth to find and give her back to you. Will you do this, Robert?"

"Yes, Ma'am, I will."

"Good! Now you are the man I thought you, and I'll work for you with all my heart. You need sleep, my poor fellow; go, and try to forget. The captain is still alive, and as yet you are spared that sin. No, don't look there; I'll care for him. Come, Robert, for Lucy's sake."

Thank heaven for the immortality of love for when all other means of salvation failed, a spark of this vital fire softened the man's iron will until a woman's hand could bend it. He let me take from him the key, let me draw him gently away and lead him to the solitude which now was the most healing balm I could bestow. Once in his little room, he fell down on his bed and lay there as if spent with the sharpest conflict of his life. I slipped the bolt across his door and unlocked my own, flung up the window, steadied myself with a breath of air, then rushed to Doctor Franck. He came; and till dawn we worked together, saving one brother's life, and taking earnest thought how best to secure the other's liberty. When the sun came up as blithely as if it shone only upon happy homes, the Doctor went to Robert. For an hour I heard the murmur of their voices; once I caught the sound of heavy sobs, and for a time, reverent hush, as if in the silence the good man were ministering to soul as well as sense. When he departed he took Robert with him pausing to tell me he should get him off as soon as possible, but not before we met again.

Nothing more was seen of them all day; another surgeon came to see the captain, and another attendant came to fill the empty place. I tried to rest, but could not, with the thought of poor Lucy tugging at my heart, and was soon back at my post again, anxiously hoping that my contraband had not been too hastily spirited away. Just as night fell there came a tap, and, opening, I saw Robert literally "clothed and in his right mind." The Doctor had replaced the ragged suit with tidy garments, and no trace of that tempestuous night remained but deeper lines upon the forehead and the docile look of a repentant child. He did not cross the threshold, did not offer me his hand,—only took off his cap, saying with a traitorous falter in his voice,—

"God bless you, Ma'am! I'm goin'."

I put out both my hands, and held his fast.

"Good bye, Robert! Keep up good heart, and when I come home to Massachusetts we'll meet in a happier place than this. Are you quite ready, quite comfortable for your journey?"

"Yes, Ma'am, yes; the Doctor's fixed everything; I'm goin' with a friend of his; my papers are all right, an' I'm as happy as can be till I find"—-

He stopped there; then went on, with a glance into the room—

"I'm glad I didn't do it, an' I thank yer, Ma'am, fer hinderin' me,—thank yer hearty; but I'm afraid I hate him jest the same."

Of course he did; and so did I; for these faulty hearts of ours cannot turn perfect in a night, but need frost and fire, wind and rain, to ripen and make them ready for the great harvest-home. Wishing to divert his mind, I put my poor mite into his hand, and, remembering the magic of a certain little book, I gave him mine, on whose dark cover whitely shone the Virgin Mother and the Child, the grand history of whose life the book contained. The money went into Robert's pocket with a grateful murmur, the book into his bosom with a long look and a tremulous—

"I never saw MY baby, Ma'am."

I broke down then; and though my eyes were too dim to see, I felt the touch of lips upon my hands, heard the sound of departing feet, and knew my contraband was gone.

When one feels an intense dislike, the less one says about the subject of it the better; therefore I shall merely record that the captain lived,—in time was exchanged; and that, whoever the other party was, I am convinced the Government got the best of the bargain. But long before this occurred, I had fulfilled my promise to Robert; for as soon as my patient recovered strength of memory enough to make his answer trustworthy, I asked, without any circumlocution,—

"Captain Fairfax, where is Lucy?"

And too feeble to be angry, surprised, or insincere, he straightway answered,—

"Dead, Miss Dane."

"And she killed herself, when you sold Bob?"

"How the Devil did you know that?" he muttered, with an expression half-remorseful, half-amazed; but I was satisfied, and said no more.

Of course, this went to Robert, waiting far away there in a lonely home,—waiting, working, hoping for his Lucy. It almost broke my heart to do it; but delay was weak, deceit was wicked; so I sent the heavy tidings, and very soon the answer came,—only three lines; but I felt that the sustaining power of the man's life was gone.

"I thought I'd never see her any more; I'm glad to know she's out of trouble. I thank yer, Ma'am; an' if they let us, I'll fight fer yer till I'm killed, which I hope will be 'fore long."

Six months later he had his wish, and kept his word.

Every one knows the story of the attack on Fort Wagner; but we should not tire yet of recalling how our Fifty-Fourth, spent with three sleepless nights, a day's fast, and a march under the July sun, stormed the fort as night fell, facing death in many shapes, following their brave leaders through a fiery rain of shot and shell, fighting valiantly for "God and Governor Andrew,"—how the regiment that went into action seven hundred strong came out having had nearly half its number captured, killed, or wounded, leaving their young commander to be buried, like a chief of earlier times, with his body-guard around him, faithful to the death. Surely, the insult turns to honor, and the wide grave needs no monument but the heroism that consecrates it in our sight; surely, the hearts that held him nearest see through their tears a noble victory in the seeming sad defeat; and surely, God's benediction was bestowed, when this loyal soul answered, as Death called the roll, "Lord, here I am, with the brothers Thou has given me!"

The future must show how well that fight was fought; for though Fort Wagner still defies us, public prejudice is down; and through the cannon-smoke of that black night the manhood of the colored race shines before many eyes that would not see, rings in many ears that would not hear, wins many hearts that would not hitherto believe.

When the news came that we were needed, there was none so glad as I to leave teaching contrabands, the new work I had taken up, and go to nurse "our boys," as my dusky flock so proudly called the wounded of the Fifty-Fourth. Feeling more satisfaction, as I assumed my big apron and turned up my cuffs, than if dressing for the President's levee, I fell to work on board the hospital-ship in Hilton-Head harbor. The scene was most familiar, and yet strange; for only dark faces looked up at me from the pallets so thickly laid along the floor, and I missed the sharp accent of my Yankee boys in the slower, softer voices calling cheerily to one another, or answering my questions without a stout, "We'll never give it up, Ma'am, till the last Reb's dead," or "If our people's free, we can afford to die."

Passing from bed to bed, intent on making one pair of hands do the work of three, at least, I gradually washed, fed, and bandaged my way down the long line of sable heroes, and coming to the very last, found that he was my contraband. So old, so worn, so deathly weak and wan, I never should have known him but for the deep scar on his cheek. That side lay uppermost, and caught my eye at once; but even then I doubted, such an awful change had come upon him, when, turning to the ticket just above his head, I saw the name, "Robert Dane."

That both assured and touched me, for, remembering that he had no name, I knew that he had taken mine. I longed for him to speak to me, to tell how he had fared since I lost sight of him, and let me perform some little service for him in return for many he had done for me; but he seemed asleep; and as I stood reliving that strange night again, a bright lad, who lay next him softly waving an old fan across both beds, looked up and said,—

"I guess you know him, Ma'am?"

"You are right. Do you?"

"As much as any one was able to, Ma'am."

"Why do you say 'was,' as if the man were dead and gone?"

"I s'pose because I know he'll have to go. He's got a bad jab in the breast an' is bleedin' inside, the Doctor says. He don't suffer any, only gets weaker 'n' weaker every minute. I've been fannin' him this long while, an' he's talked a little; but he don't know me now, so he's most gone, I guess."

There was so much sorrow and affection in the boy's face, that I remembered something, and asked, with redoubled interest,—

"Are you the one that brought him off? I was told about a boy who nearly lost his life in saving that of his mate?"

I dare say the young fellow blushed, as any modest lad might have done; I could not see it, but I heard the chuckle of satisfaction that escaped him, as he glanced from his shattered arm and bandaged side to the pale figure opposite.

"Lord, Ma'am, tha's nothin'; we boys always stan' by one another, an' I warn't goin' to leave him to be tormented any more by them cussed Rebs. He's been a slave once, though he don't look half so much like it as me, an' I was born in Boston."

He did not; for the speaker was as black as the ace of spades,—being a sturdy specimen, the knave of clubs would perhaps be a fitter representative,—but the dark freeman looked at the white slave with the pitiful, yet puzzled expression I have so often seen on the faces of our wisest men, when this tangled question of Slavery presents itself, asking to be cut or patiently undone.

"Tell me what you know of this man; for, even if he were awake, he is too weak to talk."

"I never saw him till I joined the regiment, an' no one 'peared to have got much out of him. He was a shut-up sort of feller, an' didn't seem to care for anything but gettin' at the Rebs. Some say he was the fust man of us that enlisted; I know he fretted till we were off, an' when we pitched into old Wagner, he fought like the Devil."

"Were you with him when he was wounded? How was it?"

"Yes, Ma'am. There was somethin' queer about it; for he 'peared to know the chap that killed him, an' the chap knew him. I don't dare to ask, but I rather guess one owned the other some time,— for, when they clinched, the chap sung out, 'Bob! an' Dane, 'Marster Ned!'—then they went at it."

I sat down suddenly, for the old anger and compassion struggled in my heart, and I both longed and feared to hear what was to follow.

"You see when the Colonel—Lord keep an' send him back to us!—it a'n't certain yet, you know, Ma'am, though it's two days ago we lost him—well, when the Colonel shouted, 'Rush on, boys, rush on!' Dane tore away as if he was goin' to take the fort alone; I was next him, an' kept close as we went through the ditch an' up the wall. Hi! warn't that a rusher!" and the boy flung up his well arm with a whoop, as if the mere memory of that stirring moment came over him in a gust of irrepressible excitement.

"Were you afraid?" I said,—asking the question women often put, and receiving the answer they seldom fail to get.

"No, Ma'am!"—emphasis on the "Ma'am,"—"I never thought of anything but the damn Rebs, that scalp, slash, an' cut our ears off, when they git us. I was bound to let daylight into one of 'em at least, an' I did. Hope he liked it!"

"It is evident that you did, and I don't blame you in the least. Now go on about Robert, for I should be at work."

"He was one of the fust up; I was just behind, an' though the whole thing happened in a minute, I remember how it was, for all I was yellin' an' knockin' round like mad. Just where we were, some sort of an officer was wavin' his sword an' cheerin' on his men; Dane saw him by a big flash that come by; he flung away his gun, give a leap, an' went at that feller as if he was Jeff, Beauregard, an' Lee, all in one. I scrabbled after as quick as I could, but was only up in time to see him git the sword straight through him an' drop into the ditch. You needn't ask what I did next, Ma'am, for I don't quite know myself; all I'm clear about is, that I managed somehow to pitch that Reb into the fort as dead as Moses, git hold of Dane, an' bring him off. Poor old feller! We said we went in to live or die; he said he went in to die, an' he's done it."

I had been intently watching the excited speaker; but as he regretfully added those last words I turned again, and Robert's eyes met mine,—those melancholy eyes, so full of an intelligence that proved he had heard, remembered, and reflected with that preternatural power which often outlives all other faculties. He knew me, yet gave no greeting; was glad to see a woman's face, yet had no smile wherewith to welcome it; felt that he was dying, yet uttered no farewell. He was too far across the river to return or linger now; departing thought, strength, breath, were spent in one grateful look, one murmur of submission to the last pang he could ever feel. His lips moved, and, bending to them, a whisper chilled my cheek, as it shaped the broken words,—

"I would have done it,—but it's better so,—I'm satisfied."

Ah! well he might be,—for, as he turned his face from the shadow of the life that was, the sunshine of the life to be touched it

with a beautiful content, and in the drawing of a breath my contraband
found wife and home, eternal liberty and God.

"Scarlet Stockings"

Putnam's Magazine, July 1869

Chapter 1: How They Walked into Lennox's Life

"Come out for a drive, Harry?"

"Too cold."

"Have a game of billiards?"

"Too tired."

"Go and call on the Fairchilds?"

"Having an unfortunate prejudice against country girls, I respectfully decline."

"What will you do then?"

"Nothing, thank you."

And settling himself more luxuriously upon the couch, Lennox closed his eyes, and appeared to slumber tranquilly. Kate shook her head, and stood regarding her brother, despondently, till a sudden idea made her turn toward the window, exclaiming abruptly,

"Scarlet stockings, Harry!"

"Where?" and, as if the words were a spell to break the deepest daydream, Lennox hurried to the window, with an unusual expression of interest in his listless face.

"I thought that would succeed! She isn't there, but I've got you up, and you are not to go down again," laughed Kate, taking possession of the sofa.

"Not a bad maneuver. I don't mind; it's about time for the one interesting event of the day to occur, so I'll watch for myself, thank you," and Lennox took the easy chair by the window with a shrug and a yawn.

"I'm glad any thing does interest you," said Kate, petulantly, "though I don't think it amounts to much, for, though you perch yourself at the window every day to see that girl pass, you don't care enough about it to ask her name."

"I've been waiting to be told."

"It's Belle Morgan, the Doctor's daughter, and my dearest friend."

"Then, of course, she is a blue-belle?"

"Don't try to be witty or sarcastic with her, for she will beat you at that."

"Not a dumb-belle then?"

"Quite the reverse; she talks a good deal, and very well too, when she likes."

"She is very pretty; has anybody the right to call her 'Ma belle'?"

"Many would be glad to do so, but she won't have any thing to say to them."

"A Canterbury belle in every sense of the word then?"

"She might be, for all Canterbury loves her, but she isn't fashionable, and has more friends among the poor than among the rich."

"Ah, I see, a diving-belle, who knows how to go down into a sea of troubles, and bring up the pearls worth having."

"I'll tell her that, it will please her. You are really waking up, Harry," and Kate smiled approvingly upon him.

"This page of 'Belle's Life' is rather amusing, so read away," said Lennox, glancing up the street, as if he awaited the appearance of the next edition with pleasure.

"There isn't much to tell; she is a nice, bright, energetic, warm-hearted dear; the pride of the Doctor's heart, and a favorite with every one, though she is odd."

"How odd?"

"Does and says what she likes, is very blunt and honest, has ideas and principles of her own, goes to parties in high dresses, won't dance round dances, and wears red stockings, though Mrs. Plantagenet says it's fast."

"Rather a jolly little person, I fancy. Why haven't we met her at some of the tea-fights and muffin-worries we've been to lately?"

"It may make you angry, but it will do you good, so I'll tell. She didn't care enough about seeing the distinguished stranger to come; that's the truth."

"Sensible girl, to spare herself hours of mortal dullness, gossip, and dyspepsia," was the placid reply.

"She has seen you, though, at church and dawdling about town, and she called you 'Sir Charles Coldstream' on the spot. How does that suit?" asked Kate, maliciously.

"Not bad, I rather like that. Wish she'd call some day, and stir us up."

"She won't; I asked her, but she said she was very busy, and told Jessy Tudor, she wasn't fond of peacocks."

"I don't exactly see the connection."

"Stupid boy! She meant you, of course."

"Oh, I'm peacocks, am I?"

"I don't wish to be rude, but I really do think you are vain of your good looks, elegant accomplishments, and the impression you make wherever you go. When it's worthwhile you exert yourself, and are altogether fascinating, but the 'I come —see—and—conquer' air you put on, spoils it all for sensible people."

"It strikes me that Miss Morgan has slightly infected you with her oddity as far as bluntness goes. Fire away, it's rather amusing to be abused when one is dying of ennui."

"That's grateful and complimentary to me, when I have devoted myself to you ever since you came. But every thing bores you, and the only sign of interest you've shown is in those absurd red hose. I should like to know what the charm is," said Kate, sharply.

"Impossible to say; accept the fact calmly as I do, and be grateful that there is one glimpse of color, life, and spirit in this aristocratic tomb of a town."

"You are not obliged to stay in it!" fiercely.

"Begging your pardon, my dove, but I am. I promised to give you my enlivening society for a month, and a Lennox keeps his word, even at the cost of his life."

"I'm sorry I asked such a sacrifice; but I innocently thought that after being away for five long years, you might care to see your orphan sister," and the dove produced her handkerchief with a plaintive sniff.

"Now, my dear creature, don't be melodramatic, I beg of you," cried her brother, imploringly. "I wished to come, I pined to embrace you, and I give you my word, I don't blame you for the stupidity of this confounded place."

"It never was so gay as since you came, for every one has tried to make it pleasant for you," cried Kate, ruffled at his indifference to the hospitable efforts of herself and friends. "But you don't care for any of our simple amusements, because you are spoilt by the flattery, gayety, and nonsense of foreign society. If I didn't know it was half affectation, I should be in despair, you are so blase and absurd. It's always the way with men, if one happens to be handsome, accomplished, and talented, he puts on as many airs, and is as vain as any silly girl."

"Don't you think if you took breath, you'd get on faster, my dear?" asked the imperturbable gentleman, as Kate paused with a gasp.

"I know it's useless for me to talk, as you don't care a straw what I say, but it's true, and some day you'll wish you had done something worth doing all these years. I was so proud of you, so fond of you, that I can't help being disappointed, to find you with no more ambition than to kill time comfortably, no interest in any thing but your own pleasures, and only energy enough to amuse yourself with a pair of scarlet stockings."

Pathetic as poor Kate's face and voice were, it was impossible to help laughing at the comical conclusion of her lament. Lennox tried to hide the smile on his lips by affecting to curl his moustache with care, and to gaze pensively out as if touched by her appeal.

But he wasn't, oh, bless you, no! She was only his sister, and, though she might have talked with the wisdom of Solomon, and the eloquence of Demosthenes, it wouldn't have done a particle of good. Sisters do very well to work for one, to pet one, and play confidante when one's love affairs need feminine wit to conduct them, but when they begin to reprove, or criticize or moralize, it won't do, and can't be allowed, of course. Lennox never snubbed anybody, but blandly extinguished them by a polite acquiescence in all their affirmations, for the time being, and then went on his own way as if nothing had been said.

"I dare say you are right; I'll go and think over your very sensible advice," and, as if roused to unwonted exertion by the stings of an accusing conscience, he left the room abruptly.

"I do believe I've made an impression at last! He's actually gone out to think over what I've said. Dear Harry, I was sure he had a heart, if one only knew how to get at it!" and with a sigh of satisfaction Kate went to the window to behold the "dear Harry" going briskly down the street after a pair of scarlet stockings. A spark of anger kindled in her eyes as she watched him, and when he vanished, she still stood knitting her brows in deep thought, for a grand idea was dawning on her.

It was a dull town; no one could deny that, for everybody was so intensely proper and well-born, that nobody dared to be jolly. All the houses were square, aristocratic mansions with Revolutionary elms in front and spacious coach-houses behind. The knockers had a supercilious perk to their bronze or brass noses, the dandelions on the lawns had a highly connected air, and the very pigs were evidently descended from "our first families." Stately dinner-parties, decorous dances, moral picnics, and much tea-pot gossiping were the social resources of the place. Of course, the young people flirted, for the diversion is apparently irradicable even in the "best society," but it was done with a propriety which was edifying to behold.

One can easily imagine that such a starched state of things would not be particularly attractive to a traveled young gentleman like Lennox, who, as Kate very truly said, had been spoilt by the flattery, luxury, and gayety of foreign society. He did his best, but by the end of the first week ennui claimed him for its own, and passive endurance was all that was left him. From perfect despair he was rescued by the scarlet stockings, which went tripping by one day as he stood at the window, planning some means of escape.

A brisk, blithe-faced girl passed in a gray walking suit with a distracting pair of high-heeled boots and glimpses of scarlet at the ankle. Modest, perfectly so, I assure you, were the glimpses, but the feet were so decidedly pretty that one forgot to look at the face appertaining thereunto. It wasn't a remarkably lovely face, but it was a happy, wholesome one, with all sorts of good little dimples in cheek and chin, sunshiny twinkles in the black eyes, and a decided, yet lovable look about the mouth that was quite satisfactory. A busy, bustling little body she seemed to be, for sack-pockets and muff were full of bundles, and the trim boots tripped briskly over the ground, as if the girl's heart were as light as her heels. Somehow this active, pleasant figure seemed to wake up the whole street, and leave a streak of sunshine behind it, for every one nodded as it passed, and the primmest faces relaxed into smiles, which lingered when the girl had gone.

"Uncommonly pretty feet—she walks well, which American girls seldom do—all waddle or prance, nice face, but the boots are French, and it does my heart good to see 'em."

Lennox made these observations to himself as the young lady approached, nodded to Kate at another window, gave a quick but comprehensive glance at himself and trotted round the corner, leaving the impression on his mind that a whiff of fresh spring air had blown through the street in spite of the December snow. He didn't trouble himself to ask who it was, but fell into the way of lounging in the bay-window at about three p.m., and watching the gray and scarlet figure pass with its blooming cheeks, bright eyes, and elastic step. Having nothing else to do, he took to petting this new whim, and quite depended on the daily stirring-up which the sight of the energetic damsel gave him. Kate saw it all, but took no notice till the day of the little tiff above recorded; after that she was as soft as a summer sea, and by some clever stroke had Belle Morgan to tea that very week.

Lennox was one of the best tempered fellows in the world, but the "peacocks" did rather nettle him because there was some truth in the insinuation; so he took care to put on no airs or try to be fascinating in the presence of Miss Belle. In truth he soon forgot himself entirely, and enjoyed her oddities with a relish, after the prim proprieties of the other young ladies who had simpered and sighed before him. For the first time in his life, the "Crusher," as his male friends called him, got crushed; for Belle, with the subtle skill of a quick-witted, keen-sighted girl, soon saw and condemned the elegant affectations which others called foreign polish. A look, a word, a gesture from a pretty woman is often more eloquent and impressive than moral essays or semi-occasional twinges of conscience, and in the presence of one satirical little person, Sir Charles Coldstream soon ceased to deserve the name.

Belle seemed to get over her hurry and to find time for occasional relaxation, but one never knew in what mood he might find her, for the weathercock was not more changeable than she. Lennox liked that, and found the muffin-worries quite endurable with this *sauce piquante* to relieve their insipidity. Presently he discovered that he was suffering for exercise, and formed the wholesome habit of promenading the town about three p.m.; Kate said, to follow the scarlet stockings.

Chapter 2: Where They Led Him

"Whither away, Miss Morgan?" asked Lennox, as he overtook her one bitter cold day.

"I'm taking my constitutional."
"So am I."

"With a difference," and Belle glanced at the blue-nosed, muffled-up gentleman strolling along beside her with an occasional shiver and shrug.

"After a winter in the south of France one don't find arctic weather like this easy to bear," he said, with a disgusted air.

"I like it, and do my five or six miles a day, which keeps me in what fine ladies call 'rude health,'" answered Belle, walking him on at a pace which soon made his furs a burden.

She was a famous pedestrian, and a little proud of her powers, but she outdid all former feats that day, and got over the ground in gallant style. Something in her manner put her escort on his mettle, and his usual lounge was turned into a brisk march which set his blood dancing, face glowing, and spirits effervescing as they had not done for many a day.

"There! You look more like your real self now," said Belle, with the first sign of approval she had ever vouchsafed him, as he rejoined her after a race to recover her veil, which the wind whisked away over hedge and ditch.

"Are you sure you know what my real self is?" he asked, with a touch of the "conquering hero" air.

"Not a doubt of it. I always know a soldier when I see one," returned Belle, decidedly.

"A soldier! That's the last thing I should expect to be accused of," and Lennox looked both surprised and gratified.

"There's a flash in your eye and a ring in your voice, occasionally, which made me suspect that you had fire and energy enough if you only chose to show it, and the spirit with which you have just executed the 'Morgan Quick step' proves that I was right," returned Belle, laughing.

"Then I am not altogether a 'peacock?'" said Lennox, significantly, for during the chat, which had been as brisk as the walk, Belle had given his besetting sins several sly hits, and he couldn't resist one return shot, much as her unexpected compliment pleased him.

Poor Belle blushed up to her forehead, tried to look as if she did not understand, and gladly hid her confusion behind the recovered veil without a word.

There was a decided display both of the "flash" and the "ring," as Lennox looked at the suddenly subdued young lady, and, quite satisfied with his retaliation, gave the order—"Forward, march!" which brought them to the garden-gate breathless, but better friends than before.

The next time the young people met, Belle was in such a hurry that she went round the corner with an abstracted expression which was quite a triumph of art. Just then, off tumbled the lid of the basket she carried, and Lennox, rescuing it from a puddle, obligingly helped readjust it over a funny collection of bottles, dishes, and tidy little rolls of all sorts.

"It's very heavy, mayn't I carry it for you?" he asked, in an insinuating manner.

"No, thank you," was on Belle's lips, but observing that he was got up with unusual elegance to pay calls, she couldn't resist the temptation of making a beast of burden of him, and took him at his word.

"You may, if you like. I've got more bundles to take from the store, and another pair of hands won't come amiss."

Lennox lifted his eyebrows, also the basket, and they went on again, Belle very much absorbed in her business, and her escort wondering where the dickens she was going with all that rubbish. Filling his unoccupied hand with sundry brown paper parcels, much to the detriment of the light kid that covered it, Belle paraded him down the main street before the windows of the most aristocratic mansions, and then dived into a dirty back-lane, where the want and misery of the town was decorously kept out of sight.

"You don't mind scarlet fever, I suppose?" observed Belle, as they approached the unsavory residence of Biddy O'Brien.

"Well, I'm not exactly partial to it," said Lennox, rather taken aback.

"You needn't go in if you are afraid, or speak to me afterwards, so no harm will be done—except to your gloves."

"Why do you come here, if I may ask? It isn't the sort of amusement I should recommend," he began, evidently disapproving of the step.

"Oh, I'm used to it, and like to play nurse where father plays doctor. I'm fond of children, and Mrs. O'Brien's are little dears," returned Belle, briskly, threading her way between ash-heaps and mud-puddles as if bound to a festive scene.

"Judging from the row in there, I should infer that Mrs. O'Brien had quite a herd of little dears."

"Only nine."

"And all sick?"

"More or less."

"By Jove! It's perfectly heroic in you to visit this hole in spite of dirt, noise, fragrance, and infection," cried Lennox, who devoutly wished that the sense of hearing were temporarily denied him.

"Bless you, it's the sort of thing I enjoy, for there's no nonsense here; the work you do is pleasant if you do it heartily, and the thanks you get are worth having, I assure you."

She put out her hand to relieve him of the basket, but he gave it an approving little shake, and said briefly—

"Not yet, I'm coming in."

It's all very well to rhapsodize about the exquisite pleasure of doing good, to give carelessly of one's abundance, and enjoy the delusion of having remembered the poor. But it is a cheap charity, and never brings the genuine satisfaction which those know who give their mite with heart as well as hand, and truly love their neighbor as themselves. Lennox had seen much fashionable benevolence, and laughed at it even while he imitated it, giving generously when it wasn't inconvenient. But this was a new sort of thing entirely, and in spite of the dirt, the noise, and the smells, he forgot the fever, and was glad he came when poor Mrs. O'Brien turned from her sick babies, exclaiming, with Irish fervor at sight of Belle, "The Lord love ye, darlin, for remimberin us when ivery one, barrin' the doctor, and the praste, turns the cowld shouldther in our throuble!"

"Now if you really want to help, just keep this child quiet while I see to the sickest ones," said Belle, dumping a stout infant on to his knee, thrusting an orange into his hand, and leaving him aghast, while she unpacked her little messes, and comforted the maternal bird.

With the calmness of desperation, her aid-de-camp put down his best beaver on the rich soil which covered the floor, pocketed his Paris kids, and making a bib of his cambric handkerchief, gagged young Pat deliciously with bits of orange whenever he opened his mouth to roar. At her first leisure moment, Belle glanced at him to see how he was getting on, and found him so solemnly absorbed in his task that she went off into a burst of such infectious merriment that the O'Briens, sick and well, joined in it to a man.

"Good fun, isn't it?" she asked, turning down her cuffs when the last spoonful of gruel was administered.

"I've no doubt of it, when one is used to the thing. It comes a little hard at first, you know," returned Lennox, wiping his forehead, with a long breath, and seizing his hat as if quite ready to tear himself away.

"You've done very well for a beginner; so kiss the baby and come home," said Belle approvingly.

"No, thank you," muttered Lennox, trying to detach the bedaubed innocent. But little Pat had a grateful heart, and falling upon his new nurse's neck with a rapturous crow clung there like a burr.

"Take him off! Let me out of this! He's one too many for me!" cried the wretched young man in comic despair.

Being freed with much laughter, he turned and fled, followed
by a shower of blessings, from Mrs. O'Brien.

As they came up again into the pleasant highways, Lennox
said, awkwardly for him, "The thanks of the poor are excellent things
to have, but I think I'd rather receive them by proxy. Will you kindly
spend this for me in making that poor soul comfortable?"

But Belle wouldn't take what he offered her, she put it back,
saying earnestly,

"Give it yourself; one can't buy blessings, they must be
earned or they are not worth having. Try it, please, and if you find it a
failure, then I'll gladly be your almoner."

There was a significance in her words which he could not fail
to understand. He neither shrugged, drawled, nor sauntered now, but
gave her a look in which respect and self-reproach were mingled, and
left her, simply saying, "I'll try it, Miss Morgan."

"Now isn't she odd?" whispered Kate to her brother, as Belle
appeared at a little dance at Mrs. Plantagenet's in a high-necked dress,
knitting away on an army-sock, as she greeted the friends who
crowded round her.

"Charmingly so. Why don't you do that sort of thing when
you can?" answered her brother, glancing at her thin, bare shoulders
and hands, rendered nearly useless by the tightness of the gloves.

"Gracious, no! It's natural to her to do so, and she carries it
off well; I couldn't, therefore I don't try, though I admire it in her. Go
and ask her to dance, before she is engaged."
"She doesn't dance round dances you know."

"She is dreadfully prim about some things and so free and
easy about others, I can't understand it, do you?"

"Well, yes, I think I do. Here's Forbes coming for you, I'll go
and entertain Belle by a quarrel."
He found her in a recess out of the way of the rushing and
romping, busy with her work, yet evidently glad to be amused.

"I admire your adherence to principles, Miss Belle, but don't you find it a little hard to sit still while your friends are enjoying themselves?" he asked, sinking luxuriously into the lounging chair beside her.

"Yes, very," answered Belle with characteristic candor. "But father don't approve of that sort of exercise, so I console myself with something useful till my chance comes."

"Your work can't exactly be called ornamental," said Lennox, looking at the big sock.

"Don't laugh at it, sir, it is for the foot of the brave fellow who is going to fight for me and his country."

"Happy fellow! May I ask who he is?" and Lennox sat up with an air of interest.

"My substitute; I don't know his name, for father has not got him yet, but I'm making socks, and towels, and a comfort-bag for him, so that when found he may be off at once."

"You really mean it?" cried Lennox.

"O course I do; I can't go myself, but I *can* buy a pair of strong arms to fight for me, and I intend to do it. I only hope he'll have the right sort of courage and be a credit to me."

"What do you call the right sort of courage?" asked Lennox, soberly.

"That which makes a man ready and glad to live or die for a principle. There's a chance for heroes now, if there ever was. When do you join your regiment?" she added abruptly.

"Haven't the least idea," and Lennox subsided again.

"But you intend to do so, of course?"

"Why should I?"

Belle dropped her work. "Why should you? What a question! Because you have health, and strength and courage, and money to help on the good cause, and every man should give his best, and not dare to stay at home when he is needed."

"You forget that I am an Englishman, and we rather prefer to be strictly neutral just now."

"You are only half English, and for your mother's sake you should be proud and glad to fight for the North," cried Belle warmly.

"I don't remember my mother."

"That's evident!"

"But I was about to add, I've no objection to lend a hand if it isn't too much trouble to get off," said Lennox indifferently, for he liked to see Belle's color rise, and her eyes kindle while he provoked her.

"Do you expect to go South in a bandbox? You'd better join one of the kid-glove regiments, they say the dandies fight well when the time comes."

"I've been away so long, the patriotic fever hasn't seized me yet, and as the quarrel is none of mine, I think, perhaps I'd better take care of Kate, and let you fight it out among yourselves. Here's the Lancers, may I have the honor?"

But Belle, being very angry at this luke-warmness, answered in her bluntest manner.

"Having reminded me that you are a 'strictly neutral' Englishman, you must excuse me if I decline; I dance only with loyal Americans," and rolling up her work with a defiant flourish, she walked away, leaving him to lament his loss and wonder how he could retrieve it. She did not speak to him again till he stood in the hall waiting for Kate, then Belle came down in the charming little red hood, and going straight up to him with her hand out, a repentant look, and a friendly smile, said frankly—
"I was very rude; I want to beg pardon of the English, and shake hands with the American half."

So peace was declared, and lasted unbroken for the remaining week of his stay, when he proposed to take Kate to the city for a little gayety. Miss Morgan openly approved the plan, but secretly felt as if the town was about to be depopulated, and tried to hide her melancholy in her substitute's socks. They were not large enough, however, to absorb it all, and when Lennox went to make his adieu, it was perfectly evident that the Doctor's Belle was out of tune. The young gentleman basely exulted over this, till she gave him something to think about by saying gravely,

"Before you go, I feel as if I ought to tell you something, since Kate won't. If you are offended about it, please don't blame her; she meant it kindly and so did I." Belle paused as if it was not an easy thing to tell, and then went on quickly, with her eyes upon her work.

"Three weeks ago Kate asked me to help her in a little plot, and I consented, for the fun of the thing. She wanted something to amuse and stir you up, and finding that my queer ways diverted you, she begged me to be neighborly and let you do what you liked. I didn't care particularly about amusing you, but I did think you needed rousing, so for her sake I tried to do it, and you very good-naturedly bore my lecturing. I don't like deceit of any kind, so I confess, but I can't say I'm sorry, for I really think you are none the worse for the teasing and teaching you've had."

Belle didn't see him flush or frown as she made her confession, and when she looked up he only said, half gratefully, half reproachfully,

"I'm a good deal the better for it, I dare say, and ought to be very thankful for our friendly exertions. But two against one was hardly fair, now was it?"

"No, it was sly and sinful in the highest degree, but we did it for your good, so I know you'll forgive us, and as a proof of it sing one or two of my favorites for the last time."

"You don't deserve any favor, but I'll do it to show you how much more magnanimous men are than women."

Not at all loth to improve his advantages, Lennox warbled his most melting lays *con amore*, watching, as he sung, for any sign of sentiment in the girlish face opposite. But Belle wouldn't be

sentimental; and sat rattling her knitting-needles industriously, though
"The Harbor Bar was Moaning" dolefully, though "Douglas" was
touchingly "tender and true," and the "Wind of the Summer Nigh"
sighed romantically through the sitting-room.

"Much obliged. Must you go?" she said, without a sign of soft
confusion as he rose.

"I must, but I shall come again before I leave the country.
May I?" he asked, holding her hand.

"If you come in a uniform."

"Good night, Belle," tenderly. "Good-bye Sir Charles," with a
wicked twinkle of the eye, which lasted till he closed the hall door,
growling irefully,

"I thought I'd had some experience, but one never can
understand these women."

Canterbury did become a desert to Belle after her dear friend
had gone; (of course the dear friend's brother had nothing to do with
the desolation), and as the weeks dragged slowly, Belle took to reading
poetry, practicing plaintive ballads, and dawdling over her work at a
certain window which commanded a view of the railway station and
hotel.

"You're dull, my dear, run up to town with me tomorrow, and
see your young man off," said the Doctor, one evening as Belle sat
musing with a half-mended red stocking in her hand.

"My young man?" she ejaculated, turned with a start and a
blush.

"Your substitute, child. Stephens attended to the business for
me, and he's off tomorrow. I began to tell you about the fellow last
week, but you were wool-gathering, so I stopped."

"Yes, I remember, it was all very nice. Goes tomorrow, does
he? I'd like to see him, but do you think we can both leave home at
once? Some one might come you know, and I fancy it's going to

snow," said Belle, putting her face behind the curtain to inspect the weather.

"You'd better go, the trip will do you good, you can take your things to Tom Jones, and see Kate on the way; she's got back from Philadelphia."

"Has she! I'll go, then; it will please her, and I do need change. You are an old dear, to think of it;" and giving her father a hasty glimpse of a suddenly excited countenance, Belle slipped out of the room to prepare her best array with a most reckless disregard of the impending storm.

It didn't snow on the morrow, and up they went to see the — th regiment off. Belle did not see "her young man," however, for while her father went to carry him her comforts and a patriotic nosegay of red and white flowers, tied up with a smart blue ribbon, she called on Kate. But Miss Lennox was engaged, and sent an urgent request that her friend would call in the afternoon. Much disappointed and a little hurt, Belle then devoted herself to the departing regiment, wishing she was going with it, for she felt in a war-like mood. It was past noon when a burst of martial music, the measured tramp of many feet, and enthusiastic cheers announced that "the boys" were coming. From the balcony where she stood with her father, Belle looked down upon the living stream that flowed by like a broad river with a steely glitter above the blue. All her petty troubles vanished at the sight, her heart beat high, her face glowed, her eyes filled, and she waved her hat as zealously as if she had a dozen friends and lovers in the ranks below.

"Here comes your man; I told him to stick the posy where it would catch my eye, so I could point him out to you. Look, it's the tall fellow at the end of the front line," said the Doctor in an excited tone, as he pointed and beckoned.

Belle looked and gave a little cry, for there, in a private's uniform, with her nosegay at his buttonhole, and on his face a smile she never forgot, was Lennox! For an instant she stood staring at him as pale and startled as if he were a ghost, then the color rushed into her face, she kissed both hands to him, and cried bravely, "Good-bye, good-bye, God bless you, Harry!" and immediately laid her head on her father's shoulder, sobbing as if her heart was broken.

When she looked up, her substitute was lost in the undulating mass below, and for her the spectacle was over.

"Was it really he? Why wasn't I told? What does it all mean?" she demanded, looking bewildered, grieved, and ashamed.

"He's really gone, my dear. It's a surprise of his, and I was bound over to silence. Here, this will explain the joke, I suppose," and the Doctor handed her a cocked-hat note, done up like a military order.

"A Roland for your Oliver, Mademoiselle! I came home for the express purpose of enlisting, and only delayed a month on Kate's account. If I ever return, I will receive my bounty at your hands. Till then please comfort Kate, think as kindly as you can of 'Sir Charles,' and sometimes pray a little prayer for

"Your unworthy

"Substitute."

Belle looked very pale and meek when she put her note in her pocket, but she only said, "I must go and comfort Kate," and the Doctor gladly obeyed, feeling that the joke was more serious than he had imagined.

The moment her friend appeared, Miss Lennox turned on her tears, and "played away" pouring forth lamentations, reproaches and regrets in a steady stream.

"I hope you are satisfied now, you cruel girl!" she began, refusing to be kissed. "You've sent him off with a broken heart to rush into danger and be shot, or get his arms and legs spoilt. You know he loved you and wanted to tell you so, but you wouldn't let him, and now you've driven him away, and he's gone as an insignificant private with his head shaved, and a heavy knapsack breaking his back, and a horrid gun that will be sure to explode, and he *would* wear those immense blue socks you sent, for he adores you, and you only teased and laughed at him, my poor deluded, deserted brother!" And quite overwhelmed by the afflicting picture, Kate lifted up her voice and wept again.

"I *am* satisfied; for he's done what I hoped he would, and he's none the less a gentleman because he's a private and wears my socks. I pray they will keep him safe and bring him home to us when he has done his duty like a man, as I know he will. I'm proud of my brave substitute, and I'll try to be worthy of him," cried Belle, kindling beautifully as she looked out into the wintry sunshine with a new softness in the eyes that still seemed watching that blue-coated figure marching away to danger, perhaps death.

"It's ill playing with edged tools; we meant to amuse him and we may have sent him to destruction. I'll never forgive you for your part, never!" said Kate, with the charming inconsistency of her sex.

But Belle turned away her wrath by a soft answer, as she whispered, with a tender choke in her voice, "We both love him, dear; let's comfort one another."

Chapter 3: What Became of Them

Private Lennox certainly had chosen pretty hard work, for the —th was not a "kid-glove" regiment by any means; fighting in mid-winter was not exactly festive, and camps do not abound in beds of roses even at the best of times. But Belle was right in saying she knew a soldier when she saw him, for now that he was thoroughly waked up, he proved that there was plenty of courage, energy, and endurance in him.

It's my private opinion that he might now and then have slightly regretted the step he had taken, had it not been for certain recollections of a sarcastic tongue and a pair of keen eyes, not to mention the influence of one of the most potent rulers of the human heart, namely, the desire to prove himself worthy of the respect, if nothing more, of somebody at home. Belle's socks did seem to keep him safe, and lead him straight in the narrow path of duty. Belle's comfort-bag was such in very truth, for not one of the stout needles on the tricolored cushion but what seemed to wink its eye approvingly at him; not one of the tidy balls of thread that did not remind him of the little hand he coveted, and the impracticable scissors, were cherished as a good omen, though he felt that the sharpest steel that ever came from Sheffield couldn't cut his love in twain. And Belle's lessons, short as they had been, were not forgotten but seemed to have been taken up by a sterner mistress, whose rewards were greater if not so sweet as those the girl could give. There was plenty of exercise nowadays of hard work that left many a tired head asleep forever under the snow. There were many opportunities for diving "into the depths and bringing up pearls worth having" by acts of kindness among the weak, the wicked, and the suffering all about him. He learned now how to earn, not buy, the thanks of the poor, and unconsciously proved in the truest way that a private *could* be a gentleman. But best of all was the steadfast purpose "to live and die for a principle," which grew and strengthened with each month of bitter hardship, bloody strife, and dearly-bought success. Life grew earnest to him, time seemed precious, self was forgotten, and all that was best and bravest rallied round the flag on which his heart inscribed the motto, "Love and Liberty."

Praise and honor he could not fail to win, and had he never gone back to claim his bounty he would have earned the great "Well done," for he kept his oath loyally, did his duty manfully, and loved his lady faithfully, like a knight of the chivalrous times. He knew nothing of her secret, but wore her blue ribbon like an order, never went into battle without first, like many another poor fellow, kissing something which he carried next his heart, and with each day of absence felt himself a better man, and brave soldier, for the fondly foolish romance he had woven about the scarlet stockings.

Belle and Kate did comfort one another, not only with tears and kisses, but with womanly work which kept hearts happy and hands busy. How Belle bribed her to silence will always remain the ninth wonder of the world, but though reams of paper passed between brother and sister during those twelve months not a hint was dropped on one side in reply to artful inquiries from the other. Belle never told her love in words, but she stowed away an unlimited quantity of the article in the big boxes that went to gladden the eyes and—alas for romance!—the stomach of Private Lennox. If pickles could typify passion, cigars prove constancy, and gingerbread reveal the longings of the soul, then would the above-mentioned gentleman have been the happiest of lovers. But camp-life had doubtless dulled his finer intuitions, for he failed to understand the new language of love, and gave away these tender tokens with lavish prodigality. Concealment preyed a trifle on Belle's damask cheek it must be confessed, and the keen eyes grew softer with the secret tears that sometimes dimmed them; the sharp tongue seldom did mischief now, but uttered kindly words to every one as if doing penance for the past, and a sweet seriousness toned down the lively spirit which was learning many things in the sleepless nights that followed when the "little prayer" for the beloved substitute was done.

"I'll wait and see if he is all I hope he will be, before I let him know. I shall read the truth the instant I see him, and if he has stood the test I'll run into his arms and tell him everything," she said to herself with delicious thrills at the idea; but you may be sure she did nothing of the sort when the time came.

A rumor flew though the town one day that Lennox had arrived; upon receipt of which joyful tidings Belle had a panic and hid herself in the garret. But when she had quaked, and cried, and peeped, and listened for an hour or two, finding that no one came to hunt her up, she composed her nerves and descended to pass the afternoon in the parlor and a high state of dignity. All sorts of reports reached her—he was mortally wounded, he had been made a major or a colonel, or a general, no one knew exactly which; he was dead, was going to be married, and hadn't come at all. Belle fully expiated all her small sins by the agonies of suspense she suffered that day, and when at last a note came from Kate begging her "to drop over to see Harry," she put her pride in her pocket and went at once.

The drawing-room was empty and in confusion, there was a murmur of voices upstairs, a smell of camphor in the air, and an empty wine glass on the table where a military cap was lying. Belle's heart sunk, and she covertly kissed the faded blue coat as she stood waiting breathlessly, wondering if Harry had any arms for her to run into. She heard the chuckling Biddy lumber up and announce her, then a laugh and a half fond, half exulting—"Ah, ha, I thought she'd come!"

That spoilt it all; Belle took out her pride instantly, set her teeth, rubbed a quick color into her white cheeks, and snatching up a newspaper, sat herself down with as expressionless a face as it was possible for an excited young woman to possess. Lennox came running down —"Thank heaven, his legs are safe!" sighed Belle, with her eyes glued to the price of beef. He entered with both hands extended, which relieved her mind upon another point, and he beamed upon her, looking so vigorous, manly, and martial that she cried within herself, "My beautiful brown soldier!" even while she greeted him with an unnecessarily brief, "How do you do, Mr. Lennox?"

The sudden eclipse which passed over his joyful countenance would have been ludicrous if it hadn't been pathetic; but he was used to hard knocks now, and bore this, his hardest, like a man. He shook hands heartily, and as Belle sat down again (not to betray that she was trembling a good deal), he stood at ease before her, talking in a way which soon satisfied her that he *had* borne the test, and that bliss was waiting for her round the corner. But she had made it such a sharp corner she couldn't turn it gracefully, and while she pondered how to do so he helped her with a cough. She looked up quickly, discovering all at once that he was very thin, rather pale in spite of the nice tan, and breathed hurriedly as he stood with one hand in his breast.

"Are you ill, wounded, in pain?" she asked, forgetting herself entirely.

"Yes, all three," he answered, after a curious look at her changing color and anxious eyes.

"Sit down—tell me about it—can I do any thing?" and Belle began to plump up the pillows on the couch with nervous eagerness.

"Thank you, I'm past help," was the mournful reply, accompanied by a hollow cough which made her shiver.

"Oh, don't say so! Let me bring father; he is very skillful. Shall I call Kate?"

"He can do nothing; Kate doesn't know this, and I beg you won't tell her. I got a shot in the breast and made light of it, but it will finish me sooner or later. I don't mind telling you, for you are one of the strong, cool sort, you know, and are not affected by such things. But Kate is so fond of me, I don't want to shock and trouble her yet a while. Let her enjoy my little visit, and after I'm gone you can tell her the truth."

Belle had sat like a statue while he spoke with frequent pauses and an involuntary clutch or two at the suffering breast. As he stopped and passed his hand over his eyes, she said slowly, as if her white lips were stiff,

"Gone! Where?"

"Back to my place. I'd rather die fighting than fussed and wailed over by a parcel of women. I expected to stay a week or so, but a battle is coming sooner than we imagined, so I'm away again tomorrow. As I'm not likely ever to come back, I just wanted to ask you to stand by poor Kate when I'm finished, and to say good-bye to you, Belle, before I go." He put out his hand, but holding it fast in both her own, she laid her tearful face down on it, whispering imploringly,

"Oh, Harry, stay!"

Never mind what happened for the next ten minutes; suffice it to say that the enemy having surrendered, the victor took possession with great jubilation and showed no quarter.

"Bang the field piece, toot the fife, and beat the rolling drum, for ruse number three has succeeded! Come down, Kate, and give us your blessing," called Lennox, taking pity on his sister, who was anxiously awaiting the denouement on the stairs.

In she rushed, and the young ladies laughed and cried, kissed and talked tumultuously, while their idol benignantly looked on, vainly endeavoring to repress all vestiges of unmanly emotion.

"And you are not dying, really truly?" cried Belle, when fair weather set in after the flurry.

"Bless your dear heart, no! I'm as sound as a nut, and haven't a wound to boast of, except this ugly slash on the head."

"It's a splendid wound, and I'm proud of it," and Belle set a rosy little seal on the scar which quite reconciled her lover to the disfigurement of his handsome forehead. "You've learned to fib in the army, and I'm disappointed in you," she added, trying to look reproachful and failing entirely.

"No, only the art of strategy. You quenched me by your frosty reception, and I thought it was all up till you put the idea of playing invalid into my head. It succeeded so well that I piled on the agony, resolving to fight it out on that line, and if I failed again to make a masterly retreat. You gave a lesson in deceit once, so don't complain if I turned the tables and made your heart ache for a minute, as you've made mine for a year."

Belle's spirit was rapidly coming back, so she gave him a capital imitation of his French shrug, and drawled out in his old way—

"I have my doubts abut that, mon ami."

"What do you say to this—and this—and this?" he retorted, pulling out and laying before her with triumphant flourish, a faded blue ribbon, fat pincushion with a hole through it, and a dainty-painted little picture of a pretty girl in scarlet stockings.

"There, I've carried those treasures in my breast-pocket for a year, and I'm firmly convinced that they have all done their part toward keeping me safe. The blue ribbon bound me fast to you, Belle; the funny cushion caught the bullet that otherwise might have finished me, and the blessed little picture was my comfort during those dreadful marches, my companion on picket-duty with treachery and danger all about me, and my inspiration when the word 'Charge!' went down the line, for in the thickest of the night I always saw the little gray figure beckoning me on to my duty."

"Oh, Harry, you won't go back to all those horrors, will you? I'm sure you've done enough, and may rest now and enjoy your reward," said Kate, trying not to feel that "two is company and three is none."

"I've enlisted for the war, and shall not rest till either it or I come to an end. As for my reward, I had it when Belle kissed me."

"You are right, I'll wait for you, and love you all the better for the sacrifice," whispered Belle. "I only wish I could share your hardships, dear, for while you fight and suffer I can only love and pray."

"Waiting is harder than working to such as you, so be contented with your share, for the thought of you will glorify the world generally for me. I'll tell you what you can do while I'm away; it's both useful and amusing, so it will occupy and cheer you capitally. Just knit lots of red hose, because I don't intend you to wear any others hereafter, Mrs. Lennox."

"Mine are not worn out yet," laughed Belle, getting merry at the thought.

"No matter for that, those are sacred articles, and henceforth must be treasured as memorials of our love. Frame and hang 'em up; or, if the prejudices of society forbid that flight of romance, lay them carefully away where moths can't devour nor thieves steal 'em, so that years hence, when my descendants praise me for any virtues I may possess, any good I may have done, or any honor I may have earned, I can point to those precious relics and say proudly,

"My children, for all that I am, or hope to be, you must thank your honored mother's scarlet stockings."

Harriet Prescott Spofford

(1835-1921)

Born April 3, 1835, in Calais, Maine, Harriet Prescott Spofford comes from a distinguished family with New England roots that can be traced back over two hundred years. As the oldest of five children—four daughters and one son—of Sarah Bridges and Joseph Prescott, Spofford learned at an early age the meaning of financial instability. At age fourteen, her father left the household to seek a better livelihood in Oregon. When he returned seven years later in 1856, his fortunes were not better and his health was worse.

During her father's absence she lived with her mother, three sisters, four aunts, her grandmother, and one brother. Despite the family's limited financial resources, Spofford received a good education. In her early years and when finances permitted, she attended sporadically Miss Porter's private school. When her father left for the West in 1849, her mother moved the family to Newburyport, Massachusetts, where they lived with a married sister and her husband. In Newburyport, Spofford had the opportunity to study at the Putnam Free School which had been founded a year earlier. Spofford's school encouraged reading, and here her literary interests blossomed. In Newburyport, she met Thomas Higginson who remained a lifelong friend and who encouraged the literary pursuits of the youth by awarding prizes for best poetry and prose. At age eighteen in 1853, Harriet's family moved again, this time to Derry, New Hampshire. Here, Harriet completed her formal education by attending the distinguished Pinkerton Academy, which had been established in 1815 but excluded women in 1821, only readmitting them in 1853. Prescott stands out in the nineteenth century as a woman writer with a high level of formal education.

In 1865 at age thirty, she married Richard Spofford, a lawyer and poet. For many years, they lived alternately in Washington, D.C., and Newburyport where he was professionally active. When her husband died in 1888, a group of women friends increasingly became the center of her intellectual and social life. After her husband's death, she continued to write. In 1921 at age eighty–six she died and was buried at Newburyport.

In a literary career that spans six decades in two centuries, Spofford began writing at age twenty to help support her family. In 1858 at age twenty-three, she submitted her first story, "In a Cellar," to *The Atlantic Monthly*. In 1860, she published her first novel, *Sir Rohan's Ghost.* Over the years Spofford wrote hundreds of short stories, poems, novellas, essays, children's stories, personal reminiscences and novels. Unquestionably, her short stories demonstrate best her literary skill and are her claim to fame. Along with other women included in this collection, Spofford realistically portrays many aspects of nineteenth-century New England life. Besides writing about the New England towns she knew so well, she explores the lives of women and their relationships. Her ability to capture the essence of New England character through dialect and description earned her the praise of Henry James and William Dean Howells.

In "Miss Moggaridge's Provider," a story first published in the January 1871 issue of *The Atlantic Monthly*, Spofford focuses on the lives of what appear to be two very different women and their very different views regarding religion. Central to the conflict between these women is the application of law and love. Having grown up in a parsonage with her father as a Calvinistic preacher, the outspoken and feisty Miss Moggaridge has seen his strict application of law and knows the potential destructiveness of it. In her case, in fact, her own brother has been cut off from the family. Spofford's portrayal of Moggaridge's father is a good example of what Donna Campbell refers to in the fiction from this time as having " . . . misguidedly idealistic characters, particularly ministers and the organized religion that they represent, [which] function more as bastions of moral legalism than as sources of spiritual comfort" (*Resisting Regionalism.* [Athens: Ohio University Press, 1997], p. 59). What we see explored, among other things, in this story is the transition from the power and authority of men, and particularly ministers, to a "feminized" American culture celebrating love, compassion, and charity. As a result of her background, Miss Moggaridge gravitates toward love as the compass in her life. Miss Keturah, on the other hand, follows the law (has been indoctrinated?) and idealizes Moggaridge's father. With masterful character development, irony, and her use of humor, Spofford captures the conflict that threatens the very relationship between these two women and surprises us with an ending that shows us how much the two are alike.

Selected Primary Works

Sir Rohan's Ghost: A Romance, 1860; *Azarian: An Episode*, 1864; *New England Legends*, 1871; *The Servant Girl Question*, 1881; *House and Hearth*, 1891; *A Scarlet Poppy, and Other Stories*, 1894; *The King's Easter*, 1912; *A Little Book of Friends*, 1916; *The Elder's People*, 1920.

"Miss Moggaridge's Provider"

The Atlantic Monthly, January 1871

The way in which people interested themselves in Miss Moggaridge's affairs would have been a curiosity in itself anywhere but in the sea coast town where Miss Moggaridge lived. But there it had become so much a matter of course for one neighbor to discuss the various bearings of all the incidents in another neighbor's life, and,— if unexplained facts still remained, to supply the gap from fancy,—in addition to the customary duty of keeping the other neighbor's conscience, that it never struck a soul among all the worthy tribes there that they were doing anything at all out of the way of gossiping, wondering, conjecturing, and declaring this, that, and the other, about Miss Moggaridge's business after a fashion that would have made any one but herself perfectly wild.

But Miss Moggaridge was a placid old soul, and as the fact of her neighbor's gossip implied a censure which perhaps she felt to be not altogether undeserved, while, on the other hand, their wonder was not entirely uncomplimentary, she found herself able to disregard them altogether, and in answer to query, complaint, or expostulation concerning her wicked waste which was to make woful want, always met her interlocutor with the sweet and gentle words, "The Lord will provide."

Poor Miss Moggaridge's father had been that extraordinary phenomenon, a clergyman possessed not only of treasure in Heaven, but of the rustier and more corruptible treasure of this world's goods,—an inherited treasure, by the way, which he did not have time to scatter to the four winds in person, as it was left to him by an admirer (to whom his great sermon on the Seventh Seal had brought spiritual peace), but a few years before his death, which happened suddenly; and the property was consequently divided according to his last will and testament between two of his three children, giving them each a modest competency, but leaving the third to shift for himself as he had always done. The first thing which Miss Moggaridge did with her freedom and her money was to imitate the example of the "fearless son of Ginger Blue," and try a little travel, to the great scandal of souls in her native borough who found no reason why Miss Moggaridge should want to see any more of the world than that borough presented

to her, and never shared her weak and wicked desire to see what sort
of region it was that lay on the other side of the bay and the breakers.

"The idea, Ann!" said Miss Keturah Meteyard, a well-to-do
spinster whose farm and stock, and consequently whose opinions, were
the pride of the place,—"the idea of your beginning at your time of life
to kite round like a young girl. The eyes of the fool are in the ends of
the earth," quoted Miss Keturah, with a long sigh. "For my part, the
village is good enough for me!"

"And for me too, Kitty," said Miss Moggaridge. "I am not
going any great distance; I—I am going to see Jack."

Now Jack was the scapegrace Moggaridge, who had run away
to sea and therewith to the bad; and the stern clergyman, his father,
having satisfied his mind on the point that there was no earthly
reclamation possible for Jack, had with true old style rigor commenced
and carried on the difficult work of tearing the boy out of his heart,
that since Heaven had elected Jack to damnation there might be no
carnal opposition on his own part through the weak bonds of the flesh;
and Jack's name had not been spoken in that house from which he fled
for many a year before the old man was gathered to his fathers. For all
that, every now and then a letter came to Miss Ann and another went
from her in reply, and her father with an inconsistency very mortifying
but highly human saw them come and saw them go, convinced that he
should hear from Ann whatever news need might be for him to hear;
and so it came to pass that Miss Ann knew of Jack's whereabouts, and
that Miss Keturah, hearing her intent of seeking them, Miss Keturah
with one eye on the community and one on her old pastor, held up her
hands a brief instant in holy horror before memory twitched them
down again.

"Ann!" said she, solemnly,—"Ann, do you know what you
are doing?"

"Doing?" said Miss Moggaridge. "In going to see Jack, do
you mean? Certainly I do. A Christian duty."

"And what," said Miss Keturah,—"what constitutes you a
better judge of Christian duty than your sainted father, a Christian
minister for fifty years breaking the bread of life in this parish?"

"Very well," said Miss Moggaridge, unable to answer such an argument as that,—for Miss Keturah fought like those armies that put their prisoners in the front, so that a shot from Miss Moggaridge must necessarily have demolished her father the clergyman,—"very well," said his faithful daughter, "perhaps not a Christian duty; we will say not; but, at any rate, a natural duty."

"And you dare to set a natural duty, a duty of our unregenerate condition, above the duties of such as are set apart from the world."

"My dear Kitty," said Miss Moggaridge, "I am not sure that we ever are or ever should be set apart from the world; that we are not placed here to work in it and with it till our faith and our example leaven it."

"Ann Moggaridge!" said the other, springing to her feet, with a vixenish scarlet in her yellow face, a color less Christian perhaps than that of her remarks, "this is rank heresy, and I won't stay to hear it!"

"O pooh, Kitty," said Miss Moggaridge, listening to the denunciation of her opinions with great good humor, "we've gone all through that a hundred times. Sit down again,—we'll leave argument to the elders,—I want to talk about something else."

"Something else?" with a change as easy as Harlequin's.

"Yes, I want to talk to you about that corner meadow. It just takes a jog out of your land, and I've an idea you'd like to buy it. Now say so, freely, if you would."

"Humph! What has put that into your head, I'd like to know? You've refused a good price for it, you and your father, every spring for ten years, to my knowledge. You want," said Miss Keturah, facing about with uplifted forefinger like an accusing angel,—in curl-papers and brown gingham, — "you want the ready money to go and see Jack with!"

"Well, yes. I don't need the meadow and I do need the money; for when you have everything tied up in stocks, you can't always get at it, you know."

"That's very shiftless of you, Ann Moggaridge," said Miss Keturah. "When the money's gone, it's gone, but there the meadow'll always be."

"Bless your heart, for the matter of that, I've made up my mind to get rid of all the farm."

"Get rid of the farm!"

"Yes. I'm not well enough nor strong enough to carry it on by myself, now father's gone, and his means are divided. Your place would make me blush like a fever beside it. No, I couldn't keep it to advantage; so I think I shall let you take the corner meadow, if you want it, and Squire Purcell will take the rest."

"And what will you do with yourself when you come back from—from Jack, if you really mean to go?"

"O, board with the Squire or anywhere; the Lord will provide a place; perhaps with you," added Miss Moggaridge, archly.

"No, indeed," said Miss Keturah, "not with me! We never should have any peace of our lives. There isn't a point in all the Westminster catechism that we don't differ about, and we should quarrel as to means of grace at every meal we sat down to. Besides which, you would fret me to death with your obstinacy when you are notoriously wrong,—as in this visit to Jack, for instance."

"Jack needs me, Kitty. I must go to him."

"It is your spiritual pride that must go and play the good Samaritan!"

"Jack and I used to be the dearest things in the world to each other when we were children, you know," said Miss Ann, gently. "We had both our pleasures and our punishments together. The severity of our home drove him off,—I don't know what it drove him to. I waited, because father claimed my first duty; now, I must do what can be done to help Jack into the narrow path again."

"The severity of your home!" said Miss Keturah, who had heard nothing since that; "of such a home as yours, such a Christian home with—with—"

"The benefit of clergy," laughed Miss Moggaridge.

"Ann you're impious!" exclaimed Miss Keturah, bringing down her umbrella hard enough to blunt its ferule. "Much such a spirit as that will do to bring Jack back! It isn't your place to bring him back either. You've had no call to be a missionary, and it's presumption in you to interfere with the plain will of Providence. You will go your own gait of course, but you sha'n't go without knowing that I and every friend you have disapprove of the proceeding. And it's another step to total beggary, for the upshot of it all will be that Jack coaxes and wheedles your money."

"My money?" said Miss Ann. "There will be no need of any coaxing and wheedling; it's as much his as mine."

"His!"

"I know father expected me to do justice, and so he didn't trouble himself. I should feel I was wronging him in his grave if I refused."

"And what is Luke going to do, may I ask?" inquired Miss Keturah, with grim stolidity.

"Because Luke won't give up any of his, is no reason why I shouldn't."

"Luke won't? That's like him. Sensible. Sensible! He won't give the Lord's substance to the ungodly."

"So he says. But I'm afraid not to the godly either. I'm afraid he wouldn't even to me if I stood in want, though perhaps I oughtn't to say so."

"Not if you'd wasted all you have on Jack, certainly."

"I shall divide my property with Jack as a measure of simple justice, Kitty," said Miss Moggaridge, firmly. "It is as much his as mine, as I said."

"And when it's all gone," continued Miss Keturah, "what is to become of you then?"

"When it's all gone? O, there's no danger of that."

"There's danger of anything between your butter-fingers, Ann. So if it should happen, what then?"

"The Lord will provide," said Miss Ann, sweetly.

"The Lord helps them that help themselves," said Miss Keturah. "Well, I'm gone. I'd wrestle longer with you if it was any use,—you're as set as Lot's wife. I suppose," she said, turning round after she had reached the door, "you'll come and see me before you go. I've—I've something you might take Jack; you know I've been knitting socks all the year and we've no men-folks," and then she was gone.

Poor Miss Keturah,—a good soul after her own fashion, which was not Miss Moggaridge's fashion,—once she had expected the wicked Jack to come home from sea and marry her; and the expectation and the disappointment together had knit a bond between her and his sister that endured a great deal of stretching and striving. The neighbors said that she had pious spells; but if that were so, certainly these spells were sometimes so protracted as almost to become chronic and in fact frequently to assume the complexion of a complaint; but they never hindered her from driving a bargain home to the head, from putting royal exactions on the produce of her dairy, from sending her small eggs to market, and from disputing every bill, from the tax-man's to the tithes, that ever was presented at her door. But it is probable that somewhere down under that crust of hers there was a drop of honey to regard the adventurous seeker, and Miss Ann always declared that she knew where to find it.

So Miss Moggaridge went away from the sea-coast for some seasons, and the tides ebbed and flowed, and the moons waxed and waned, and the years slipped off after each other, and the villagers found other matter for their gossip; and the most of them had rather forgotten her, when some half-dozen years later she returned, quite old and worn and sad, having buried the wretched Jack, and a goodly portion of her modest fortune with him, and bringing back nothing but his dog as a souvenir, of his existence,—a poor little shivering hound that in no wise met the public approbation.

But Miss Moggaridge did not long allow her old acquaintance to remain unaware of her return among them. The very day after her arrival a disastrous fire in the village had left a family destitute and shelterless; and, heading a subscription-list with a moderate sum, she went round with it in person, as she had been wont to do in the old times, till the sight of her approaching shadow had caused the stingy man to flee. And now, with every rebuff she met, every complaint of hard times, bad bargains, poor crops, she altered the figures against her own name for those of a larger amount, till by nightfall the forlorn family had the means of being comfortable again, through the goodness of the village and Miss Moggaridge; for had not the village given the cipher, whatever might be the other figures which Miss Moggaridge had of herself prefixed thereto? True to her instinct, Miss Keturah Meteyard waylaid her old friend next day. "I've heard all about it, Ann, so you needn't pretend ignorance," she began. "And you may think it very fine, but I call it totally unprincipled. Are you Croesus, or Rothschild, or the Queen of Sheba come again, to be running to the relief of all the lazy and shiftless folks in the country? Everybody is talking about it; everybody's wondering at you, Ann!"

"Everybody may reimburse me, Kitty, just as soon as they please."

"Perhaps they will, when they're angels. The idea of your—"

"But Kitty, I couldn't see those poor Morrises without a roof over them; and if you want the truth," said Miss Moggaridge, turning like the trodden worm, "I can't imagine how you could. Why, where on earth could they go?"

"There was no need of seeing them without a roof. The neighbors'd have taken them in till they rebuilt the place. Perhaps that would have spurred Morris up enough to make an exertion, which he never did in his life. If he'd been one atom forehanded, he'd have had something laid by in bank to fall back on at such a time. I declare, I've no patience!" cried Miss Keturah, with nobody to dispute her. "And any one would be glad of those two girls as help," she continued. "Great lazy, hulking, fine ladies they are! And the first thing they'll do with your money will be to buy an ingrain carpet and a looking-glass and a couple of silk gowns, whether there's enough left for a broom and a dish-cloth or not. Go?" cried Miss Keturah, now quite to the climax of her virtuous indignation. "They could go to the poorhouse, where you'll go if some of your friends don't take you in hand and have a guardian appointed over you!"

But Miss Moggaridge only laughed and kissed her censor good-bye, and made up her mind to save the sum of her prodigality out of her own expenses in some way; by giving up her nice boarding-place, perhaps, and boarding herself in two or three rooms of a house she still owned, where she could go without groceries and goodies, for instance, in such things as fruit and sugar and butter and eggs and all the dainties to be concocted therewith; for bread and meat and milk would keep body and soul together healthily, she reasoned, and acted on her reasoning. But instead of making good, by this economy, the sum she had extracted from her hoard, she presently found that the saving thus accomplished had been used upon the outfit of a poor young minister going to preach to the Queen of Madagascar. Miss Keturah was not so loud in her disapproval of this as of some of Miss Moggaridge's other less eccentric charities; but as giving away in any shape was not agreeable to her, she could not help remarking that, if she were Miss Moggaridge, she should feel as if she had lent a hand to help cast him into a fiery furnace, for that would undoubtedly be the final disposition of the unfortunate young minister by the wicked savages of the island whither he was bound. She herself only bestowed upon him some of her knitted socks to walk the furnace in. What she did cavil at much more was the discovery that Miss Moggaridge was living alone. "Without help, Ann Moggaridge!" she said, laying her hands along her knees in an attitude of fine Egyptian despair. "And pinching yourself to the last extremity, I'll be bound, for these Morrises and young ministers and what not! What would your father say to see it? And if you should be sick in the middle of the night and no one near to hear you call—"

"The Lord'll provide for me, Kitty," said Miss Moggaridge, for the thousandth time.

"He won't provide a full-grown servant-girl, springing up out of nothing."

"But there's no need of worry, dear, with such health as mine."

"It's tempting Providence!"

"Tempting Providence to what?"

"Ann!" said Miss Keturah, severely, "I don't understand how any one as good as you,—for you are good in spite of your faults—"

"There is none good but One," Miss Moggaridge gently admonished her.

"As good as you," continued Miss Keturah, obliviously, "and enjoying all your lifelong privileges, can indulge in levity and so often go so near the edge of blasphemy, without a shudder."

"Dear Kitty," said Miss Ann, laughing, "we shall never agree, though we love each other so much; so where is the use? For my part, I think it blasphemy to suppose Providence could be tempted."

"Ann! Ann!" said Miss Keturah, solemnly. "Don't indulge such thoughts. They will lead you presently into doubting the existence of a personal Devil! And now," continued she, reverting to the original topic, "I sha'n't go away till you promise me to take in help, so that you needn't die alone in the night, and be found stiff in the morning by a stranger!" And poor Miss Moggaridge had to promise, at last, though it upset all her little scheme of saving in groceries and firewood and wages, and went to her heart sorely.

It was not very long after this expostulation of Miss Keturah's that, a stout-armed serving-woman having been added to Miss Moggaridge's family, another more singular addition made itself on the night when a ship was nipped among the breakers behind which the town had entrenched itself, and went to pieces just outside the cove of stiller water, at whose head stood the house in which were Miss Moggaridge's rooms. Of all the freighting lives on board that doomed craft, one thing alone ever came to shore,—a bird, that, as Miss Moggaridge peered from the door which Bridget held open for her, fluttered through the tumultuous twilight air and into her arms. Miss Moggaridge left Bridget to set her back to the door and push it inch by inch, till one triumphant slam proclaimed victory over the elements, while hastening in herself to bare her foundling before the fire. It was a parrot, drenched with the wave and the weather in spite of his preening oils, shivering in her hands, and almost ready to yield to firelight and warmth the remnant of life that survived his battling flight. Miss Moggaridge bestowed him in a basket of wool in a corner of the heated hearth, placed milk and crumbs at hand, and no more resumed her knitting and soft-voiced psalm-singing, but fidgeted about the darkened windows and wondered concerning the poor souls who, since they never could make shore again themselves, had given the bird the liberty of his wing. She was attracted again to the fireside by a long whistle of unspeakable relief, and, turning, saw the bird preening and pluming, stepping from the basket, treading daintily down the tiles, and waddling to and fro before the blessed blaze, while he chuckled to himself unintelligibly, but quite as if he had practiced the cunningest trick over storm and shipwreck that could have been devised. Bridget would have frowned the intruder down, and did eventually give warning "along of the divil's imp," as she called him; but Miss Moggaridge was as pleased as a child; it was the only thing of the sort in the village, and what a means to attract the little people whom she loved, and at the same time to administer to them diluted doses of the moral law! Had she chosen, to be sure, it would have been one of the great gray African things she had read of, that spread a scarlet tail and seem the phoenix of some white-ashed brand in which the smoldering fire yet sparkles. But this was a little fellow with scarlet on his shoulders and his wings, a golden cap on his head, and it would have been hard to say whether the glistening mantle over his back were emerald crusted with gold or gold enamelled with emerald, so much did every single feather shine like a blade of green grass full of flint. While she looked, and admired, and wished, nevertheless, that it were gray, another door was pushed gently open and Folly entered,—Jack's slim white hound, as much a miracle of beauty in his own way—made at the bird with native instinct, then paused with equally native cowardice, and looked at Miss Moggaridge and wagged his tail, as who should say, "Praise my forbearance." But the parrot, having surveyed Master Folly on this side and on that from a pair of eyes like limpid jewels, opened his mouth and barked. Nothing else was needed; the phantom of the gray parrot disappeared whence he came; more intelligence no child could have shown. Miss Moggaridge caught him up, received a vicious bite for her pains, but, notwithstanding, suffered him to cling upon her fingers, tightly grasping which, he looked down upon the hound, flapped his gorgeous wings and crowed; then he went through an astonishing series of barnyard accomplishments, winding up by vigorously grinding no end of coffee in his throat, having released one claw with which to turn round and round the invisible handle of an imaginary mill, and finally ending in a burst and clatter of the most uproarious side-splitting laughter. Having done this, he had exhausted his repertory, and never for all the time during which he delighted the heart of Miss Moggaridge and forced Miss Keturah to regard him as a piece of supernatural sin created by the Evil One in mockery of the creation of man, so that had she but been a good Catholic she would have crossed herself before him, and, without being an ancient Persian, did frequently propitiate him after the fashion of the Ahrimanian worship, —never during all that time did he catch a new sound or alter an articulate syllable to denote from what nationality—Spanish, Portuguese, or Dutch—he had received his earliest lessons. But he had done enough. Folly, never particularly brilliant in his wits, and, being a hound, not more strongly developed in his affections, was given hearth-room on sufferance for his lissome limbs, and on general grounds of compassion for himself and Jack together; but the parrot, luring one on with perpetual hopes of new attainment, and born of the tropical sun that made a perpetual mirage in her imagination, became cherished society, and had not only a shining perch, but a nest in Miss Moggaridge's affections as well,—a nest that cost her dearly some years afterward.

But before the town had much more than done wondering at Miss Moggaridge's parrot, and telling all the gossipry of his deeds and misdeeds,—of the way he picked the lock of his cage, walked up the walls, tearing off the papering as he went, bit big splinters from the window-blinds, drove away every shadow of a cat, and made general havoc, Miss Moggaridge gave such occasion for a fresh onslaught of tongues, that the bird was half forgotten.

It was when her name was found to have been endorsed upon her brother Luke's paper,—Luke being the resident of another place,—and in his failure the larger portion of her earthly goods was swept out of her hands. One would have supposed that Miss Moggaridge had been guilty of a forgery, and that not her own property, but the church funds, had been made away with by means of the wretched signature; and a particular aggravation of the calamity, in the eyes of her townspeople, seemed to be its clandestine character; if they had been consulted or had even been made aware that such a thing might possibly be expected, much might have been condoned.

As it was, they were glad, they were sure, that she felt able to afford such fine doings, but they had heard of such a thing as being just before you were generous, and they only hoped she wouldn't come upon the town in her old age in consequence, that was all; for much that close-fisted Luke would do for her, even if he got upon his feet again,—Luke who had been heard to remark that the loss of a cent spoiled the face of a dollar!

But Luke never got upon his feet again, and during the rest of his life he struggled along from hand to mouth, with one child binding shoes and another in the mills, a scanty board, a threadbare back; and though Miss Moggaridge was left now with nothing but a mere pittance of bank-stock over and above the possession of the house in which she reserved her rooms, yet out of the income thus remaining she still found it possible now and then to send a gold-piece to Luke,— a gold-piece which in his eyes looked large enough to eclipse the sun, while she patched and turned and furbished many a worn old garment of her own, in order that she might send a new one to her sister-in-law, of whom Miss Keturah once declared that she put her more in mind of an old shoe-knife worn down to the handle than of anything else in the world.

"As if it would make the least difference in her appearance," said Miss Keturah, who had a faculty of mousing out all these innocent crimes against society on Miss Moggaridge's part, "whether she wore calico or homespun? Dress up a split rail! And you rigging yourself out of the rag-bag so as to send her an alpaca. Why can't she work? *I* work!"

"Bless you, Kitty, doesn't she work like a slave now for the mere privilege of drawing her breath? What more can she do?"

"That's no business of mine, or yours either.   Your duty," said Miss Keturah, "your bounden duty's to take care of yourself. And here you are wearing flannels thin as vanity, because you've no money left to buy thick ones; and you'll get a cold and a cough through these Luke Moggaridges that 'll carry you out of the world; and then," exclaimed she, with an unusual quaver in her piercing tone—"then I should like to know what is to become of—"

"The Lord will provide for me, Kitty."

"So I've heard you say!" she snapped. "But I was talking about myself,—he won't provide me with another Ann Moggaridge—" And there Miss Keturah whisked herself out of sight, possibly to prevent any such catastrophe as her friend's seeing a tear in those sharp eyes of hers unused to such weak visitants.

Yet as a law of ethics is the impossibility of standing still in face of the necessity of motion, either progressive or retrograde, so Miss Moggaridge went on verifying the worst prognostications of her neighbors; and it was surmised that the way in which she had raised the money to pay for having the cataract removed from old Master Sullivan's eyes,—eyes worn out in the service of two generations of the town's children,—which she was one day found to have done, was by scrimping her store of wood and coal (Bridget's departure having long left her free to do so), so that mere apology for a fire the winter long to which she owed a rheumatism that now began to afflict her hands and feet in such a manner as to make her nearly useless in any physical effort. It was no wonder the townsfolk were incensed against her, for her conduct implied a reproof of theirs that was vexatious; why in the world couldn't she have let Master Sullivan's eyes alone? He had looked out upon the world and had seen it to his satisfaction or dissatisfaction for threescore years and over, one would have imagined he had seen enough of a place whose sins he was always bewailing!

But a worse enormity than almost any preceding ones remained yet to be perpetrated by Miss Moggaridge. It was an encroachment upon her capital, her small remaining capital, of the education of one of the Luke Moggaridges, a bright boy whom his aunt thought to be possessed of too much ability to rust away in a hand-to-hand struggle with life; ongoing, perhaps, to hear him preach some searching sermon in his grandfather's pulpit, and to surrender into safe and appreciative keeping those barrels full of sacred manuscripts which she still treasured, she had resolved to have him fitted and sent to college. Very likely the town in which the boy lived thought it a worthy action of the aunt's, but the town in which he didn't live regarded it as a piece of Quixotism on a par with all her previous proceedings, since the boy would have been as well off at a trade, Miss Moggaridge much better off, and the town plus certain tax-money now lost to it forever. It was, however, reserved for Miss Keturah to learn the whole extent of her offence before the town had done so,—to learn that she had not been spending merely all her income, dismissing Bridget, freezing herself, starving herself, but she had been drawing on her little principal till there was barely enough to buy her a yearly gown and shoes, and in order to live at all she must spend the whole remainder now, instead of waiting for any interest.

"Exactly, exactly, exactly what I prophesied!" cried Miss Keturah. "And who but you could contrive, let alone could have done, such a piece of work? You show ingenuity enough in bringing yourself to beggary to have made your fortune at a patent. You have a talent for ruin!"

"I am not afraid of beggary, Kitty," said Miss Moggaridge. "How often shall I quote the Psalmist to you, 'I have been young and now am old; yet have I never seen the righteous forsaken, nor his seed begging bread.'"

"I know that, Ann. I say it over oftener than you do, for it's the only thing that leaves me any hope for you." And Miss Keturah kept a silent meditation for a few moments. "As if it wasn't just as well," she broke forth at length, "for that Luke Moggaridge boy to dig potatoes or make shoes, as to preach bad sermons, or kill off patients, or make confusion worse confounded in a lawsuit."

Whether Miss Moggaridge thought it a dreadful world where every one spoke the truth to his neighbor, or not, she answered, pleasantly, "Kitty dear, I should have consulted you as to that—"

"As to what? Shoes or sermons? He might have made good shoes."

"Only," continued Miss Moggaridge, meekly but determinedly, "only you make such a breeze if you think differently, that I felt it best to get him through college first."

"Why couldn't he get himself through?"

"Well, he's sickly."

"O dear Lord, as if there weren't enough of that kind! Serve Heaven because he can't serve the flesh! Taking dyspepsia and blue devils for faith and works!"

"You mustn't now, Kitty, you mustn't. I meant for us all to advise together concerning the choice of profession after his graduation. For he has a real talent, he'll do us credit."

"Well," said Miss Keturah, a little mollified, "it might have been wise. It might have saved you a pretty penny. I might have lent the young man the money he needed, and it would have done him no harm to feel that he was to refund it when he was able."

"That is exactly what I have done, Kitty. And I never thought of letting any one else, even you,—though I'd rather it should be you than any one,—while I was able. And I'm sure I can pinch along any way till he can pay me; and if he never can pay me, he can take care of me, for he is a noble boy, a noble boy."

"And what if he shouldn't live to do anything of the sort?"

"O, I can't think of such a thing."

"He mightn't, though. There's many a hole in the skimmer."

"I don't know. I don't know what I should do. But there, no matter, I shall be taken care of some way, come what will. I always have been. The Lord will provide."

"Well, now, Ann, I'm going to demand one thing by my right as your next friend, and one caring a great deal more about you than all the Lukes in the world. You won't lend that boy, noble or otherwise, another penny, but you'll let him keep school and work his way through his profession himself."

"No indeed, Kitty! That would make it six or seven years before he got his profession. There are only a few hundreds left, so they may as well go with the others."

"Light come, light go," sniffed Miss Keturah. "If you'd had to work for that money—What, I repeat, what in the mean time is to become of you?"

"Don't fear for me; the Lord will provide."

"The poorhouse will, you mean! Why in the name of wonder can't he work his way up, as well as his betters?"

"Well, the truth is, Kitty, he's—he's engaged. And of course he wants to be married. And—"

But Miss Keturah had risen from her chair and stalked out, and slammed the door behind her, without another syllable.

Poor Miss Moggaridge. It was but little more than a twelve month after this conversation that her noble boy was drowned while bathing; and half broken-hearted,—for she had grown very fond of him through his constant letters and occasional visits,—she never called to mind how her money, principal and interest and education, had gone down with him and left her absolutely penniless, save for the rent of the residue of the house where she kept her two or three rooms. But Miss Keturah did.

Miss Moggaridge was now, moreover, quite unable to do a thing to help herself. Far too lame in her feet to walk and in her hands to knit, she was obliged to sit all day in her chair doing nothing, and having her meals brought to her by the family, and her rooms kept in order, in payment of the rent; while her time was enlivened only by the children who dropped in to see the parrot,—an entertainment ever new; by a weekly afternoon of Mrs. Morris's, who came and did up all the little odd jobs of mending on which she could lay her willing hands; by the calls of Master Sullivan, glowering at the world out of a pair of immense spectacles, through which he read daily chapters of the Psalms to her; and by the half-loving, half-quarreling visits of Miss Keturah. She used to congratulate herself in those days over the possession of the parrot. "I should forget my tongue if I hadn't him and the hound to talk with," she used to say, in answer to Miss Keturah's complaints of the screeching with which the bird always greeted her. "He is a capital companion. When I see him so gay and good-natured, imprisoned in his cage with none of his kind near, I wonder at myself for repining over my confinement in so large and airy a room as this, where I can look out on the sea all day long." And she bent her head down for the bird to caress, and loved him none the less on the next day,—when Miss Keturah would have been glad to wring his neck—for the crowning disaster of her life which he brought about that very evening.

For the mischievous fellow, working open the door of his cage, as he had done a thousand times before, while Miss Moggaridge sat nodding in her chair, had clambered with bill and claw here and there about the room, calling in the aid of his splendid wings when need was, till, reaching a match-safe and securing a card of matches in his bill with which he made off, pausing only on the top of a pile of religious newspapers, on a table beneath the chintz window-curtains, to pull them into a multitude of splinters; and the consequence was that presently his frightened screams woke the helpless Miss Moggaridge to a dim, half-suffocated sense that the world was full of smoke, and to find the place in flames, and the neighbors rushing in and carrying her and the parrot clinging to her, to a place of safety, upon which Miss Keturah swooped down directly and had her removed to her own house and installed in the bedroom adjoining the best-room, without asking her so much as whether she would or no.

"Well, Ann," said Miss Keturah, rising from her knees after their evening prayers, "it's the most wonderful deliverance I ever heard anything about."

"It is indeed," sobbed the poor lady, still quivering with her excitement. "And, under Heaven, I may thank Poll for it," she said, looking kindly at the crestfallen bird on the chair's arm, whose screams had alarmed the neighbors.

"Indeed you may!" the old Adam coming uppermost again,—strange they never called it the old Eve,—"indeed you may,—thank him for any mischief,—picking out a baby's eyes or setting a house afire, it's all one to him. But there's no great loss without some small gain; and there's one thing in it I'm truly grateful for, you can't waste any more money, Ann Moggaridge, for you haven't got any more to waste!"

"Why, Kitty, there's the land the house stood on, that will bring something,"—profoundly of the conviction that her possession was the widow's cruse, and with no idea of ever taking offense at anything that Miss Keturah said.

"Yes, something. But you'll never have it," said Miss Keturah, grimly. "For I'm going to buy that land myself, and never pay you a cent for it; so you can't give that away! And now you're here, I'm going to keep you, Ann; for you're no more fit to be trusted with yourself than a baby. And I shall see that you have respectable gowns and thick flannels and warm socks and the doctor. You'll have this room, and I the one on the other side that I've always had; and we'll have your chair wheeled out in the daytimes; and I think we shall get along very well together for the rest of our lives, if you're not as obstinate and unreasonable—"

"O Kitty," said Miss Moggaridge, looking up with streaming eyes that showed how great, although unspoken, her anxiety had become, and how great the relief from that dread of public alms which we all share alike,—"O Kitty! I had just as lief have everything from you as not! I had rather owe—"

"There's no owing in the case!" said Miss Keturah, tossing her head to the infinite danger of the kerosene from the whirlwind made by her ribbons.

"O there is! There is!" sobbed Miss Moggaridge. "Debts, too, I never can pay! You've always stood my next best friend to Heaven, dear; and didn't I say," she cried, with a smile breaking like sunshine through her tears,—"didn't I say the Lord would provide?"

Sarah Orne Jewett

(1849-1909)

Descending on both sides from pre-Revolution families, Sarah Orne Jewett was the second of three daughters born to Theodore Herman and Caroline Frances Perry Jewett on September 3, 1849. As a child she grew up in the home of her paternal grandfather, Captain Theodore F. Jewett, in South Berwick, Maine, a home she maintained until her death in 1909.

Although Jewett hoped to become a doctor like her father, poor health prevented her from achieving that goal. Poor health also limited her formal education as a child but fostered a close relationship with her father as she accompanied him on his rounds throughout the rural towns and villages of the South Berwick area. Through her relationship with her father came her early schooling as well as her appreciation for the people, the life, and the culture of the rural seacoast communities. Although she later attended Miss Raynes's School and graduated from the Berwick Academy in 1865, Jewett admitted that her best education came from the numerous trips she took with her father. Those trips also supplied her with sufficient material for her literature.

Although she never married, her secure economic position permitted the indulgence of her love: writing. Influenced by Harriet Beecher Stowe's 1862 publication of *The Pearl of Orr's Island,* Jewett began to write about the coastal towns and villages she knew so well after her graduation from Berwick Academy in 1865. Her first significant regional publication, "The Shore House," appeared in 1873 in *The Atlantic Monthly.*

As her writing developed so also did her circle of friends. In the early 1880s when James T. Fields, the Boston publisher, died, Jewett's relationship with Fields's wife, Annie, developed into what became known as a "Boston marriage." The strong bond between the two women led to their travel throughout the eastern United States as well as Europe. In addition, Jewett and Fields spent a great portion of each year alternating between Boston and Jewett's family home in

South Berwick. Their circle of friends included John Greenleaf Whittier, Thomas Bailey Aldrich, and Celia Thaxter. In addition, they met, visited, or corresponded with other writers included in this collection: Rose Terry Cooke, Harriet Beecher Stowe, Mary Wilkins Freeman.

In a career spanning more than three decades, Jewett wrote stories for children, nine collections of stories, and five novels. Besides the influence of Stowe in her writing, her mother's influence can be inferred as Jewett focuses again and again in her fiction on the relationship between women, particularly between mothers and daughters. Action in her stories is limited; instead, she focuses in detail on the region, and the relationship of characters to the region and to one another. Her primary concern is character development and the significance of relationships.

Jewett's best-known work is her 1896 novel, *The Country of the Pointed Firs*. In it she focuses on an unidentified visitor-writer from the city who comes to a Maine coastal village and spends the summer with the feisty widow and herbalist, Almira Todd. From the narrative perspective of an outsider, then, we are introduced to the charming and eccentric people of Dunnet Landing. Here we meet Mrs. Todd's mother, Mrs. Blackett, who lives on Green Island with her bachelor son, William. In addition, we meet Captain Littlepage, an old sea captain who longs for the past as well as lives in it. Other characters also live in a more comfortable past. Elijah, the old fisherman, dedicates his life to preserving his dead wife's memory; Joanna Todd, victim of a bad love affair, lives in self-imposed exile on another island. Unquestionably, Jewett's novel conveys the significance of relationships as she explores the moods, emotions, and bonds that give one a sense of permanence and meaning in a transitory life.

In 1901, Jewett received an honorary doctorate from Bowdoin College, the first woman ever to be recognized in such fashion by Bowdoin. Jewett's writing career came to an end in 1902 when she fell from her carriage on her fifty-third birthday. The fall left her with permanent head and spinal injuries for the remainder of her life. In June 1909, she suffered a stroke and three months later died of a cerebral hemorrhage in her ancestral South Berwick home.

The three stories included in this collection reflect Jewett's changing views in the 1870s and 1880s, reflections probably of her own situation in those decades. In "A Lost Lover," first published in *The Atlantic Monthly* in March 1878, Jewett focuses on strong individuals and the independence of women in the character of Horatia Dane. Left alone at an early age as a result of her lover being lost at sea, Horatia Dane could have let this loss destroy her. She doesn't; instead, she seems to have been energized by the loss. With her strength, independence, and ability to overcome hardship, her character reflects the family home she lives in: "This was a high, square house, with a row of pointed windows in its roof, a peaked porch in front, with some lilac-bushes around it, and down by the road was a long, orderly procession of poplars, like a row of sentinels standing guard." Like her home, she is an imposing and strong person.

By the 1880s as Jewett's friendship with Annie Fields's developed, she increasingly moved to examine in her fiction the idea of a female community and a matriarchy that provides emotional and moral support. "Marsh Rosemary," Jewett's story published in the May 1886 issue of *The Atlantic Monthly* illustrates this change. Ann Floyd, the central character of the story, defines the importance of female friendship and community bonds after her much younger husband deserts her. Ann's strength comes from her bonds within the community: "She was ready to go to any household that needed help, and in spite of her ceaseless industry with her needle she found many a chance to do good, and help her neighbors to life and carry the burdens of their lives."

Between these two stories and the shift of focus from the strong, independent woman that "A Lost Lover" illustrates to the emphasis in "Marsh Rosemary" on the significance of relationships and bonds between women, comes the transitional "Tom's Husband," a story that examines marriage. In many ways, the story reflects the redefinition of gender behavior and relationships taking place in the late nineteenth century. Elaine Showalter suggests that women's culture was breaking down from the inside as we moved from a focus on relationship, female bonding, and sisterhood to "work, mobility, sexual autonomy and power outside the female sphere" (*Tradition and Change in American Women's Writing*. [New York: Oxford, 1991], p. 15).

First published in *The Atlantic Monthly* in February of 1882, "Tom's Husband" reflects widespread feminist interest in the marriage question during the 1880s. Besides examining marriage in this story, Jewett also explores gender roles, and not just the traditional roles prescribed for women by their culture but also the roles prescribed for men. In many ways the marriage of Tom and Mary in "Tom's Husband" reflects the "Boston marriage" of Jewett and Annie Fields. As Jewett's recent biographer, Paula Blanchard, describes the Jewett-Fields relationship, it was a marriage of the best kind—a partnership offering mutual love and support, free of any assumption of power usually associated with traditional male-female marriages (*Sarah Orne Jewett*. [New York: Addison-Wesley, 1994], p. 153). In a story most unusual for the time and certainly modern, Jewett endorses an egalitarian marriage in "Tom's Husband."

Selected Primary Works

Deephaven, 1877; *Old Friends and New*, 1879; *Country By-Ways*, 1881; *A Country Doctor*, 1884; *A Marsh Island*, 1885; *A White Heron, and Other Stories*, 1886; *The King of Folly Island, and Other People*, 1888; *Strangers and Wayfarers*, 1890; *Tales of New England*, 1890; *The Country of the Pointed Firs*, 1896; *The Queen's Twin, and Other Stories*, 1899.

"A Lost Lover"

The Atlantic Monthly, March 1878

For a great many years it had been understood in Longfield that Miss Horatia Dane once had a lover, and that he had been lost at sea. By little and little, in one way and another, her acquaintances had found out or made up the whole story; and Miss Dane stood in the position, not of an unmarried woman exactly, but rather of having spent most of her life in a long and lonely widowhood. She looked like a person with a history, strangers often said (as if we each did not have a history); and her own unbroken reserve about this romance of hers gave everybody the more respect for it.

The Longfield people paid willing deference to Miss Dane: her family had always been one that could be liked and respected, and she was the last that was left in the old home of which she was so fond. This was a high, square house, with a row of pointed windows in its roof, a peaked porch in front, with some lilac-bushes around it; and down by the road was a long, orderly procession of poplars, like a row of sentinels standing guard. She had lived here alone since her father's death, twenty years before. She was a kind, just woman, whose pleasures were of a stately and sober sort; and she seemed not unhappy in her loneliness, though she sometimes said gravely that she was the last of her family, as if the fact had a great sadness for her.

She had some middle-aged and elderly cousins living at a distance, and they came occasionally to see her; but there had been no young people staying in the house for many years until this summer, when the daughter of her youngest cousin had written to ask if she might come to make a visit. She was a motherless girl of twenty, both older and younger than her years. Her father and brother, who were civil engineers, had taken some work upon the line of a railway in the far Western country. Nelly had made many long journeys with them before and since she had left school, and she had meant to follow them now, after she had spent a fortnight with the old cousin whom she had not seen since her childhood. Her father had laughed at the visit as a freak, and warned her of the dullness and primness of Longfield; but the result was that the girl found herself very happy in the comfortable home. She was still her own free, unfettered, lucky, and sunshiny self; and the old house was so much pleasanter for the girlish face and life, that Miss Horatia had, at first timidly and then most heartily, begged her to stay for the whole summer, or even the autumn, until her father was ready to come East. The name of Dane was very dear to Miss Horatia, and she grew fonder of her guest. When the village-people saw her glance at the girl affectionately, as they sat together in the family-pew of a Sunday, or saw them walking together after tea, they said it was a good thing for Miss Horatia; how bright she looked; and no doubt she would leave all her money to Nelly Dane, if she played her cards well.

But we will do Nelly justice, and say that she was not mercenary: she would have scorned such a thought. She had grown to have a great love for her cousin Horatia, and she liked to please her. She idealized her, I have no doubt; and her repression, her grave courtesy and rare words of approval, had a great fascination for a girl who had just been used to people who chattered, and were upon most intimate terms with you directly, and could forget you with equal ease. And Nelly liked having so admiring and easily pleased an audience as Miss Dane and her old servant Melissa. She liked to be queen of her company: she had so many gay, bright stories of what had happened to herself and her friends. Beside, she was clever with her needle, and had all those practical gifts which elderly women approve so heartily in girls. They liked her pretty clothes; she was sensible and economical and busy; they praised her to each other and to the world, and even stubborn old Andrew, the man, to whom Miss Horatia herself spoke with deference, would do anything she asked. Nelly would by no means choose so dull a life as this for the rest of her days; but she enjoyed it immensely for the time being. She instinctively avoided all that would shock the grave dignity and old-school ideas of Miss Dane; and somehow she never had felt happier or better satisfied with life. Perhaps it was because she was her best and most lady-like self. It was not long before she knew the village-people almost as well as Miss Dane did, and she became a very great favorite, as a girl so easily can who is good-natured and pretty, and well versed in city fashions; who has the tact and cleverness that come to such a nature from going about the world and knowing many people.

She had not been in Longfield many weeks before she heard something of Miss Dane's love-story; for one of her new friends said, in a confidential moment, "Does your cousin ever speak to you about the young man to whom she was engaged to be married?" and Nelly answered, "No," with great wonder, and not without regret at her own ignorance. After this she kept her eyes and ears open for whatever news of this lover's existence might be found.

At last it happened one day that she had a good chance for a friendly talk with Melissa; for who should know about the family affairs better than she? Miss Horatia had taken her second-best parasol, with a deep fringe, and had gone majestically down the street to do some morning errands which she could trust to no one. Melissa was shelling peas at the shady kitchen-doorstep, and Nelly came strolling round from the garden, along the clean-swept flag-stones, and sat down to help her. Melissa moved along, with a grim smile, to make room for her. "You needn't bother yourself," said she: "I've nothing else to do. You'll green your fingers all over." But she was evidently pleased to have company.

"My fingers will wash," said Nelly, "and I've nothing else to do either. Please push the basket this way a little, or I shall scatter the pods, and then you will scold." She went to work busily, while she tried to think of the best way to find out the story she wished to hear.

"There!" said Melissa, "I never told Miss H'ratia to get some citron, and I settled yesterday to make some pound-cake this forenoon after I got dinner along a piece. She's most out o' mustard too; she's set about having mustard to eat with her beef, just as the old colonel was before her. I never saw any other folks eat mustard with their roast beef; but every family has their own tricks. I tied a thread round my left-hand little finger purpose to remember that citron, before she came down this morning. I hope I ain't losing my fac'lties." It was seldom that Melissa was so talkative as this at first. She was clearly in a talkative mood.

"Melissa," asked Nelly, with great bravery, after a minute or two of silence, "who was it that my cousin Horatia was going to marry? It's odd that I shouldn't know; but I don't remember father's ever speaking of it, and I shouldn't think of asking her."

"I s'pose it'll seem strange to you," said Melissa, beginning to shell the peas a great deal faster, "but, as many years as I have lived in this house with her,—her mother, the old lady, fetched me up,—I never knew Miss H'ratia to say a word about him. But there! she knows I know, and we've got an understanding on many things we never talk over as some folks would. I've heard about it from other folks. She was visiting her great-aunt in Salem when she met with him. His name was Carrick, and it was presumed they was going to be married when he came home from the voyage he was lost on. He had the promise of going out master of a new ship. They didn't keep company long: it was made up of a sudden, and folks here didn't get hold of the story till some time after. I've heard some that ought to know say it was only talk, and they never were engaged to be married no more than I am."

"You say he was lost at sea?" asked Nelly.

"The ship never was heard from. They supposed she was run down in the night out in the South Seas somewhere. It was a good while before they gave up expecting news; but none ever come. I think she set everything by him, and took it very hard losing of him. But there! she'd never say a word. You're the freest-spoken Dane I ever saw; but you may take it from your mother's folks. I know he gave her that whale's tooth with the ship drawn on it that's on the mantel-piece in her room; she may have a sight of other keepsakes, for all I know, but it ain't likely;" and here there was a pause, in which Nelly grew sorrowful as she thought of the long waiting for tidings of the missing ship, and of her cousin's solitary life. It was very odd to think of prim Miss Horatia's being in love with a sailor. There was a young lieutenant in the navy whom Nelly herself liked dearly, and he had gone away on a long voyage. "Perhaps she's been just as well off," said Melissa. "She's dreadful set, y'r cousin H'ratia is, and sailors is high-tempered men. I've heard it hinted that he was a fast fellow; and if a woman's got a good home like this, and's able to do for herself, she'd better stay there. I ain't going to give up a certainty for an uncertainty, —that's what I always tell 'em," added Melissa, with great decision, as if she were besieged by lovers; but Nelly smiled inwardly as she thought of the courage it would take to support any one who wished to offer her companion his heart and hand. It would need desperate energy to scale the walls of that garrison.

The green peas were all shelled presently, and Melissa said gravely that she should have to be lazy now until it was time to put in the meat. She wasn't used to being helped, unless there was extra work, and she calculated to have one piece of work join on to another. However, it was no account, and she was obliged for the company; and Nelly laughed merrily as she stood washing her hands in the shining old copper basin at the sink. The sun would not be round that side of the house for a long time yet, and the pink and blue morning-glories were still in their full bloom and freshness. They grew over the window, twined on strings exactly the same distance apart. There was a box crowded full of green houseleeks down at the side of the door: they were straying over the edge, and Melissa stooped stiffly down with an air of disapproval at their untidiness. "They straggle all over everything," said she, "and they're no kind of use, only Miss's mother she set everything by 'em. She fetched 'em from home with her when she was married, her mother kep' a box, and they came from England. Folks used to say they was good for bee stings." Then she went into the inner kitchen, and Nelly went slowly away along the flag-stones to the garden from whence she had come. The garden-gate opened with a tired creak, and shut with a clack; and she noticed how smooth and shiny the wood was where the touch of so many hands had worn it. There was a great pleasure to this girl in finding herself among such old and well-worn things. She had been for a long time in cities or at the West; and among the old fashions and ancient possessions of Longfield it seemed to her that everything had its story, and she liked the quietness and unchangeableness with which life seemed to go on from year to year. She had seen many a dainty or gorgeous garden, but never one that she had liked so well as this, with its herb-bed and its broken rows of currant-bushes, its tall stalks of white lilies, and its wandering rose-bushes and honeysuckles, that had bloomed beside the straight paths for so many more summers than she herself had lived. She picked a little bouquet of late red roses, and carried it into the house to put on the parlor table. The wide hall-door was standing open, with its green outer blinds closed, and the old hall was dim and cool. Miss Horatia did not like a glare of sunlight, and she abhorred flies with her whole heart. Nelly could hardly see her way through the rooms, it had been so bright out of doors; but she brought the tall champagne-glass of water from the dining-room and put the flowers in their place. Then she looked at two silhouettes which stood on the mantel in carved ebony frames. They were portraits of an uncle of Miss Dane and his wife. Miss Dane had thought Nelly looked like this uncle the evening before. She could not see the likeness herself; but the pictures suggested something else, and she turned suddenly, and went hurrying up the stairs to Miss Horatia's own room, where she remembered to have seen a group of silhouettes fastened to the wall. There were seven or eight, and she looked at the young men among them most carefully; but they were all marked with the name of Dane: they were Miss Horatia's uncles and brothers, and our friend hung them on their little brass hooks again with a feeling of disappointment.

Perhaps her cousin had a quaint miniature of the lover, painted on ivory, and shut in a worn red morocco case; she hoped she should get a sight of it some day. This story of the lost sailor had a wonderful charm for the girl. Miss Horatia had never been so interesting to her before. How she must have mourned for the lover, and missed him, and hoped there would yet be news from the ship! Nelly thought she would tell her own little love-story some day, though there was not much to tell yet, in spite of there being so much to think about. She built a little castle in Spain as she sat in the front window-seat of the upper hall, and dreamed pleasant stories for herself until the sharp noise of the front gate-latch waked her; and she looked out through the blind to see her cousin coming up the walk.

Miss Horatia looked hot and tired, and her thoughts were not of any fashion of romance. "It is going to be very warm," said she. "I have been worrying ever since I have been gone, because I forgot to ask Andrew to pick those white currants for the minister's wife. I promised that she should have them early this morning. Would you go out to the kitchen, and ask Melissa to step in for a moment, my dear?"

Melissa was picking over red currants to make a pie, and rose from her chair with a little unwillingness. "I guess they could wait until afternoon," said she, as she came back. "Miss H'ratia's in a fret because she forgot about sending some white currants to the minister's. I told her that Andrew had gone to have the horses shod, and wouldn't be back till near noon. I don't see why part of the folks in the world should kill themselves trying to suit the rest. As long as I haven't got any citron for the cake, I suppose I might go out and pick 'em," added Melissa ungraciously. "I'll get some to set away for tea anyhow."

Miss Dane had a letter to write after she had rested from her walk; and Nelly soon left her in the dark parlor, and went back to the sunshiny garden to help Melissa, who seemed to be taking life with more than her usual disapproval. She was sheltered by an enormous gingham sunbonnet.

"I set out to free my mind to your cousin H'ratia this morning," said she, as Nelly crouched down at the opposite side of the bush where she was picking; "but we can't agree on that p'int, and it's no use. I don't say nothing. You might 's well ask the moon to face about and travel the other way as to try to change Miss H'ratia's mind.

I ain't going to argue it with her, it ain't my place; I know that as well as anybody. She'd run her feet off for the minister's folks any day, and though I do say he's a fair preacher, they haven't got a speck o' consideration nor fac'lty; they think the world was made for them, but I think likely they'll find out it wasn't; most folks do. When he first was settled here, I had a fit o' sickness, and he come to see me when I was getting over the worst of it. He did the best he could; I always took it very kind of him; but he made a prayer, and he kep' sayin' 'this aged handmaid,' I should think, a dozen times. Aged handmaid!" said Melissa scornfully: "I don't call myself aged yet, and that was more than ten years ago. I never made pretensions to being younger than I am; but you'd 'a' thought I was a topplin' old creatur' going on a hundred."

Nelly laughed; Melissa looked cross, and moved on to the next currant-bush. "So that's why you don't like the minister?" But the question did not seem to please.

"I hope I never should be set against a preacher by such as that," and Nelly hastened to change the subject, but there was to be a last word. "I like to see a minister that's solid minister right straight through, not one of these veneered folks. But old Parson Croden spoilt me for setting under any other preaching."

"I wonder," said Nelly, after a little, "if Cousin Horatia has any picture of that Captain Carrick."

"He wasn't captain," said Melissa. "I never heard that it was any more than they talked of giving him a ship next voyage."

"And you never saw him? he never came here to see her?"

"Bless you, no! She met with him at Salem, where she was spending the winter, and he went right away to sea. I've heard a good deal more about it of late years than I ever did at the time. I suppose the Salem folks talked about it enough. All I know is, there was other good matches that offered to her since, and couldn't get her, and I suppose it was on account of her heart's being buried in the deep with *him;*" and this unexpected bit of sentiment, spoken in Melissa's grummest tone, seemed so funny to her young companion, that she bent very low to pick from a currant-twig close to the ground, and could not ask any more questions for some time.

"I have seen her a sight o' times when I knew she was thinking about him," Melissa went on presently, this time with a tenderness in her voice that touched Nelly's heart. "She's been dreadful lonesome. She and the old colonel, her father, wasn't much company to each other, and she always kep' everything to herself. The only time she ever said a word to me was one night six or seven years ago this Christmas. They got up a Christmas-tree in the vestry, and she went, and I did too; I guess everybody in the whole church and parish that could crawl turned out to go. The children they made a dreadful racket. I'd ha' got my ears took off if I had been so forth-putting when I was little. I was looking round for Miss H'ratia 'long at the last of the evening, and somebody said they'd seen her go home. I hurried, and I couldn't see any light in the house; and I was afraid she was sick or something. She come and let me in, and I see she had been a-cryin'. I says, 'Have you heard any bad news?' But she says, 'No,' and began to cry again, real pitiful. 'I never felt so lonesome in my life,' says she, 'as I did down there. It's a dreadful thing to be left all alone in the world.' I did feel for her; but I couldn't seem to say a word. I put some pine-chips I had handy for morning on the kitchen-fire, and I made her up a cup o' good hot tea quick 's I could, and took it to her; and I guess she felt better. She never went to bed till three o'clock that night. I couldn't shut my eyes till I heard her come upstairs. There! I set everything by Miss H'ratia. I haven't got no folks either. I was left an orphan over to Deerfield, where Miss's mother come from, and she took me out o' the town-farm to bring up. I remember, when I come here, I was so small I had a box to stand up on when I helped wash the dishes. There's nothing I ain't had to make me comfortable, and I do just as I'm a mind to, and call in extra help every day of the week if I give the word; but I've had my lonesome times, and I guess Miss H'ratia knew."

Nelly was very much touched by this bit of a story, it was a new idea to her that Melissa should have so much affection and be so sympathetic. People never will get over being surprised that chestnut-burrs are not as rough inside as they are outside, and the girl's heart warmed toward the old woman who had spoken with such unlooked-for sentiment and pathos. Melissa went to the house with her basket, and Nelly also went in, but only to put on another hat, and see if it were straight, in a minute spent before the old mirror, and then she hurried down the long elm-shaded street to buy a pound of citron for the cake. She left it on the kitchen-table when she came back, and nobody ever said anything about it; only there were two delicious

pound-cakes—a heart and a round—on a little blue china plate beside
Nelly's plate at tea.

After tea Nelly and Miss Dane sat in the front-doorway, the
elder woman in a high-backed arm-chair, and the younger on the
doorstep. The tree-toads and crickets were tuning up heartily, the stars
showed a little through the trees, and the elms looked heavy and black
against the sky. The fragrance of the white lilies in the garden blew
through the hall. Miss Horatia was tapping the ends of her fingers
together. Probably she was not thinking of anything in particular. She
had had a very peaceful day, with the exception of the currants; and
they had, after all, gone to the parsonage some time before noon.
Beside this, the minister had sent word that the delay made no trouble;
for his wife had unexpectedly gone to Downton to pass the day and
night. Miss Horatia had received the business-letter for which she had
been looking for several days; so there was nothing to regret deeply for
that day, and there seemed to be nothing for one to dread on the
morrow.

"Cousin Horatia," asked Nelly, "are you sure you like having
me here? Are you sure I don't trouble you?"

"Of course not," said Miss Dane, without a bit of sentiment in
her tone: "I find it very pleasant having young company, though I am
used to being alone; and I don't mind it so much as I suppose you
would."

"I should mind it very much," said the girl softly.

"You would get used to it, as I have," said Miss Dane. "Yes,
dear, I like having you here better and better. I hate to think of your
going away." And she smoothed Nelly's hair as if she thought she
might have spoken coldly at first, and wished to make up for it. This
rare caress was not without its effect.

"I don't miss father and Dick so very much," owned Nelly
frankly, "because I have grown used to their coming and going; but
sometimes I miss people—Cousin Horatia, did I ever say anything to
you about George Forest?"

"I think I remember the name," answered Miss Dane.

"He is in the navy, and he has gone a long voyage, and—I think everything of him. I missed him awfully; but it is almost time to get a letter from him."

"Does your father approve of him?" asked Miss Dane, with great propriety. "You are very young yet, and you must not think of such a thing carelessly. I should be so much grieved if you threw away your happiness."

"Oh! we are not really engaged," said Nelly, who felt a little chilled. "I suppose we are, too: only nobody knows yet. Yes, father knows him as well as I do, and he is very fond of him. Of course I should not keep it from father; but he guessed at it himself. Only it's such a long cruise, Cousin Horatia,—three years, I suppose, away off in China and Japan."

"I have known longer voyages than that," said Miss Dane, with a quiver in her voice; and she rose suddenly, and walked away, this grave, reserved woman, who seemed so contented and so comfortable. But when she came back, she asked Nelly a great deal about her lover, and learned more of the girl's life than she ever had before. And they talked together in the pleasantest way about this pleasant subject, which was so close to Nelly's heart, until Melissa brought the candles at ten o'clock, that being the hour of Miss Dane's bed-time.

But that night Miss Dane did not go to bed at ten; she sat by the window in her room, thinking. The moon rose late; and after a little while she blew out her candles, which were burning low. I suppose that the years which had come and gone since the young sailor went away on that last voyage of his had each added to her affection for him. She was a person who clung the more fondly to youth as she left it the farther behind.

This is such a natural thing: the great sorrows of our youth sometimes become the amusements of our later years; we can only remember them with a smile. We find that our lives look fairer to us, and we forget what used to trouble us so much when we look back. Miss Dane certainly had come nearer to truly loving the sailor than she had any one else; and the more she had thought of it, the more it became the romance of her life. She no longer asked herself, as she often had done in middle life, whether, if he had lived and had come home, she would have loved and married him. She had minded less and less, year by year, knowing that her friends and neighbors thought her faithful to the love of her youth. Poor, gay, handsome Joe Carrick! how fond he had been of her, and how he had looked at her that day he sailed away out of Salem Harbor on the ship Chevalier! If she had only known that she never should see him again, poor fellow!

But, as usual, her thoughts changed their current a little at the end of her reverie. Perhaps, after all, loneliness was not so hard to bear as other sorrows. She had had a pleasant life; God had been very good to her, and had spared her many trials, and granted her many blessings. She would try and serve him better. "I am an old woman now," she said to herself. "Things are better as they are; I can get on by myself better than most women can, and I never should have liked to be interfered with."

Then she shut out the moonlight, and lighted her candles again, with an almost guilty feeling. "What should I say if Nelly sat up till nearly midnight looking out at the moon?" thought she. "It is very silly; but it is such a beautiful night. I should like to have her see the moon shining through the tops of the trees."

But Nelly was sleeping the sleep of the just and sensible in her own room.

Next morning at breakfast Nelly was a little conscious of there having been uncommon confidences the night before, but Miss Dane was her usual calm and somewhat formal self, and proposed their making a few calls after dinner, if the weather were not too hot. Nelly at once wondered what she had better wear. There was a certain black grenadine which Miss Horatia had noticed with approval, and she remembered that the lower ruffle needed hemming, and made up her mind that she would devote most of the time before dinner to that and to some other repairs. So, after breakfast was over, she brought the dress downstairs, with her work-box, and settled herself in the dining-room. Miss Dane usually sat there in the morning; it was a pleasant room, and she could keep an unsuspected watch over the kitchen and Melissa, who did not need watching in the least. I dare say it was for the sake of being within the sound of a voice.

Miss Dane marched in and out that morning; she went upstairs, and came down again, and she was busy for a while in the parlor. Nelly was sewing steadily by a window, where one of the blinds was a little way open, and tethered in its place by a string. She hummed a tune to herself over and over:

> "What will you do, love, when I am going,
> With white sails flowing, the seas beyond?"

And old Melissa, going to and fro at her work in the kitchen, grumbled out bits of an ancient psalm-tune at intervals. There seemed to be some connection between these fragments in her mind; it was like a ledge of rock in a pasture, that sometimes runs under the ground, and then crops out again. I think it was the tune of Windham.

Nelly found that there was a good deal to be done to the grenadine dress when she looked it over critically, and became very diligent. It was quiet in and about the house for a long time, until suddenly she heard the sound of heavy footsteps coming in from the road. The side-door was in a little entry between the room where Nelly sat and the kitchen, and the new-comer knocked loudly. "A tramp," said Nelly to herself; while Melissa came to open the door, wiping her hands hurriedly on her apron.

"I wonder if you couldn't give me something to eat," said the man.

"I suppose I could," answered Melissa. "Will you step in?" Beggars were very few in Longfield, and Miss Dane never wished anybody to go away hungry from her house. It was off the grand highway of tramps, but they were by no means unknown.

Melissa searched among her stores, and Nelly heard her putting one plate after another on the kitchen-table, and thought that the breakfast promised to be a good one, if it were late.

"Don't put yourself out," said the man, as he moved his chair nearer. "I put up at an old barn three or four miles above here last night, and there didn't seem to be very good board there."

"Going far?" inquired Melissa concisely.

"Boston," said the man. "I'm a little too old to travel afoot. Now, if I could go by water, it would seem nearer. I'm more used to the water. This is a royal good piece o' beef. I suppose you couldn't put your hand on a mug of cider?" This was said humbly, but the tone failed to touch Melissa's heart.

"No, I couldn't," said she decisively; so there was an end of that, and the conversation seemed to flag for a time.

Presently Melissa came to speak to Miss Dane, who had just come downstairs. "Could you stay in the kitchen a few minutes?" she whispered. "There's an old creatur' there that looks foreign. He came to the door for something to eat, and I gave it to him; but he's miser'ble looking, and I don't like to leave him alone. I'm just in the midst o' dressing the chickens. He'll be through pretty quick, according to the way he's eating now."

Miss Dane followed her without a word; and the man half rose, and said, "Good-morning, madam!" with unusual courtesy. And, when Melissa was out of hearing, he spoke again: "I suppose you haven't any cider?" to which his hostess answered, "I couldn't give you any this morning," in a tone that left no room for argument. He looked as if he had had a great deal too much to drink already.

"How far do you call it from here to Boston?" he asked, and was told that it was eighty miles.

"I'm a slow traveler," said he: "sailors don't take much to walking." Miss Dane asked him if he had been a sailor. "Nothing else," replied the man, who seemed much inclined to talk. He had been eating like a hungry dog, as if he were half-starved,—a slouching, red-faced, untidy-looking old man, with some traces of former good looks still to be discovered in his face. "Nothing else. I ran away to sea when I was a boy, and I followed it until I got so old they wouldn't ship me even for cook." There was something in his being for once so comfortable—perhaps it was being with a lady like Miss Dane, who pitied him—that lifted his thoughts a little from their usual low level. "It's drink that's been the ruin of me," said he. "I ought to have been somebody. I was nobody's fool when I was young. I got to be mate of a first-rate ship, and there was some talk o' my being captain before long. She was lost that voyage, and three of us were all that was saved; we got picked up by a Chinese junk. She had the plague aboard of her, and my mates died of it, and I was sick. It was a hell of a place to be in. When I got ashore I shipped on an old bark that pretended to be coming round the Cape, and she turned out to be a pirate. I just went to the dogs, and I've gone from bad to worse ever since."

"It's never too late to mend," said Melissa, who came into the kitchen just then for a string to tie the chickens.

"Lord help us, yes, it is!" said the sailor. "It's easy for you to say that. I'm too old. I ain't been master of this craft for a good while." And he laughed at his melancholy joke.

"Don't say that," said Miss Dane.

"Well, now, what could an old wrack like me do to earn a living? and who 'd want me if I could? You wouldn't. I don't know when I've been treated so decent as this before. I'm all broke down." But his tone was no longer sincere; he had fallen back on his profession of beggar.

"Couldn't you get into some asylum or—there's the Sailors' Snug Harbor, isn't that for men like you? It seems such a pity for a man of your years to be homeless and a wanderer. Haven't you any friends at all?" And here, suddenly, Miss Dane's face altered, and she grew very white; something startled her. She looked as one might who saw a fearful ghost.

"No," said the man; "but my folks used to be some of the best in Salem. I haven't shown my head there this good while. I was an orphan. My grandmother brought me up. Why, I didn't come back to the States for thirty or forty years. Along at the first of it I used to see men in port that I used to know; but I always dodged 'em, and I was way off in outlandish places. I've got an awful sight to answer for. I used to have a good wife when I was in Australia. I don't know where I haven't been, first and last. I was always a hard fellow. I've spent as much as a couple o' fortunes, and here I am. Devil take it!"

Nelly was still sewing in the dining-room; but, soon after Miss Dane had gone out to the kitchen, one of the doors between had slowly closed itself with a plaintive whine. The round stone that Melissa used to keep it open had been pushed away. Nelly was a little annoyed: she liked to hear what was going on; but she was just then holding her work with great care in a place that was hard to sew; so she did not move. She heard the murmur of voices, and thought, after a while, that the old vagabond ought to go away by this time. What could be making her cousin Horatia talk so long with him? It was not like her at all. He would beg for money, of course, and she hoped Miss Horatia would not give him a single cent.

It was some time before the kitchen-door opened, and the man came out with clumsy, stumbling steps. "I'm much obliged to you," he said, "and I don't know but it is the last time I'll get treated as if I was a gentleman. Is there anything I could do for you round the place?" he asked hesitatingly and as if he hoped that his offer would not be accepted.

"No," answered Miss Dane. "No, thank you. Good-by!" and he went away.

I said he had been lifted a little above his low life; he fell back again directly before he was out of the gate. "I'm blessed if she didn't give me a ten-dollar bill!" said he. "She must have thought it was a one. I'll get out o' call as quick as I can, hope she won't find it out, and send anybody after me." Visions of unlimited drinks, and other things in which the old sailor found pleasure, flitted through his stupid mind. "How the old lady stared at me once!" he thought. "Wonder if she was anybody I used to know? 'Downton?' I don't know as I ever heard of the place." And he scuffed along the dusty road; and that night he was very drunk, and the next day he went wandering on, God only knows where.

But Nelly and Melissa both had heard a strange noise in the kitchen, as if some one had fallen, and had found that Miss Horatia had fainted dead away. It was partly the heat, she said, when she saw their anxious faces as she came to herself; she had had a little headache all the morning; it was very hot and close in the kitchen, and the faintness had come upon her suddenly. They helped her walk into the cool parlor presently, and Melissa brought her a glass of wine, and Nelly sat beside her on a footstool as she lay on the sofa, and fanned her. Once she held her cheek against Miss Horatia's hand for a minute, and she will never know as long as she lives what a comfort she was that day.

Every one but Miss Dane forgot the old sailor-tramp in this excitement that followed his visit. Do you guess already who he was?

But the certainty could not come to you with the chill and horror it did to Miss Dane. There had been something familiar in his look and voice from the first, and then she had suddenly known him, her lost lover. It was an awful change that the years had made in him. He had truly called himself a wreck: he was like some dreary wreck in its decay and utter ruin, its miserable ugliness and worthlessness, falling to pieces in the slow tides of a lifeless southern sea.

And he had once been her lover, Miss Dane thought many times in the days that came after. Not that there was ever anything asked or promised between them, but they had liked each other dearly, and had parted with deep sorrow. She had thought of him all these years so tenderly; she had believed always that his love had been even greater than her own, and never once had doubted that the missing ship Chevalier had carried with it down into the sea a heart that was true to her.

By little and little this all grew familiar, and she accustomed herself to the knowledge of her new secret. She shuddered at the thought of the misery of a life with him, and she thanked God for sparing her such shame and despair. The distance between them seemed immense. She had been a person of so much consequence among her friends, and so dutiful and irreproachable a woman. She had not begun to understand what dishonor is in the world; her life had been shut in by safe and orderly surroundings. It was a strange chance that had brought this wanderer to her door. She remembered his wretched untidiness. She would not have liked even to touch him. She had never imagined him grown old: he had always been young to her. It was a great mercy he had not known her; it would have been a most miserable position for them both; and yet she thought, with sad surprise, that she had not known she had changed so entirely. She thought of the different ways their roads in life had gone; she pitied him; she cried about him more than once; and she wished that she could know he was dead. He might have been such a brave, good man, with his strong will and resolute courage. God forgive him for the wickedness which his strength had been made to serve! "God forgive him!" said Miss Horatia to herself sadly over and over again. She wondered if she ought to have let him go away, and so have lost sight of him; but she could not do anything else. She suffered terribly on his account; she had a pity, such as God's pity must be, for even his willful sins.

So her romance was all over with; yet the towns-people still whispered it to strangers, and even Melissa and Nelly never knew how she had lost her lover in so strange and sad a way in her latest years. Nobody noticed much change; but Melissa saw that the whale's tooth had disappeared from its place in Miss Horatia's room, and her old friends said to each other that she began to show her age a great deal. She seemed really like an old woman now; she was not the woman she had been a year ago.

This is all of the story; but I so often wish when a story comes to an end that I knew what became of the people afterward. Shall I tell you that Miss Horatia clings more and more fondly to her young cousin Nelly; and that Nelly will stay with her a great deal before she marries, and sometimes afterward, when the lieutenant goes away to sea? Shall I say that Miss Dane seems as well satisfied and comfortable as ever, though she acknowledges she is not so young as she used to be, and somehow misses something out of her life? It is the contentment of winter rather than that of summer: the flowers are out of bloom for her now, and under the snow. And Melissa, will not she always be the same, with a quaintness and freshness and toughness like a cedar-tree, to the end of her days? Let us hope they will live on together and be untroubled this long time yet, the two good women; and let us wish Nelly much pleasure, and a sweet soberness and fearlessness as she grows older and finds life a harder thing to understand and a graver thing to know.

"Tom's Husband"

The Atlantic Monthly, February 1882

I shall not dwell long upon the circumstances that led to the marriage of my hero and heroine; though their courtship was, to them, the only one that has ever noticeably approached the ideal, it had many aspects in which it was entirely commonplace in other people's eyes. While the world in general smiles at lovers with kindly approval and sympathy, it refuses to be aware of the unprecedented delight which is amazing to the lovers themselves.

But, as has been true in many other cases, when they were at last married, the most ideal of situations was found to have been changed to the most practical. Instead of having shared their original duties, and, as school-boys would say, going halves, they discovered that the cares of life had been doubled. This led to some distressing moments for both our friends; they understood suddenly that instead of dwelling in heaven they were still upon earth, and had made themselves slaves to new laws and limitations. Instead of being freer and happier than ever before, they had assumed new responsibilities; they had established a new household, and must fulfill in some way or another the obligations of it. They looked back with affection to their engagement; they had been longing to have each other to themselves, apart from the world, but it seemed that they never felt so keenly that they were still units in modern society. Since Adam and Eve were in Paradise, before the devil joined them, nobody has had a chance to imitate that unlucky couple. In some respects they told the truth when, twenty times a day, they said that life had never been so pleasant before; but there were mental reservations on either side which might have subjected them to the accusation of lying. Somehow, there was a little feeling of disappointment, and they caught themselves wondering —though they would have died sooner than confess it—whether they were quite so happy as they had expected. The truth was, they were much happier than people usually are, for they had an uncommon capacity for enjoyment. For a little while they were like a sail-boat that is beating and has to drift a few minutes before it can catch the wind and start off on the other tack. And they had the same feeling, too, that any one is likely to have who has been long pursuing some object of his ambition or desire. Whether it is a coin, or a picture, or a stray volume of some old edition of Shakespeare, or whether it is an office under government or a lover, when it is fairly in one's grasp there is a loss of the eagerness that was felt in pursuit. Satisfaction, even after one has dined well, is not so interesting and eager a feeling as hunger.

My hero and heroine were reasonably well established to begin with: they each had some money, though Mr. Wilson had most. His father had at one time been a rich man, but with the decline, a few years before, of manufacturing interests, he had become, mostly through the fault of others, somewhat involved; and at the time of his death his affairs were in such a condition that it was still a question whether a very large sum or a moderately large one would represent his estate. Mrs. Wilson, Tom's step-mother, was somewhat of an invalid; she suffered severely at times with asthma, but she was almost entirely relieved by living in another part of the country. While her husband lived, she had accepted her illness as inevitable, and had rarely left home; but during the last few years she had lived in Philadelphia with her own people, making short and wheezing visits only from time to time, and had not undergone a voluntary period of suffering since the occasion of Tom's marriage, which she had entirely approved. She had a sufficient property of her own, and she and Tom were independent of each other in that way. Her only other step-child was a daughter, who had married a navy officer, and had at this time gone out to spend three years (or less) with her husband, who had been ordered to Japan.

It is not unfrequently noticed that in many marriages one of the persons who choose each other as partners for life is said to have thrown himself or herself away, and the relatives and friends look on with dismal forebodings and ill-concealed submission. In this case it was the wife who might have done so much better, according to public opinion. She did not think so herself, luckily, either before marriage or afterward, and I do not think it occurred to her to picture to herself the sort of career which would have been her alternative. She had been an only child, and had usually taken her own way. Some one once said that it was a great pity that she had not been obliged to work for her living, for she had inherited a most uncommon business talent, and, without being disreputably keen at a bargain, her insight into the practical working of affairs was very clear and far-reaching. Her father, who had also been a manufacturer, like Tom's, had often said it had been a mistake that she was a girl instead of a boy. Such executive ability as hers is often wasted in the more contracted sphere of women, and is apt to be more a disadvantage than a help. She was too independent and self-reliant for a wife; it would seem at first thought that she needed a wife herself more than she did a husband. Most men like best the women whose natures cling and appeal to theirs for protection. But Tom Wilson, while he did not wish to be protected himself, liked these very qualities in his wife which would have displeased some other men; to tell the truth, he was very much in love with his wife just as she was. He was a successful collector of almost everything but money, and during a great part of his life he had been an invalid, and he had grown, as he laughingly confessed, very old-womanish. He had been badly lamed, when a boy, by being caught in some machinery in his father's mill, near which he was idling one afternoon, and though he had almost entirely out-grown the effect of his injury, it had not been until after many years. He had been in college, but his eyes had given out there, and he had been obliged to leave in the middle of his junior year, though he had kept up a pleasant intercourse with the members of his class, with whom he had been a great favorite. He was a good deal of an idler in the world. I do not think his ambition, except in the case of securing Mary Dunn for his wife, had ever been distinct; he seemed to make the most he could of each day as it came, without making all his days' works tend toward some grand result, and go toward the upbuilding of some grand plan and purpose. He consequently gave no promise of being either distinguished or great. When his eyes would allow, he was an indefatigable reader; and although he would have said that he read only for amusement, yet he amused himself with books that were well worth the time he spent over them.

The house where he lived nominally belonged to his step-mother, but she had taken for granted that Tom would bring his wife home to it, and assured him that it should be to all intents and purposes his. Tom was deeply attached to the old place, which was altogether the pleasantest in town. He had kept bachelor's hall there most of the time since his father's death, and he had taken great pleasure, before his marriage, in refitting it to some extent, though it was already comfortable and furnished in remarkably good taste. People said of him that if it had not been for his illnesses, and if he had been a poor boy, he probably would have made something of himself. As it was, he was not very well known by the towns-people, being somewhat reserved, and not taking much interest in their every-day subjects of conversation. Nobody liked him so well as they liked his wife, yet there was no reason why he should be disliked enough to have much said about it.

After our friends had been married for some time, and had outlived the first strangeness of the new order of things, and had done their duty to their neighbors with so much apparent willingness and generosity that even Tom himself was liked a great deal better than he ever had been before, they were sitting together one stormy evening in the library, before the fire. Mrs. Wilson had been reading Tom the letters which had come to him by the night's mail. There was a long one from his sister in Nagasaki, which had been written with a good deal of ill-disguised reproach. She complained of the smallness of the income of her share in her father's estate, and said that she had been assured by American friends that the smaller mills were starting up everywhere, and beginning to do well again. Since so much of their money was invested in the factory, she had been surprised and sorry to find by Tom's last letters that he had seemed to have no idea of putting in a proper person as superintendent, and going to work again. Four per cent on her other property, instead of eight, which she had been told she must soon expect, would make a great difference to her. A navy captain in a foreign port was obliged to entertain a great deal, and Tom must know that it cost them much more to live than it did him, and ought to think of their interests. She hoped he would talk over what was best to be done with their mother (who had been made executor, with Tom, of his father's will).

Tom laughed a little, but looked disturbed. His wife had said something to the same effect, and his mother had spoken once or twice in her letters of the prospect of starting the mill again. He was not a bit of a business man, and he did not feel certain, with the theories which he had arrived at of the state of the country, that it was safe yet to spend the money which would have to be spent in putting the mill in order. "They think that the minute it is going again we shall be making money hand over hand, just as father did when we were children," he said. "It is going to cost us no end of money before we can make anything. Before father died he meant to put in a good deal of new machinery, I remember. I don't know anything about the business myself, and I would have sold out long ago if I had had an offer that came anywhere near the value. The larger mills are the only ones that are good for anything now, and we should have to bring a crowd of French Canadians here; the day is past for the people who live in this part of the country to go into the factory again. Even the

Irish all go West when they come into the country, and don't come to places like this any more."

"But there are a good many of the old work-people down in the village," said Mrs. Wilson. "Jack Towne asked me the other day if you weren't going to start up in the spring."

Tom moved uneasily in his chair. "I'll put you in for superintendent, if you like," he said, half angrily, whereupon Mary threw the newspaper at him; but by the time he had thrown it back he was in good humor again.

"Do you know, Tom," she said, with amazing seriousness, "that I believe I should like nothing in the world so much as to be the head of a large business? I hate keeping house,—I always did; and I never did so much of it in all my life put together as I have since I have been married. I suppose it isn't womanly to say so, but if I could escape from the whole thing I believe I should be perfectly happy. If you get rich when the mill is going again, I shall beg for a housekeeper, and shirk everything. I give you fair warning. I don't believe I keep this house half so well as you did before I came here."

Tom's eyes twinkled. "I am going to have that glory,—I don't think you do, Polly; but you can't say that I have not been forbearing. I certainly have not told you more than twice how we used to have things cooked. I'm not going to be your kitchen-colonel."

"Of course it seemed the proper thing to do," said his wife, meditatively; "but I think we should have been even happier than we have if I had been spared it. I have had some days of wretchedness that I shudder to think of. I never know what to have for breakfast; and I ought not to say it, but I don't mind the sight of dust. I look upon housekeeping as my life's great discipline;" and at this pathetic confession they both laughed heartily.

"I've a great mind to take it off your hands," said Tom. "I always rather liked it, to tell the truth, and I ought to be a better housekeeper,—I have been at it for five years; though housekeeping for one is different from what it is for two, and one of them a woman. You see you have brought a different element into my family. Luckily, the servants are pretty well drilled. I do think you upset them a good deal at first!"

Mary Wilson smiled as if she only half heard what he was saying. She drummed with her foot on the floor and looked intently at the fire, and presently gave it a vigorous poking. "Well?" said Tom, after he had waited patiently as long as he could.

"Tom! I'm going to propose something to you. I wish you would really do as you said, and take all the home affairs under your care, and let me start the mill. I am certain I could manage it. Of course I should get people who understood the thing to teach me. I believe I was made for it; I should like it above all things. And this is what I will do: I will bear the cost of starting it, myself,—I think I have money enough, or can get it; and if I have not put affairs in the right trim at the end of a year I will stop, and you may make some other arrangement. If I have, you and your mother and sister can pay me back."

"So I am going to be the wife, and you the husband," said Tom, a little indignantly; "at least, that is what people will say. It's a regular Darby and Joan affair, and you think you can do more work in a day than I can do in three. Do you know that you must go to town to buy cotton? And do you know there are a thousand things about it that you don't know?"

"And never will?" said Mary, with perfect good humor. "Why, Tom, I can learn as well as you, and a good deal better, for I like business, and you don't. You forget that I was always father's right-hand man after I was a dozen years old, and that you have let me invest my money and some of your own, and I haven't made a blunder yet."

Tom thought that his wife had never looked so handsome or so happy. "I don't care, I should rather like the fun of knowing what people will say. It is a new departure, at any rate. Women think they can do everything better than men in these days, but I'm the first man, apparently, who has wished he were a woman."

"Of course people will laugh," said Mary, "but they will say that it's just like me, and think I am fortunate to have married a man who will let me do as I choose. I don't see why it isn't sensible: you will be living exactly as you were before you married, as to home affairs; and since it was a good thing for you to know something about housekeeping then, I can't imagine why you shouldn't go on with it now, since it makes me miserable, and I am wasting a fine business talent while I do it. What do we care for people's talking about it?"

"It seems to me that it is something like women's smoking: it isn't wicked, but it isn't the custom of the country. And I don't like the idea of your going among business men. Of course I should be above going with you, and having people think I must be an idiot; they would say that you married a manufacturing interest, and I was thrown in. I can foresee that my pride is going to be humbled to the dust in every way," Tom declared in mournful tones, and began to shake with laughter. "It is one of your lovely castles in the air, dear Polly, but an old brick mill needs a better foundation than the clouds. No, I'll look around, and get an honest man with a few select brains for agent. I suppose it's the best thing we can do, for the machinery ought not to lie still any longer; but I mean to sell the factory as soon as I can. I devoutly wish it would take fire, for the insurance would be the best price we are likely to get. That is a famous letter from Alice! I am afraid the captain has been growling over his pay, or they have been giving too many little dinners on board ship. If we were rid of the mill, you and I might go out there this winter. It would be capital fun."

Mary smiled again in an absent-minded way. Tom had an uneasy feeling that he had not heard the end of it yet, but nothing more was said for a day or two. When Mrs. Tom Wilson announced, with no apparent thought of being contradicted, that she had entirely made up her mind, and she meant to see those men who had been overseers of the different departments, who still lived in the village, and have the mill put in order at once, Tom looked disturbed, but made no opposition; and soon after breakfast his wife formally presented him with a handful of keys, and told him there was meat enough in the house for dinner; and presently he heard the wheels of her little phaeton rattling off down the road. I should be untruthful if I tried to persuade any one that he was not provoked; he thought she would at least have waited for his formal permission, and at first he meant to take another horse, and chase her, and bring her back in disgrace, and put a stop to the whole thing. But something assured him that she knew what she was about, and he determined to let her have her own way. If she failed, it might do no harm, and this was the only ungallant thought he gave her. He was sure that she would do nothing unladylike, or be unmindful of his dignity; and he believed it would be looked upon as one of her odd, independent freaks, which always had won respect in the end, however much they had been laughed at in the beginning. "Susan," said he, as that estimable person went by the door with the dust-pan, "you may tell Catherine to come to me for orders about the house, and you may do so yourself. I am going to take charge again, as I did before I was married. It is no trouble to me, and Mrs. Wilson dislikes it. Besides, she is going into business, and will have a great deal else to think of."

"Yes, sir; very well, sir," said Susan, who was suddenly moved to ask so many questions that she was utterly silent. But her master looked very happy; there was evidently no disapproval of his wife; and she went on up the stairs, and began to sweep them down, knocking the dust-brush about excitedly, as if she were trying to kill a descending colony of insects.

Tom went out to the stable and mounted his horse, which had been waiting for him to take his customary after-breakfast ride to the post-office, and he galloped down the road in quest of the phaeton. He saw Mary talking with Jack Towne, who had been an overseer and a valued workman of his father's. He was looking much surprised and pleased.

"I wasn't caring so much about getting work, myself," he explained; "I've got what will carry me and my wife through; but it'll be better for the young folks about here to work near home. My nephews are wanting something to do; they were going to Lynn next week. I don't say but I should like to be to work in the old place again. I've sort of missed it, since we shut down."

"I'm sorry I was so long in overtaking you," said Tom, politely, to his wife. "Well, Jack, did Mrs. Wilson tell you she's going to start the mill? You must give her all the help you can."

"'Deed I will," said Mr. Towne, gallantly, without a bit of astonishment.

"I don't know much about the business yet," said Mrs. Wilson, who had been a little overcome at Jack Towne's lingo of the different rooms and machinery, and who felt an overpowering sense of having a great deal before her in the next few weeks. "By the time the mill is ready, I will be ready, too," she said, taking heart a little; and Tom, who was quick to understand her moods, could not help laughing, as he rode alongside. "We want a new barrel of flour, Tom, dear," she said, by way of punishment for his untimely mirth.

If she lost courage in the long delay, or was disheartened at the steady call for funds, she made no sign; and after a while the mill started up, and her cares were lightened, so that she told Tom that before next pay day she would like to go to Boston for a few days, and go to the theatre, and have a frolic and a rest. She really looked pale and thin, and she said she never worked so hard in all her life; but nobody knew how happy she was, and she was so glad she had married Tom, for some men would have laughed at it.

"I laughed at it," said Tom, meekly. "All is, if I don't cry by and by, because I am a beggar, I shall be lucky." But Mary looked fearlessly serene, and said that there was no danger at present.

It would have been ridiculous to expect a dividend the first year, though the Nagasaki people were pacified with difficulty. All the business letters came to Tom's address, and everybody who was not directly concerned thought that he was the motive power of the reawakened enterprise. Sometimes business people came to the mill, and were amazed at having to confer with Mrs. Wilson, but they soon had to respect her talents and her success. She was helped by the old clerk, who had been promptly recalled and reinstated, and she certainly did capitally well. She was laughed at, as she had expected to be, and people said they should think Tom would be ashamed of himself; but it soon appeared that he was not to blame, and what reproach was offered was on the score of his wife's oddity. There was nothing about the mill that she did not understand before very long, and at the end of the second year she declared a small dividend with great pride and triumph. And she was congratulated on her success, and every one thought of her project in a different way from the way they had thought of it in the beginning. She had singularly good fortune: at the end of the third year she was making money for herself and her friends faster than most people were, and approving letters began to come from Nagasaki. The Ashtons had been ordered to stay in that region, and it was evident that they were continually being obliged to entertain more instead of less. Their children were growing fast too, and constantly becoming more expensive. The captain and his wife had already begun to congratulate themselves secretly that their two sons would in all probability come into possession, one day, of their uncle Tom's handsome property.

For a good while Tom enjoyed life, and went on his quiet way serenely. He was anxious at first, for he thought that Mary was going to make ducks and drakes of his money and her own. And then he did not exactly like the looks of the thing, either; he feared that his wife was growing successful as a business person at the risk of losing her womanliness. But as time went on, and he found there was no fear of that, he accepted the situation philosophically. He gave up his collection of engravings, having become more interested in one of coins and medals, which took up most of his leisure time. He often went to the city in pursuit of such treasures, and gained much renown in certain quarters as a numismatologist of great skill and experience. But at last his house (which had almost kept itself, and had given him little to do beside ordering the dinners, while faithful old Catherine and her niece Susan were his aids) suddenly became a great care to him. Catherine, who had been the main-stay of the family for many years, died after a short illness, and Susan must needs choose that time, of all others, for being married to one of the second hands in the mill. There followed a long and dismal season of experimenting, and for a long time there was a procession of incapable creatures going in at one kitchen door and out of the other. His wife would not have liked to say so, but it seemed to her that Tom was growing fussy about the house affairs, and took more notice of those minor details than he used. She wished more than once, when she was tired, that he would not talk so much about the housekeeping; he seemed sometimes to have no other thought.

In the first of Mrs. Wilson's connection with manufacturing, she had made it a rule to consult Tom on every subject of importance; but it had speedily proved to be a formality. He tried manfully to show a deep interest which he did not feel, and his wife gave up, little by little, telling him much about her affairs. She said that she liked to drop business when she came home in the evening; and at last she fell into the habit of taking a nap on the library sofa, while Tom, who could not use his eyes much by lamp-light, sat smoking or in utter idleness before the fire. When they were first married his wife had made it a rule that she should always read him the evening papers, and afterward they had always gone on with some book of history or philosophy, in which they were both interested. These evenings of their early married life had been charming to both of them, and from time to time one would say to the other that they ought to take up again the habit of reading together. Mary was so unaffectedly tired in the evening that Tom never liked to propose a walk; for, though he was not a man of peculiarly social nature, he had always been accustomed to pay an occasional evening visit to his neighbors in the village. And though he had little interest in the business world, and still less knowledge of it, after a while he wished that his wife would have more to say about what she was planning and doing, or how things were getting on. He thought that her chief aid, old Mr. Jackson, was far more in her thoughts than he. She was forever quoting Jackson's opinions. He did not like to find that she took it for granted that he was not interested in the welfare of his own property; it made him feel like a sort of pensioner and dependent, though, when they had guests at the house, which was by no means seldom, there was nothing in her manner that would imply that she thought herself in any way the head of the family. It was hard work to find fault with his wife in any way, though, to give him his due, he rarely tried.

But, this being a wholly unnatural state of things, the reader must expect to hear of its change at last, and the first blow from the enemy was dealt by an old woman, who lived near by, and who called to Tom one morning, as he was driving down to the village in a great hurry (to post a letter, which ordered his agent to secure a long-wished-for ancient copper coin, at any price), to ask him if they had made yeast that week, and if she could borrow a cupful, as her own had met with some misfortune. Tom was instantly in a rage, and he mentally condemned her to some undeserved fate, but told her aloud to go and see the cook. This slight delay, besides being killing to his dignity, caused him to lose the mail, and in the end his much-desired copper coin. It was a hard day for him, altogether; it was Wednesday, and the first days of the week having been stormy the washing was very late. And Mary came home to dinner provokingly good-natured. She had met an old school-mate and her husband driving home from the mountains, and had first taken them over her factory, to their great amusement and delight, and then had brought them home to dinner. Tom greeted them cordially, and manifested his usual graceful hospitality; but the minute he saw his wife alone he said in a plaintive tone of rebuke, "I should think you might have remembered that the girls are unusually busy to-day. I do wish you would take a little interest in things at home. The girls have been washing, and I'm sure I don't know what sort of a dinner we can give your friends. I wish you had thought to bring home some steak. I have been busy myself, and couldn't go down to the village. I thought we would only have a lunch."

Mary was hungry, but she said nothing, except that it would be all right,—she didn't mind; and perhaps they could have some canned soup.

She often went to town to buy or look at cotton, or to see some improvement in machinery, and she brought home beautiful bits of furniture and new pictures for the house, and showed a touching thoughtfulness in remembering Tom's fancies; but somehow he had an uneasy suspicion that she could get along pretty well without him when it came to the deeper wishes and hopes of her life, and that her most important concerns were all matters in which he had no share. He seemed to himself to have merged his life in his wife's; he lost his interest in things outside the house and grounds; he felt himself fast growing rusty and behind the times, and to have somehow missed a good deal in life; he felt that he was a failure. One day the thought rushed over him that his had been almost exactly the experience of most women, and he wondered if it really was any more disappointing and ignominious to him than it was to women themselves. "Some of them may be contented with it," he said to himself, soberly. "People think women are designed for such careers by nature, but I don't know why I ever made such a fool of myself."

Having once seen his situation in life from such a stand-point, he felt it day by day to be more degrading, and he wondered what he should do about it; and once, drawn by a new, strange sympathy, he went to the little family burying-ground. It was one of the mild, dim days that come sometimes in early November, when the pale sunlight is like the pathetic smile of a sad face, and he sat for a long time on the limp, frost-bitten grass beside his mother's grave.

But when he went home in the twilight his step-mother, who just then was making them a little visit, mentioned that she had been looking through some boxes of hers that had been packed long before and stowed away in the garret. "Everything looks very nice up there," she said, in her wheezing voice (which, worse than usual that day, always made him nervous); and added, without any intentional slight to his feelings, "I do think you have always been a most excellent housekeeper."

"I'm tired of such nonsense!" he exclaimed, with surprising indignation. "Mary, I wish you to arrange your affairs so that you can leave them for six months at least. I am going to spend this winter in Europe."

"Why, Tom, dear!" said his wife, appealingly. "I couldn't leave my business any way in the"—

But she caught sight of a look on his usually placid countenance that was something more than decision, and refrained from saying anything more.

And three weeks from that day they sailed.

"Marsh Rosemary"

The Atlantic Monthly, May 1886

I.

One hot afternoon in August, a single moving figure might have been seen following a straight road that crossed the salt marshes of Walpole. Everybody else had either stayed at home or crept into such shade as could be found near at hand. The thermometer marked at least ninety degrees. There was hardly a fishing-boat to be seen on the glistening sea, only far away on the hazy horizon two or three coasting schooners looked like ghostly flying Dutchmen, becalmed for once and motionless.

Ashore, the flaring light of the sun brought out the fine, clear colors of the level landscape. The marsh grasses were a more vivid green than usual, the brown tops of those that were beginning to go to seed looked almost red, and the soil at the edges of the tide inlets seemed to be melting into a black, pitchy substance like the dark pigments on a painter's palette. Where the land was higher the hot air flickered above it dizzily. This was not an afternoon that one would naturally choose for a long walk, yet Mr. Jerry Lane stepped briskly forward, and appeared to have more than usual energy. His big boots trod down the soft carpet of pussy-clover that bordered the dusty, whitish road. He struck at the stationary procession of thistles with a little stick as he went by. Flight after flight of yellow butterflies fluttered up as he passed, and then settled down again to their thistle flowers, while on the shiny cambric back of Jerry's Sunday waistcoat basked at least eight large green-headed flies in complete security.

It was difficult to decide why the Sunday waistcoat should have been put on that Saturday afternoon. Jerry had not thought it important to wear his best boots or best trousers, and had left his coat at home altogether. He smiled as he walked along, and once when he took off his hat, as a light breeze came that way, he waved it triumphantly before he put it on again. Evidently this was no common errand that led him due west, and made him forget the hot weather, and caused him to shade his eyes with his hand, as he looked eagerly at a clump of trees and the chimney of a small house a little way beyond the boundary of the marshes, where the higher ground began.

Miss Ann Floyd sat by her favorite window, sewing, twitching her thread less decidedly than usual, and casting a wistful glance now and then down the road or at the bees in her gay little garden outside. There was a grim expression overshadowing her firmly-set, angular face, and the frown that always appeared on her forehead when she sewed or read the newspaper was deeper and straighter than usual. She did not look as if she were conscious of the heat, though she had dressed herself in an old-fashioned skirt of sprigged lawn and a loose jacket of thin white dimity with out-of-date flowing sleeves. Her sandy hair was smoothly brushed; one lock betrayed a slight crinkle at its edge, but it owed nothing to any encouragement of Nancy Floyd's. A hard, honest, kindly face this was, of a woman whom everybody trusted, who might be expected to give of whatever she had to give, good measure, pressed down and running over. She was a lonely soul; she had no near relatives in the world. It seemed always as if nature had been mistaken in not planting her somewhere in a large and busy household.

The little square room, kitchen in winter and sitting-room in summer, was as clean and bare and thrifty as one would expect the dwelling-place of such a woman to be. She sat in a straight-backed, splint-bottomed kitchen chair, and always put back her spool with a click on the very same spot on the window-sill. You would think she had done with youth and with love affairs, yet you might as well expect the ancient cherry-tree in the corner of her yard to cease adventuring its white blossoms when the May sun shone! No woman in Walpole had more bravely and patiently borne the burden of loneliness and lack of love. Even now her outward behavior gave no hint of the new excitement and delight that filled her heart.

"Land sakes alive!" she says to herself presently, "there comes Jerry Lane. I expect, if he sees me settin' to the winder, he'll come in an' dawdle round till supper time!" But good Nancy Floyd smooths her hair hastily as she rises and drops her work, and steps back toward the middle of the room, watching the gate anxiously all the time. Now, Jerry, with a crestfallen look at the vacant window, makes believe that he is going by, and takes a loitering step or two onward, and then stops short; with a somewhat sheepish smile he leans over the neat picket fence and examines the blue and white and pink larkspur that covers most of the space in the little garden. He takes off his hat again to cool his forehead, and replaces it, without a grand gesture this time, and looks again at the window hopefully.

There is a pause. The woman knows that the man is sure she is there; a little blush colors her thin cheeks as she comes boldly to the wide-open front door.

"What do you think of this kind of weather?" asks Jerry Lane complacently, as he leans over the fence, and surrounds himself with an air of self-sacrifice.

"I call it hot," responds the Juliet from her balcony, with deliberate assurance, "but the corn needs sun, everybody says. I shouldn't have wanted to toil up from the shore under such a glare, if I had been you. Better come in and set awhile, and cool off," she added, without any apparent enthusiasm. Jerry was sure to come, anyway. She would rather make the suggestion than have him.

Mr. Lane sauntered in, and seated himself opposite his hostess, beside the other small window, and watched her admiringly as she took up her sewing and worked at it with great spirit and purpose. He clasped his hands together and leaned forward a little. The shaded kitchen was very comfortable, after the glaring light outside, and the clean orderliness of the few chairs and the braided rugs and the table under the clock, with some larkspur and asparagus in a china vase for decoration, seemed to please him unexpectedly. "Now just see what ways you women folks have of fixing things up smart!" he ventured gallantly.

Nancy's countenance did not forbid further compliment; she looked at the flowers herself, quickly, and explained that she had gathered them a while ago to send to the minister's sister, who kept house for him. "I saw him going by, and expected he'd be back this same road. Mis' Elton's be'n havin' another o' her dyin' spells this noon, and the deacon went by after him hot foot. I'd souse her well with stone-cold water. She never sent for me to set up with her; she knows better. Poor man, 't was likely he was right into the middle of to-morrow's sermon. 'T ain't considerate of the deacon, and when he knows he's got a fool for a wife, he needn't go round persuading other folks she's so suffering as she makes out. They ain't got no larkspur this year to the parsonage, and I was going to let the minister take this over to Amandy; but I see his wagon over on the other road, going towards the village, about an hour after he went by here."

It seemed to be a relief to tell somebody all these things after such a season of forced repression, and Jerry listened with gratifying interest. "How you do see through folks!" he exclaimed in a mild voice. Jerry could be very soft spoken if he thought best. "Mis' Elton's a die-away lookin' creatur'. I heard of her saying last Sunday, comin' out o' meetin', that she made an effort to git there once more, but she expected 't would be the last time. Looks as if she eat well, don't she?" he concluded in a meditative tone.

"Eat!" exclaimed the hostess, with snapping eyes. "There ain't no woman in town, sick or well, can lay aside the food that she does. 'T ain't to the table afore folks, but she goes seeking round in the cupboards half a dozen times a day. An' I've heard her remark 't was the last time she ever expected to visit the sanctuary as much as a dozen times within five years."

"Some places I've sailed to they'd have hit her over the head with a club long ago," said Jerry, with an utter lack of sympathy that was startling. "Well, I must be gettin' back again. Talkin' of eatin' makes us think o' supper-time. Must be past five, ain't it? I thought I'd just step up to see if there wa'n't anything I could lend a hand about, this hot day."

Sensible Ann Floyd folded her hands over her sewing, as it lay in her lap, and looked straight before her without seeing the pleading face of the guest. This moment was a great crisis in her life. She was conscious of it, and knew well enough that upon her next words would depend the course of future events. The man who waited to hear what she had to say was indeed many years younger than she, was shiftless and vacillating. He had drifted to Walpole from nobody knew where, and possessed many qualities which she had openly rebuked and despised in other men. True enough, he was good-looking, but that did not atone for the lacks of his character and reputation. Yet she knew herself to be the better man of the two, and since she had surmounted many obstacles already she was confident that, with a push here and a pull there to steady him, she could keep him in good trim. The winters were so long and lonely; her life was in many ways hungry and desolate in spite of its thrift and conformity. She had laughed scornfully when he stopped, one day in the spring, and offered to help her weed her garden; she had even joked with one of the neighbors about it. Jerry had been growing more and more friendly and pleasant ever since. His ease-loving, careless nature was like a comfortable cushion for hers, with its angles, its melancholy anticipations and self-questionings. But Jerry liked her, and if she liked him and married him, and took him home, it was nobody's business; and in that moment of surrender to Jerry's cause she arrayed herself at his right hand against the rest of the world, ready for warfare with any and all of its opinions.

She was suddenly aware of the sunburnt face and light, curling hair of her undeclared lover, at the other end of the painted table with its folded leaf. She smiled at him vacantly across the larkspur; then she gave a little start, and was afraid that her thoughts had wandered longer than was seemly. The kitchen clock was ticking faster than usual, as if it were trying to attract attention.

"I guess I'll be getting home," repeated the visitor ruefully, and rose from his chair, but hesitated again at an unfamiliar expression upon his companion's face.

"I don't know as I've got anything extra for supper, but you stop," she said, "an' take what there is. I wouldn't go back across them marshes right in this heat."

Jerry Lane had a lively sense of humor, and a queer feeling of merriment stole over him now, as he watched the mistress of the house. She had risen, too; she looked so simple and so frankly sentimental, there was such an incongruous coyness added to her usually straightforward, angular appearance, that his instinctive laughter nearly got the better of him, and might have lost him the prize for which he had been waiting these many months. But Jerry behaved like a man: he stepped forward and kissed Ann Floyd; he held her fast with one arm as he stood beside her, and kissed her again and again. She was a dear good woman. She had a fresh young heart, in spite of the straight wrinkle in her forehead and her work-worn hands. She had waited all her days for this joy of having a lover.

II.

Even Mrs. Elton revived for a day or two under the tonic of such a piece of news. That was what Jerry Lane had hung round for all summer, everybody knew at last. Now he would strike work and live at his ease, the men grumbled to each other; but all the women of Walpole deplored most the weaknesses and foolishness of the elderly

bride. Ann Floyd was comfortably off, and had something laid by for a
rainy day; she would have done vastly better to deny herself such an
expensive and utterly worthless luxury as the kind of husband Jerry
Lane would make. He had idled away his life. He earned a little money
now and then in seafaring pursuits, but was too lazy, in the shore
parlance, to tend lobster-pots. What was energetic Ann Floyd going to
do with him? She was always at work, always equal to emergencies,
and entirely opposed to dullness and idleness and even placidity. She
liked people who had some snap to them, she often avowed scornfully,
and now she had chosen for a husband the laziest man in Walpole.
"Dear sakes," one woman said to another, as they heard the news,
"there's no fool like an old fool!"

       The days went quickly by, while Miss Ann made her plain
wedding clothes. If people expected her to put on airs of youth they
were disappointed. Her wedding bonnet was the same sort of bonnet
she had worn for a dozen years, and one disappointed critic deplored
the fact that she had spruced up so little, and kept on dressing old
enough to look like Jerry Lane's mother. As her acquaintances met her
they looked at her with close scrutiny, expecting to see some outward
trace of such a silly, uncharacteristic departure from good sense and
discretion. But Miss Floyd, while she was still Miss Floyd, displayed
no silliness and behaved with dignity, while on the Sunday after a
quiet marriage at the parsonage she and Jerry Lane walked up the side
aisle to their pew, the picture of middle-aged sobriety and
respectability. Their fellow parishioners, having recovered from their
first astonishment and amusement, settled down to the belief that the
newly married pair understood their own business best, and that if
anybody could make the best of Jerry and get any work out of him, it
was his capable wife.

       "And if she undertakes to drive him too hard he can slip off to
sea, and they'll be rid of each other," commented one of Jerry's
'longshore companions, as if it were only reasonable that some refuge
should be afforded to those who make mistakes in matrimony.

       There did not seem to be any mistake at first, or for a good
many months afterward. The husband liked the comfort that came
from such good housekeeping, and enjoyed a deep sense of having
made a good anchorage in a well-sheltered harbor, after many years of
thriftless improvidence and drifting to and fro. There were some
hindrances to perfect happiness: he had to forego long seasons of

gossip with his particular friends, and the outdoor work which was expected of him, though by no means heavy for a person of his strength, fettered his freedom not a little. To chop wood, and take care of a cow, and bring a pail of water now and then, did not weary him so much as it made him practically understand the truth of weakly Sister Elton's remark that life was a constant chore. And when poor Jerry, for lack of other interest, fancied that his health was giving way mysteriously, and brought home a bottle of strong liquor to be used in case of sickness, and placed it conveniently in the shed, Mrs. Lane locked it up in the small chimney cupboard where she kept her camphor bottle and her opodeldoc and the other family medicines. She was not harsh with her husband. She cherished him tenderly, and worked diligently at her trade of tailoress, singing her hymns gayly in summer weather; for she never had been so happy as now, when there was somebody to please beside herself, to cook for and sew for, and to live with and love. But Jerry complained more and more in his inmost heart that his wife expected too much of him. Presently he resumed an old habit of resorting to the least respected of the two country stores of that neighborhood, and sat in the row of loafers on the outer steps. "Sakes alive," said a shrewd observer one day, "the fools set there and talk and talk about what they went through when they follered the sea, till when the women-folks comes tradin' they are obleeged to climb right over 'em."

But things grew worse and worse, until one day Jerry Lane came home a little late to dinner, and found his wife unusually grim-faced and impatient. He took his seat with an amiable smile, and showed in every way his determination not to lose his temper because somebody else had. It was one of the days when he looked almost boyish and entirely irresponsible. His hair was handsome and curly from the dampness of the east wind, and his wife was forced to remember how, in the days of their courtship, she used to wish that she could pull one of the curling locks straight, for the pleasure of seeing it fly back. She felt old and tired, and was hurt in her very soul by the contrast between herself and her husband. "No wonder I am aging, having to lug everything on my shoulders," she thought. Jerry had forgotten to do whatever she had asked him for a day or two. He had started out that morning to go lobstering, but he had returned from the direction of the village.

"Nancy," he said pleasantly, after he had begun his dinner, a silent and solitary meal, while his wife stitched busily by the window, and refused to look at him,—"Nancy, I've been thinking a good deal about a project."

"I hope it ain't going to cost so much and bring in so little as your other notions have, then," she responded quickly; though somehow a memory of the hot day when Jerry came and stood outside the fence, and kissed her when it was settled he should stay to supper, —a memory of that day would keep fading and brightening in her mind.

"Yes," said Jerry, humbly, "I ain't done right, Nancy. I ain't done my part for our livin'. I've let it sag right on to you, most ever since we was married. There was that spell when I was kind of weakly, and had a pain acrost me. I tell you what it is: I never was good for nothin' ashore, but now I've got my strength up I'm going to show ye what I can do. I'm promised to ship with Cap'n Low's brother, Skipper Nathan, that sails out o' Eastport in the coasting trade, lumber and so on. I shall get good wages, and you shall keep the whole on 't 'cept what I need for clothes."

"You needn't be so plaintive," said Ann in a sharp voice. "You can if you want to. I have always been able to take care of myself, but when it comes to maintainin' two, 't ain't so easy. When be you goin'?"

"I expected you would be sorry," mourned Jerry, his face falling at his outbreak. "Nancy, you needn't be so quick. 'T ain't as if I hadn't always set everything by ye, if I be wuthless."

Nancy's eyes flashed fire as she turned hastily away. Hardly knowing where she went, she passed through the open doorway, and crossed the clean green turf of the narrow side yard, and leaned over the garden fence. The young cabbages and cucumbers were nearly buried in weeds, and the currant bushes were fast being turned into skeletons by the ravaging worms. Jerry had forgotten to sprinkle them with hellebore, after all, though she had put the watering-pot into his very hand the evening before. She did not like to have the whole town laugh at her for hiring a man to do his work; she was busy from early morning until late night, but she could not do everything herself. She had been a fool to marry this man, she told herself at last, and a sullen discontent and rage that had been of slow but certain growth made her long to free herself from this unprofitable hindrance for a time, at any rate. Go to sea? Yes, that was the best thing that could happen. Perhaps when he had worked hard a while on schooner fare, he would come home and be good for something!

Jerry finished his dinner in the course of time, and then sought his wife. It was not like her to go away in this silent fashion. Of late her gift of speech had been proved sufficiently formidable, and yet she had never looked so resolutely angry as to-day.

"Nancy," he began,—"Nancy, girl! I ain't goin' off to leave you, if your heart's set against it. I'll spudge up and take right holt."

But the wife turned slowly from the fence and faced him. Her eyes looked as if she had been crying. "You needn't stay on my account," she said. "I'll go right to work an' fit ye out. I'm sick of your meachin' talk, and I don't want to hear no more of it. Ef I was a man"—

Jerry Lane looked crestfallen for a minute or two; but when his stern partner in life had disappeared within the house, he slunk away among the apple-trees of the little orchard, and sat down on the grass in a shady spot. It was getting to be warm weather, but he would go round and hoe the old girl's garden stuff by and by. There would be something going on aboard the schooner, and with delicious anticipation of future pleasure this delinquent Jerry struck his knee with his hand, as if he were clapping a crony on the shoulder. He also winked several times at the same fancied companion. Then, with a comfortable chuckle, he laid himself down, and pulled his old hat over his eyes, and went to sleep, while the weeds grew at their own sweet will, and the currant worms went looping and devouring from twig to twig.

III.

Summer went by, and winter began, and Mr. Jerry Lane did not reappear. He had promised to return in September, when he parted from his wife early in June, for Nancy had relented a little at the last, and sorrowed at the prospect of so long a separation. She had already learned the vacillations and uncertainties of her husband's character; but though she accepted the truth that her marriage had been in every way a piece of foolishness, she still clung affectionately to his assumed fondness for her. She could not believe that his marriage was only one of his makeshifts, and that as soon as he grew tired of the constraint he was ready to throw the benefits of respectable home life to the four winds. A little sentimental speech-making and a few kisses the morning he went away, and the gratitude he might well have shown for her generous care-taking and provision for his voyage won her soft heart back again, and made poor, elderly, simple-hearted Nancy watch him cross the marshes with tears and foreboding. If she could have called him back that day, she would have done so and been thankful. And all summer and winter, whenever the wind blew and thrashed the drooping elm boughs against the low roof over her head, she was as full of fears and anxieties as if Jerry were her only son and making his first voyage at sea. The neighbors pitied her for her disappointment. They liked Nancy; but they could not help saying, "I told you so." It would have been impossible not to respect the brave way in which she met the world's eye, and carried herself with innocent unconsciousness of having committed so laughable and unrewarding a folly. The loafers on the store steps had been unwontedly diverted one day, when Jerry, who was their chief wit and spokesman, rose slowly from his place, and said in pious tones, "Boys, I must go this minute. Grandma will keep dinner waiting." Mrs. Ann Lane did not show in her aging face how young her heart was, and after the schooner Susan Barnes had departed she seemed to pass swiftly from middle life and an almost youthful vigor to early age and a look of spent strength and dissatisfaction. "I suppose he did find it dull," she assured herself, with wistful yearning for his rough words of praise, when she sat down alone to her dinner, or looked up sadly from her work, and missed the amusing though unedifying conversation he was wont to offer occasionally on stormy winter nights. How much of his adventuring was true she never cared to ask. He had come and gone, and she forgave him his shortcomings, and longed for his society with a heavy heart.

One spring day there was news in the Boston paper of the loss of the schooner Susan Barnes with all on board, and Nancy Lane's best friends shook their sage heads, and declared that as far as regarded Jerry Lane, that idle vagabond, it was all for the best. Nobody was interested in any other member of the crew, so the misfortune of the Susan Barnes seemed of but slight consequence in Walpole, she having passed out of her former owners' hands the autumn before. Jerry had stuck by the ship; at least, so he had sent word then to his wife by Skipper Nathan Low. The Susan Barnes was to sail regularly between Shediac and Newfoundland, and Jerry sent five dollars to

Nancy, and promised to pay her a visit soon. "Tell her I'm layin' up somethin' handsome," he told the skipper with a grin, "and I've got some folks in Newfoundland I'll visit with on this voyage, and then I'll come ashore for good and farm it."

Mrs. Lane took the five dollars from the skipper as proudly as if Jerry had done the same thing so many times before that she hardly noticed it. The skipper gave the messages from Jerry, and felt that he had done the proper thing. When the news came long afterward that the schooner was lost, that was the next thing that Nancy knew about her wandering mate; and after the minister had come solemnly to inform her of her bereavement, and had gone away again, and she sat down and looked her widowhood in the face, there was not a sadder nor a lonelier woman in the town of Walpole.

All the neighbors came to condole with our heroine, and, though nobody was aware of it, from that time she was really happier and better satisfied with life than she had ever been before. Now she had an ideal Jerry Lane to mourn over and think about, to cherish and admire; she was day by day slowly forgetting the trouble he had been and the bitter shame of him, and exalting his memory to something near saintliness. "He meant well," she told herself again and again. She thought nobody could tell so good a story; she felt that with her own bustling, capable ways he had no chance to do much that he might have done. She had been too quick with him, and alas, alas! how much better she would know how to treat him if she only could see him again! A sense of relief at his absence made her continually assure herself of her great loss, and, false even to herself, she mourned her sometime lover diligently, and tried to think herself a broken-hearted woman. It was thought among those who knew Nancy Lane best that she would recover her spirits in time, but Jerry's wildest anticipations of a proper respect to his memory were more than realized in the first two years after the schooner Susan Barnes went to the bottom of the sea. She mourned for the man he ought to have been, not for the real Jerry, but she had loved him in the beginning enough to make her own love a precious possession for all time to come. It did not matter much, after all, what manner of man he was; she had found in him something on which to spend her hoarded affection.

IV.

Nancy Lane was a peaceable woman and a good neighbor, but she never had been able to get on with one fellow townswoman, and that was Mrs. Deacon Elton. They managed to keep each other provoked and teased from one year's end to the other, and each good soul felt herself under a moral microscope, and understood that she was judged by a not very lenient criticism and discussion. Mrs. Lane clad herself in simple black after the news came of her husband's timely death, and Mrs. Elton made one of her farewell pilgrimages to church to see the new-made widow walk up the aisle.

"She needn't tell me she lays that affliction so much to heart," the deacon's wife sniffed faintly, after her exhaustion had been met by proper treatment of camphor and a glass of currant wine, at the parsonage, where she rested a while after service. "Nancy Floyd knows she's well over with such a piece of nonsense. If I had had my health, I should have spoken with her and urged her not to take the step in the first place. She hasn't spoken six beholden words to me since that vagabond come to Walpole. I dare say she may have heard something I said at the time she married. I declare for 't, I never was so outdone as I was when the deacon came home and told me Nancy Floyd was going to be married. She let herself down too low to ever hold the place again that she used to have in folks' minds. And it's my opinion," said the sharp-eyed little woman, "she ain't got through with her pay yet."

But Mrs. Elton did not half know with what unconscious prophecy her words were freighted.

The months passed by: summer and winter came and went, and even those few persons who were misled by Nancy Lane's stern visage and forbidding exterior into forgetting her kind heart were at last won over to friendliness by her renewed devotion to the sick and old people of the rural community. She was so tender to little children that they all loved her dearly. She was ready to go to any household that needed help, and in spite of her ceaseless industry with her needle she found many a chance to do good, and help her neighbors to lift and carry the burdens of their lives. She blossomed out suddenly into a lovely, painstaking eagerness to be of use; it seemed as if her affectionate heart, once made generous, must go on spending its wealth wherever it could find an excuse. Even Mrs. Elton herself was touched by her old enemy's evident wish to be friends, and said nothing more about poor Nancy's looking as savage as a hawk. The only thing to admit was the truth that her affliction had proved a blessing to her. And it was in a truly kind and compassionate spirit that, after hearing a piece of news, the deacon's hysterical wife forbore to spread it far and wide through the town first, and went down to the Widow Lane's one September afternoon. Nancy was stitching busily upon the deacon's new coat, and looked up with a friendly smile as her guest came in, in spite of an instinctive shrug as she had seen her coming up the yard. The dislike of the poor souls for each other was deeper than their philosophy could reach.

Mrs. Elton spent some minutes in the unnecessary endeavor to regain her breath, and to her surprise found she must make a real effort before she could tell her unwelcome news. She had been so full of it all the way from home that she had rehearsed the whole interview; now she hardly knew how to begin. Nancy looked serener than usual, but there was something wistful about her face as she glanced across the room, presently, as if to understand the reason of the long pause. The clock ticked loudly; the kitten clattered a spool against the table-leg, and had begun to snarl the thread round her busy paws, and Nancy looked down and saw her; then the instant consciousness of there being some unhappy reason for Mrs. Elton's call made her forget the creature's mischief, and anxiously lay down her work to listen.

"Skipper Nathan Low was to our house to dinner," the guest began. "He's bargaining with the deacon about some hay. He's got a new schooner, Skipper Nathan has, and is going to build up a regular business of freighting hay to Boston by sea. There's no market to speak of about here, unless you haul it way over to Downer, and you can't make but one turn a day."

"'T would be a good thing," replied Nancy, trying to think that this was all, and perhaps the deacon wanted to hire her own field another year. He had underpaid her once, and they had not been on particularly good terms ever since. She would make her own bargains with Skipper Nathan, she thanked him and his wife!

"He's been down to the provinces these two or three years back, you know," the whining voice went on, and straightforward Ann Lane felt the old animosity rising within her. "At dinner time I wasn't able to eat much of anything, and so I was talking with Cap'n Nathan, and asking him some questions about them parts; and I spoke something about the mercy 't was his life should ha' been spared when that schooner, the Susan Barnes, was lost so quick after he sold out his part of her. And I put in a word, bein' 's we were neighbors, about how edifyin' your course had be'n under affliction. I noticed then he'd looked sort o' queer whilst I was talkin', but there was all the folks to the table, and you know he's a very cautious man, so he spoke of somethin' else. 'T wa'n't half an hour after dinner, I was comin' in with some plates and cups, tryin' to help what my stren'th would let me, and says he, 'Step out a little ways into the piece with me, Mis' Elton. I want to have a word with ye.' I went, too, spite o' my neuralgy, for I saw he'd got somethin' on his mind. 'Look here,' says he, 'I gathered from the way you spoke that Jerry Lane's wife expects he's dead.' Certain, says I, his name was in the list o' the Susan Barnes's crew, and we read it in the paper. 'No,' says he to me, 'he ran away the day they sailed; he wasn't aboard, and he's livin' with another woman down to Shediac.' Them was his very words."

Nancy Lane sank back in her chair, and covered her horror-stricken eyes with her hands. "'T ain't pleasant news to have to tell," Sister Elton went on mildly, yet with evident relish and full command of the occasion. "He said he seen Jerry the morning he came away. I thought you ought to know it. I'll tell you one thing, Nancy: I told the skipper to keep still about it, and now I've told you, I won't spread it no further to set folks a-talking. I'll keep it secret till you say the word. There ain't much trafficking betwixt here and there, and he's dead to you, certain, as much as if he laid up here in the burying-ground."

Nancy had bowed her head upon the table; the thin sandy hair was streaked with gray. She did not answer one word; this was the hardest blow of all.

"I'm much obliged to you for being so friendly," she said after a few minutes, looking straight before her now in a dazed sort of way, and lifting the new coat from the floor, where it had fallen. "Yes, he's dead to me,—worse than dead, a good deal," and her lip quivered. "I can't seem to bring my thoughts to bear. I've got so used to thinkin'— No, don't you say nothin' to the folks, yet. I'd do as much for you." And Mrs. Elton knew that the smitten fellow-creature before her spoke the truth, and forebore.

Two or three days came and went, and with every hour the quiet, simple-hearted woman felt more grieved and unsteady in mind and body. Such a shattering thunderbolt of news rarely falls into a human life. She could not sleep; she wandered to and fro in the little house, and cried until she could cry no longer. Then a great rage spurred and excited her. She would go to Shediac, and call Jerry Lane to account. She would accuse him face to face; and the woman whom he was deceiving, as perhaps he had deceived her, should know the baseness and cowardice of this miserable man. So, dressed in her respectable Sunday clothes, in the gray bonnet and shawl that never had known any journeys except to meeting, or to a country funeral or quiet holiday-making, Nancy Lane trusted herself for the first time to the bewildering railway, to the temptations and dangers of the wide world outside the bounds of Walpole.

Two or three days later still, the quaint, thin figure familiar in Walpole highways flitted down the street of a provincial town. In the most primitive region of China this woman could hardly have felt a greater sense of foreign life and strangeness. At another time her native good sense and shrewd observation would have delighted in the experiences of this first week of travel, but she was too sternly angry and aggrieved, too deeply plunged in a survey of her own calamity, to take much notice of what was going on about her. Later she condemned the unworthy folly of the whole errand, but in these days the impulse to seek the culprit and confront him was irresistible.

The innkeeper's wife, a kindly creature, urged this puzzling guest to wait and rest and eat some supper, but Nancy refused, and without asking her way left the brightly lighted, flaring little public room, where curious eyes already offended her, and went out into the damp twilight. The voices of the street boys sounded outlandish, and she felt more and more lonely. She longed for Jerry to appear for protection's sake; she forgot why she sought him, and was eager to shelter herself behind the flimsy bulwark of his manhood. She rebuked herself presently with terrible bitterness for a womanish wonder whether he would say, "Why, Nancy, girl!" and be glad to see her. Poor woman, it was a work-laden, serious girlhood that had been hers, at any rate. The power of giving her whole self in unselfish, enthusiastic, patient devotion had not belonged to her youth only; it had sprung fresh and blossoming in her heart as every new year came and went.

One might have seen her stealing through the shadows, skirting the edge of a lumber-yard, stepping among the refuse of the harbor side, asking a question timidly now and then of some passer-by. Yes, they knew Jerry Lane,—his house was only a little way off; and one curious and compassionate Scotchman, divining by some inner sense the exciting nature of the errand, turned back, and offered fruitlessly to go with the stranger. "You know the man?" he asked. "He is his own enemy, but doing better now that he is married. He minds his work, I know that well; but he's taken a good wife." Nancy's heart beat faster with honest pride for a moment, until the shadow of the ugly truth and reality made it sink back to heaviness, and the fire of her smoldering rage was again kindled. She would speak to Jerry face to face before she slept, and a horrible contempt and scorn were ready for him, as with a glance either way along the road she entered the narrow yard, and went noiselessly toward the window of a low, poor-looking house, from whence a bright light was shining out into the night.

Yes, there was Jerry, and it seemed as if she must faint and fall at the sight of him. How young he looked still! The thought smote her like a blow. They never were mates for each other, Jerry and she. Her own life was waning; she was an old woman.

He never had been so thrifty and respectable before; the other woman ought to know the savage truth about him, for all that! But at that moment the other woman stooped beside the supper table, and lifted a baby from its cradle, and put the dear, live little thing into its father's arms. The baby was wide awake, and laughed at Jerry, who laughed back again, and it reached up to catch at a handful of the curly hair which had been poor Nancy's delight.

The other woman stood there looking at them, full of pride and love. She was young, and trig, and neat. She looked a brisk, efficient little creature. Perhaps Jerry would make something of himself now; he always had it in him. The tears were running down Nancy's cheeks; the rain, too, had begun to fall. She stood there watching the little household sit down to supper, and noticed with eager envy how well cooked the food was, and how hungrily the master of the house ate what was put before him. All thoughts of ending the new wife's sin and folly vanished away. She could not enter in and break another heart; hers was broken already, and it would not matter. And Nancy Lane, a widow indeed, crept away again, as silently as she had come, to think what was best to be done, to find alternate woe and comfort in the memory of the sight she had seen.

The little house at the edge of the Walpole marshes seemed full of blessed shelter and comfort the evening that its forsaken mistress came back to it. Her strength was spent; she felt much more desolate now that she had seen with her own eyes that Jerry Lane was alive than when he was counted among the dead. An uncharacteristic disregard of the laws of the land filled this good woman's mind. Jerry had his life to live, and she wished him no harm. She wondered often how the baby grew. She fancied sometime the changes and conditions of the far-away household. Alas! she knew only too well the weakness of the man, and once, in a grim outburst of impatience, she exclaimed, "I'd rather others should have to cope with him than me!"

But that evening, when she came back from Shediac, and sat in the dark for a long time, lest Mrs. Elton should see the light and risk her life in the evening air to bring unwelcome sympathy,—that evening, I say, came the hardest moment of all, when the Ann Floyd, tailoress, of so many virtuous, self-respecting years, whose idol had turned to clay, who was shamed, disgraced, and wronged, sat down alone to supper in the little kitchen.

She had put one cup and saucer on the table; she looked at them through bitter tears. Somehow a consciousness of her solitary age, her uncompanioned future, rushed through her mind; this failure of her best earthly hope was enough to break a stronger woman's heart.

Who can laugh at my Marsh Rosemary, or who can cry, for that matter? The gray primness of the plant is made up of a hundred colors if you look close enough to find them. This same Marsh Rosemary stands in her own place, and holds her dry leaves and tiny blossoms steadily toward the same sun that the pink lotus blooms for, and the white rose.

Mary Wilkins Freeman

(1852-1930)

Mary Ella Wilkins Freeman, the older of two daughters, was born to Warren E. and Eleanor Lothrop Wilkins on October 31, 1852, in Randolph, Massachusetts. In many ways Randolph, serves as a model of what was happening in New England communities throughout the later nineteenth century and is reflected in the writers' fiction. A typical New England manufacturing community, Randolph was noted in the 1850s for its shoe exports to Australia. With the outbreak of the Civil War in the 1860s, the town faced hard times, and Freeman's family did what numerous other New England families did during these decades: they moved. In 1867, when Freeman was fifteen, the family relocated to Brattleboro, Vermont, and Freeman's father, who had been a carpenter in Randolph, now opened a mercantile business in Brattleboro. Again, Freeman's family experience mirrors what was happening in so many other households in New England during the Brattleboro years. Her father's business failed, and the family was forced to move in with the Reverend Thomas Pickman Tyler household, where Freeman's mother became the live-in housekeeper.

In 1870, Freeman graduated from Brattleboro High School. She then spent one year at Mount Holyoke Female Seminary, the same school that Emily Dickinson briefly attended. Used to close ties with friends from Randolph and Brattleboro as well as with her sister and mother and her mother's extended family, Freeman experienced major losses even before she began to write. Evelyn Sawyer, her close friend in Brattleboro, married and moved away. Freeman's sister died in 1876 when Freeman was twenty four, her mother died in 1880 when Mary was twenty eight, and her father died three years later in 1883. In addition to these personal losses within a short period of time, Freeman's unreciprocated love for Reverend Tyler's son left her distraught. In a tribute after her mother died, Freeman adopted her mother's name, Eleanor, as her middle name.

Too late to benefit the family economically, Freeman published her first significant fiction in *Harper's Bazaar* shortly before her father's death. In 1884, after the loss of three family members, Freeman returned to Randolph, Massachusetts, to live with her very good friend from her Randolph school days, Mary Wales, and her family. Freeman's life at this point reflects the lives of other New England women who establish close friendships and bonds with other women. In this collection of writers, for example, Harriet Prescott Spofford's very close association with a circle of female friends began after her husband's death in 1888 and continued until her own death in 1921. Similarly, in the early 1880s when James T. Fields, the Boston publisher and husband of Annie Fields, died, Annie Fields established what became known as a "Boston marriage" with Sarah Orne Jewett, a relationship that continued until Jewett's death in 1909. In Freeman's own case, the relationship with her good friend, Mary Wales, lasted for more than fifteen years.

After an acquaintanceship lasting a decade, including a three-year vacillation on the question of marriage, in 1902 Freeman, at the age of forty–nine, married Charles Manning Freeman, a Columbia University medical doctor. In the early years, the marriage appears to have been a good one; however, by 1909 alcohol problems began to plague Charles Freeman. Although Charles had been treated for his drinking problems during 1909, by 1919 the situation had deteriorated to the point where Mary Wilkins committed her husband to the New Jersey State Hospital for the Insane to be treated for alcoholism. Freeman obtained a formal separation from him before his death in 1923. Mary Eleanor Wilkins Freeman died of a heart attack at the age of seventy–seven on March 13, 1930, in Metuchen, New Jersey, where she had settled after her marriage.

Freeman rejected a career in teaching to focus on her goal to become a writer, and from her first significant publication in *Harper's Bazaar* shortly before her father's death in 1883, she enjoyed a literary career which spanned nearly fifty years. In that period of time she wrote fifteen collections of short stories, sixteen novels, one play, and eight volumes of prose and poetry for children. Of the various genres she attempted, her best writing appeared in her short stories during the decades of the 1880s and 1890s.

In her fiction from the last two decades of the nineteenth century, Freeman writes about the rural New England mill towns and villages that are comparable to the town she grew up in: Randolph, Massachusetts. Randolph, a typical New England community fourteen miles from Boston, gave Freeman her sense of locale: harsh winters, raw springs, the community church, the school. Randolph also provided her a sense of community: strong bonds between women, homogeneity, hardship, the eccentricities and oddities of human character. In her fiction, Freeman depicts the common and ordinary experiences in the lives of men and women of the New England region she knew intimately. Although the lives, events, and situations of her fiction appear as being typical, Freeman transcends them to show the universal truths of human character and daily living. Perry Westbrook, one of her biographers, observes the accuracy of Freeman's depiction of New England life. "In several volumes of short stories and three or four novels, she has caught the flavor of that life as no other author has." (*Mary Wilkins Freeman*. [New York: Twayne, 1967], p. 15).

Without question, Freeman captures the essence of place. And long before terms such as "feminism" and "liberation" became part of our culture through consciousness–raising in the 1960s and '70s, Freeman concerned herself with the status and role of women. In her fiction we find portrayals of strong, defiant, and rather unconventional women. On the one hand, she creates independent women as central characters who challenge the traditional sex roles prescribed by their culture. On the other hand, narrators of the stories, and sometimes minor figures in the stories, display ambivalence toward the very roles portrayed by the central characters. Often, in fact, the narrators seem to prefer that the females follow more conventional behavior. As a result, we have a dichotomy between the characters' and narrators' attitudes toward conventional sex roles.

In the three stories included in this collection, the central characters reflect quintessential New England characteristics: determination, independence, strength of conviction, and courage in the face of overwhelming opposition. Published first in the October 1884 issue of *Harper's New Monthly* magazine, "A Gatherer of Simples" centers around Aurelia Flower, a woman described as "strongly built" with a complexion of a "hard red tinge" from exposure to sun and wind. In many ways the story suggests the perversion of New England values. Aurelia grows up in a home that offers little love. Instead of celebrating a strong mother-daughter relationship, Freeman in this story depicts a mother who is "hard" and "silent," a woman who emphasizes work and is successful but finds no satisfaction in her success. Instead of a strong, supportive father,

Freeman depicts an insecure and weak man who Aurelia remembers as being "gloomy," "melancholy," and "hard-working," a person who commits suicide in her childhood. Out of what could be considered a dysfunctional family background comes a study of a survivor in the character of Aurelia. Turning from the loneliness and despair that she knows only too well in the human world, Aurelia finds comfort through nature as an herbalist. However, only when given the opportunity to raise a small child does she realize the extent of the emptiness in her life. Through the young child, Aurelia is given the opportunity to break the bonds of despair, loneliness, and isolation and is given a second chance at the love and relationship denied in her own childhood.

Duty, family status, class and social distinctions, thwarted young love, independence, isolation, and obsession are some of the ideas central to "Evelina's Garden," a story Freeman first published in *Harper's New Monthly* magazine in June 1896. Evelina, the central character, comes from the community's most prominent family. Although she is attracted to Thomas Merriam, her sense of status and "maidenly decorum" prevents her from acting on those feelings. As a result, Thomas marries someone else and Evelina turns away from the community to become excessively reclusive. Over the remaining years of a long life, Evelina's passion becomes her garden. The results of isolation and obsession become even more apparent at her death when she wills her cousin, also named Evelina, what amounts to a substantial fortune, with the condition that she remain single and devote her life to caring for the garden. Although the surviving Evelina has strong feelings for and intends to marry Thomas Merriam's son, the village minister, he breaks off the relationship with Evelina out of a sense of duty. Only when Evelina demonstrates courageous independence and "kills" the garden by pouring hot water and salt over the plants does she break the bonds of isolation and obsession of past generations. Ideas in this story remind one of "Rappaccini's Daughter" by Hawthorne where he deals with isolation, thwarted love, and perversion of values.

"The Revolt of Sophia Lane," the final story in this collection was published by Freeman in the December 1903 issue of *Harper's New Monthly*. In certain respects, Sophia, the central character reminds us of Mother in another "revolt" story by Freeman: "The Revolt of Mother." Like Mother, Sophia is strong willed, determined, and independent. Like Mother's strong and nurturing relationship with her daughter, Sophia has a similar relationship with her niece. Although Mother and Sophia in the two stories supposedly have the best intentions and best interests at heart, in many ways, they could be viewed as controlling, domineering, and "smothering" in their relationships with the younger females. "The Revolt of Sophia Lane" is a lighter story compared with the other two stories by Freeman in this collection. In Freeman's use of humor in "The Revolt of Sophia Lane," one see another connection with "The Revolt of Mother." In their defiance of community values as well as in their independence and determination, the actions by both Mother in "The Revolt of Mother" and Sophia in "The Revolt of Sophia Lane" appear extreme and even comical. Although comic as she loads the sleigh in bitter December weather and returns Christmas gifts because of their impracticality even before the holiday, Sophia's action is disarmingly blunt, and she does make her point. Freeman knows well and shares with her audience the idiosyncrasies of New England life and characters.

Selected Primary Works

A Humble Romance, and Other Stories, 1887; *A New England Nun, and Other Stories,* 1891; *Pembroke,* 1894; *The People of Our Neighborhood,* 1898; *Silence, and Other Stories,* 1898; *By the Light of the Soul,* 1906; *Edgewater People,* 1918.

"A Gatherer of Simples"

Harper's New Monthly, October 1884

A damp air was blowing up, and the frogs were beginning to peep. The sun was setting in a low red sky. On both sides of the road were rich green meadows intersected by little canal-like brooks. Beyond the meadows on the west was a distant stretch of pine woods, that showed dark against the clear sky. Aurelia Flower was going along the road toward her home, with a great sheaf of leaves and flowers in her arms. There were the rosy spikes of hardhack; the great white corymbs of thoroughwort, and the long blue racemes of lobelia. Then there were great bunches of the odorous tansy and pennyroyal in with the rest.

Aurelia was a tall, strongly built woman: she was not much over thirty, but she looked older. Her complexion had a hard red tinge from exposure to sun and wind, and showed seams as unreservedly as granite. Her face was thin, and her cheek-bones high. She had a profusion of auburn hair, showing in a loose slipping coil, beneath her limp black straw hat. Her dress, as a matter of fashion, was execrable; in point of harmony with her immediate surroundings, very well, though she had not thought of it in that way. There was a green under-skirt, and a brown over-skirt and basque of an obsolete cut. She had worn it for a good many years just so, and never thought of altering it. It did not seem to occur to her that though her name was Flower, she was not really a flower in regard to apparel, and had not its right of unchangeableness in the spring. When the trees hung out their catkins, she flaunted her poor old greens and browns under them, rejoicing, and never dreamed but what they looked all right. As far as dress went, Aurelia was a happy woman. She went along the road to-night at a good pace, her armful of leaves and blossoms nodding; her spare muscular limbs bore her along easily. She had been over a good many miles since noon, but she never thought of being tired.

Presently she came in sight of her home, a square unpainted building, black with age. It stood back a little from the road on a gentle slope. There were three great maple trees in front of the house; their branches rustled against the roof. On the left was a small garden; some tall poles thickly twined with hops were prominent in it.

Aurelia went round to the side door of the house with her armful of green things. The door opened directly into the great kitchen. One on entering would have started back as one would on seeing unexpected company in a room. The walls were as green as a lady's bower with bunches and festoons of all sorts of New England herbs. There they hung, their brave blossoms turning gray and black, giving out strange half-pleasant, half-disgusting odors. Aurelia took them in like her native air. "It's good to get home," murmured she to herself, for there was no one else; she lived alone.

She took off her hat and disposed of her burden; then she got herself some supper. She did not build a fire in the cooking stove, for she never drank tea in warm weather. Instead, she had a tumbler of root-beer which she had made herself. She set it out on one end of her kitchen table with a slice of coarse bread and a saucer of cold beans. She sat down to it and ate with a good appetite. She looked better with her hat off. Her forehead was an important part of her face; it was white and womanly, and her reddish hair lay round it in pretty curves; then her brown eyes, under very strongly arched brows, showed to better advantage. Taken by herself, and not compared with other women, Aurelia was not so bad-looking; but she never was taken by herself in that way, and nobody had ever given her any credit for comeliness. It would have been like looking at a jack-in-the-pulpit and losing all the impression that had ever been made on one by roses and hyacinths, and seeing absolutely nothing else but that one flower's fine green and brown lines; it is doubtful if it would be done.

She had finished her supper, and was sorting her fresh herbs, when the door opened and a woman walked in. She had no bonnet on her head; she was a neighbor, and this was an unceremonious little country place.

"Good evenin', 'Relia," said she. There was an important look on her plain face, as if there was more to follow.

"Good evenin', Mis' Atwood. Take a chair."

"Been herbin' again?"

"Yes; I went out a little while this afternoon."

"Where'd you go?—upon Green Mountain?"

"No; I went over to White's Woods. There were some kinds there I wanted."

"You don't say so! That's a matter of six miles, ain't it? Ain't you tired?"

"Lor', no," said Aurelia. "I reckon I'm pretty strong, or mebbe the smell of the herbs keeps me up;" and she laughed.

So did the other. "Sure enough—well, mebbe it does. I never thought of that. But it seems like a pretty long tramp to me, though my bein' so fleshy may make a difference. I could have walked it easier once."

"I shouldn't wonder if it did make a difference. I ain't got much flesh to carry round to tire me out."

"You're always pretty well, too, ain't you, 'Relia?"

"Lor', yes; I never knew what 'twas to be sick. How's your folks, Mis' Atwood? Is Viny any better than she was?"

"I don't know as she is, much. She feels pretty poorly most of the time. I guess I'll hev you fix some more of that root-beer for her. I thought that seemed to liven her up a little."

"I've got a jug of it all made, down-cellar, and you can take it when you go home, if you want to."

"So I will, if you've got it. I was in hopes you might hev it."

The important look had not vanished from Mrs. Atwood's face, but she was not the woman to tell important news in a hurry, and have the gusto of it so soon over. She was one of the natures who always dispose of bread before pie. Now she came to it, however.

"I heard some news to-night, 'Relia," said she.

Aurelia picked out another spray of hardhack. "What was it?"

"Thomas Rankin's dead."

Aurelia clutched the hardhack mechanically. "You don't mean it, Mis' Atwood! When did he die? I hadn't heard he was sick."

"He wasn't, long. Had a kind of a fit this noon, and died right off. The doctor—they sent for Dr. Smith from Alden—called it sunstroke. You know 'twas awful hot, and he'd been out in the field to work all the mornin'. I think 'twas heart trouble; it's in the Rankin family; his father died of it. Doctors don't know everything."

"Well, it's a dreadful thing," said Aurelia. "I can't realize it. There he's left four little children, and it ain't more'n a year since Mis' Rankin died. It ain't a year, is it?"

"It ain't a year into a month and sixteen days," said Mrs. Atwood, solemnly. "Viny and I was countin' of it up just before I come in here."

"Well, I guess 'tisn't, come to think of it. I couldn't have told exactly. The oldest of those children ain't more than eight, is she?"

"Ethelind is eight, coming next month; Viny and I was reckinin' it up. Then Edith is six, and Isadore is five, and Myrtie ain't but two, poor little thing."

"What do you s'pose will be done with 'em?"

"I don't know. Viny an' me was talking of it over, and got it settled that *her* sister, Mis' Loomis, over to Alden, would hev to hev 'em. It'll be considerable for her, too, for she's got two of her own, and I don't s'pose Sam Loomis has got much. But I don't see what else can be done. Of course strangers ain't goin' to take children when there is folks."

"Wouldn't his mother take 'em?"

"What, old-lady Sears? Lor', no. You know she was dreadful put out 'bout Thomas marryin' where he did, and declared he shouldn't hev a cent of her money. It was all her second husband's, anyway. John Rankin wasn't worth anything. She won't do anything for 'em. She's livin' in great style down near the city, they say. Got a nice house, and keeps help. She might hev 'em just as well as not, but she won't. She's a hard woman to get along with, anyhow. She nagged both her husbands to death, an' Thomas never had no peace at home. Guess that was one reason why he was in such a hurry to get married. Mis' Rankin was a good-tempered soul, if she wasn't quite so drivin' as some."

"I do feel dreadfully to think of those children," said Aurelia.

"'Tis hard; but we must try an' believe it will be ruled for the best. I s'pose I must go, for I left Viny all alone."

"Well, if you must, I'll get that root-beer for you, Mis' Atwood. I shall keep thinking 'bout those children all night."

A week or two after that, Mrs. Atwood had some more news; but she didn't go to Aurelia with it, for Aurelia was the very sub-essence of it herself. She unfolded it gingerly to her daughter Lavinia— a pale, peaked young woman, who looked as if it would take more than Aurelia's root-beer to make her robust. Aurelia had taken the youngest Rankin child for her own, and Mrs. Atwood had just heard of it.

"It's true," said she; "I see her with it myself. Old-lady Sears never so much as sent a letter, let alone not coming to the funeral, and Mis' Loomis was glad enough to get rid of it."

Viny drank in the story as if it had been so much nourishing jelly. Her too narrow life was killing her as much as anything else.

Meanwhile Aurelia had the child, and was actively happy, for the first time in her life, to her own naive astonishment, for she had never known that she was not so before. She had naturally strong affections, of an outward rather than an inward tendency. She was capable of much enjoyment from pure living, but she had never had anything to be so very fond of. She could only remember her father as a gloomy, hard-working man, who never noticed her much. He had a melancholy temperament, which resulted in a tragical end when Aurelia was a mere child. When she thought of him, the same horror which she had when they brought him home from the river crept over her now. They had never known certainly just how Martin Flower had come to die; but folks never spoke of him to Aurelia and her mother, and the two never talked of him together. They knew that everybody said Martin Flower had drowned himself; they felt shame and a Puritan shrinking from the sin.

Aurelia's mother had been a hard, silent woman before; she grew more hard and silent afterward. She worked hard, and taught Aurelia to. Their work was peculiar; they hardly knew themselves how they had happened to drift into it; it had seemed to creep in with other work, till finally it usurped it altogether. At first, after her husband's death, Mrs. Flower had tried millinery; she had learned the trade in her youth. But she made no headway then in sewing rose-buds and dainty bows on to bonnets; it did not suit with tragedy. The bonnets seemed infected with her own mood; the bows lay flat with stern resolve, and the rose-buds stood up fiercely; she did not please her customers, even among those uncritical country folk, and they dropped off. She had always made excellent root-beer, and had had quite a reputation in the neighborhood for it. How it happened she could not tell, but she found herself selling it; then she made hop yeast, and sold that. Then she was a woman of a fertile brain, and another project suggested itself to her.

She and Aurelia ransacked the woods thereabouts for medicinal herbs, and disposed of them to druggists in a neighboring town. They had a garden of some sorts too—the different mints, thyme, lavender, coriander, rosemary, and others. It was an unusual business for two women to engage in, but it increased, and they prospered according to their small ideas. But Mrs. Flower grew more and more bitter with success. What regrets and longing that her husband could have lived and shared it, and been spared his final agony, she had in her heart, nobody but the poor woman herself knew; she never spoke of them. She died when Aurelia was twenty, and a woman far beyond her years. She mourned for her mother, but although she never knew it, her warmest love had not been called out. It had been barely possible. Mrs. Flower had not been a lovable mother; she had rarely spoken to Aurelia but with cold censure for the last few years. People whispered that it was a happy release for the poor girl when her mother died; they had begun to think she was growing like her husband, and perhaps was not "just right."

Aurelia went on with the business with calm equanimity, and made even profits every year. They were small, but more than enough for her to live on, and she paid the last dollar of the mortgage which had so fretted her father, and owned the old house clear. She led a peaceful, innocent life, with her green herbs for companions; she associated little with the people around, except in a business way. They came to see her, but she rarely entered their houses. Every room in her house was festooned with herbs; she knew every kind that grew in the New England woods, and hunted them out in their season and brought them home; she was a simple sweet soul, with none of the morbid melancholy of her parents about her. She loved her work, and the green-wood things were to her as friends, and the healing qualities of sarsaparilla and thoroughwort, and the sweetness of thyme and lavender, seemed to have entered into her nature, till she almost could talk with them in that way. She had never thought of being unhappy; but now she wondered at herself over this child. It was a darling of a child; as dainty and winsome a girl baby as ever was. Her poor young mother had had a fondness for romantic names, which she had bestowed, as the only heritage within her power, on all her children. This one was Myrtilla—Myrtie for short. The little thing clung to Aurelia from the first, and Aurelia found that she had another way of loving besides the way in which she loved lavender and thoroughwort. The comfort she took with the child through the next winter was unspeakable. The herbs were banished from the south room, which was turned into a nursery, and a warm carpet was put on the floor, that the baby might not take cold. She learned to cook for the baby—her own diet had been chiefly vegetarian. She became a charming nursing mother. People wondered. "It does beat all how handy 'Relia is with that baby," Mrs. Atwood told Viny.

Aurelia took even more comfort with the little thing when spring came, and she could take her out with her; then she bought a little straw carriage, and the two went after herbs together. Home they would come in the tender spring twilight, the baby asleep in her carriage, with a great sheaf of flowers beside her, and Aurelia with another over her shoulder.

She felt all through that summer as if she was too happy to last. Once she said so to one of the neighbors. "I feel as if it wa'n't right for me to be so perfectly happy," said she. "I feel some days as if I was walkin' an' walkin' an' walkin' through a garden of sweet-smellin' herbs, an' nothin' else; an' as for Myrtie, she's a bundle of myrtle an' camphor out of King Solomon's garden. I'm so afraid it can't last."

Happiness had seemed to awake in Aurelia a taint of her father's foreboding melancholy. But she apparently had no reason for it until early fall. Then returning with Myrtie one night from a trip to the woods, she found an old lady seated on her door-step, grimly waiting for her. She was an old woman and tremulous, but still undaunted and unshaken as to her spirit. Her tall, shrunken form was loaded with silk and jet. She stood up as Aurelia approached wondering, and her dim old eyes peered at her aggressively through fine gold spectacles, which lent an additional glare to them.

"I suppose you are Miss Flower?" began the old lady, with no prefatory parley.

"Yes," said Aurelia, trembling.

"Well, my name's Mrs. Matthew Sears, an' I've come for my grandchild there."

Aurelia turned very white. She let her herbs slide to the ground. "I—hardly understand—I guess," faltered she. "Can't you let me keep her?"

"Well, I guess I won't have one of my grandchildren brought up by an old yarb-woman—not if I know it!"

The old lady sniffed. Aurelia stood looking at her. She felt as if she had fallen down from heaven, and the hard reality of the earth had jarred the voice out of her. Then the old lady made a step toward the carriage, and caught up Myrtie in her trembling arms. The child screamed with fright. She had been asleep. She turned her little frightened face toward Aurelia, and held out her arms, and cried, "Mamma! mamma! mamma!" in a perfect frenzy of terror. The old lady tried to hush her in vain. Aurelia found her voice then. "You'd better let me take her and give her her supper," she said, "and when she is asleep again I will bring her over to you."

"Well," said the old lady, doubtfully. She was glad to get the frantic little thing out of her arms, though.

Aurelia held her close and hushed her, and she subsided into occasional convulsive sobs, and furtive frightened glances at her grandmother.

"I s'pose you are stopping at the hotel," said Aurelia.

"Yes, I am," said the old lady, stoutly. "You kin bring her over as soon as she's asleep." Then she marched off with uncertain majesty.

Some women would have argued the case longer, but Aurelia felt that there was simply no use in it. The old lady was the child's grandmother: if she wanted her, she saw no way but to give her up. She never thought of pleading, she was so convinced of the old lady's determination.

She carried Myrtie into the house, gave her her supper, washed her, and dressed her in her little best dress. Then she took her up in her lap and tried to explain to her childish mind the change that was to be made in her life. She told her she was going to live with her grandmother, and she must be a good little girl, and love her, and do just as she told her to. Myrtie sobbed with unreasoning grief, and clung to Aurelia; but she wholly failed to take the full meaning of it all in.

She was still fretful and bewildered by her rude awakening from her nap. Presently she fell asleep again, and Aurelia laid her down while she got together her little wardrobe. There was a hop pillow in a little linen case, which Myrtie had always slept on; she packed that up with the other things.

Then she rolled the little sleeping girl up in a blanket, laid her in her carriage, and went over to the hotel. It was not much of a hotel—merely an ordinary two-story house, where two or three spare rooms were ample accommodation for the few straggling guests who came to this little rural place. It was only a few steps from Aurelia's house. The old lady had the chamber of honor, a large square room on the first floor, opening directly on to the piazza. In spite of all Aurelia's care, Myrtie woke up and began to cry when she was carried in. She had to go off and leave her screaming piteously after her. Out on the piazza, she uttered the first complaint, almost, of her life, to the hostess, Mrs. Simonds, who had followed her there.

"Don't feel bad, 'Relia," said the woman, who was almost crying herself. "I know it's awful hard, when you was taking so much comfort. We all feel for you."

Aurelia looked straight ahead. She had the bundle of little clothes and the hop pillow in her arms; the old lady had said, in a way that would have been funny if it had not been for the poor heart that listened, that she didn't want any yarb pillows, nor any clothes scented with yarbs nuther.

"I don't mean to be wicked," said Aurelia, "but I can't help thinking that Providence ought to provide for women. I wish Myrtie was mine."

The other woman wiped her eyes at the hungry way in which she said "mine."

"Well, I can't do anything; but I'm sorry for you, if that's all. You'd make enough sight better mother for Myrtie than that cross old woman. I don't b'lieve she more'n half wants her, only she's sot. She doesn't care anything about having the other children; she's going to leave them with Mis' Loomis; but she says her grandchildren ain't going to be living with strangers, an' she ought to hev been consulted. After all you've done for the child, to treat you as she has to-night, she's the most ungrateful—I know one thing; I'd charge her for Myrtie's board—a good price, too."

"Oh, I don't want anything of that sort," said poor Aurelia dejectedly, listening to her darling's sobs. "You go in an' try to hush her, Mis' Simonds. Oh!"

"So I will! her grandmother can't do anything with her, poor little thing! I've got some peppermints. I do believe she's spankin' her—the—"

Aurelia did not run in with Mrs. Simonds; she listened outside till the pitiful cries hushed a little; then she went desolately home.

She sat down in the kitchen, with the little clothes in her lap. She did not think of going to bed; she did not cry or moan to herself; she just sat there still. It was not very late when she came home— between eight and nine. In about half an hour, perhaps, she heard a sound outside that made her heart leap—a little voice, crying pitifully, and saying, between the sobs, "Mamma! mamma!"

Aurelia made one spring to the door. There was the tiny creature in her little night gown, shaking all over with cold and sobs.

Aurelia caught her up, and all her calm was over. "Oh, you darling! you darling! you darling!" she cried, covering her little cold body all over with kisses. "You sha'n't leave me—you sha'n't'! you sha'n't! Little sweetheart—all I've got in the world. I guess they sha'n't take you away when you don't want to go. Did you cry, and mamma go off and leave you? Did they whip you? They never shall again—never! never! There, there, blessed, don't cry; mamma'll get you all warm, and you shall go to sleep on your own little pillow. Oh, you darling! darling! darling!"

Aurelia busied herself about the child, rubbing the little numb limbs, and getting some milk heated. She never asked how she came to get away; she never thought of anything except that she had her. She stopped every other minute to kiss her and croon to her; she laughed and cried. Now she gave way to her feelings; she was almost beside herself. She had the child all warm and fed and comforted by the kitchen fire, when she heard steps outside, and she knew at once what was coming, and a fierce resolve sprang up in her heart: they should not have that child again to-night. She cast a hurried glance around; there was hardly a second's time. In the corner of the kitchen was a great heap of herbs which she had taken down from the walls where they had been drying; the next day she had intended to pack them and send them off. She caught up Myrtie and covered her with them. "Lie still, darling!" she whispered. "Don't make a bit of noise, or your grandmother will get you again." Myrtie crouched under them, trembling.

Then the door opened; Mr. Simonds stood there with a lantern. "That little girl's run away," he began—"slipped out while the old lady was out of the room a minute. Beats all how such a little thing knew enough. She's here, ain't she?"

"No," said Aurelia, "she ain't."

"You don't mean it?"
"Yes."

"Ain't you seen her, though?"

"No."

Mr. Simonds, who was fat and placid, began to look grave. "Then, all there is about it, we've got to have a hunt," said he. "'Twon't do to have that little tot out in her night-gown long. We hadn't a thought but that she was here. Must have lost her way."

Aurelia watched him stride down the yard. Then she ran after him. "Mr. Simonds!" He turned. "I told you a lie. Myrtie's in the corner of the kitchen under a heap of herbs."

"Why, what on earth—"

"I wanted to keep her so to-night." Aurelia burst right out in loud sobs.

"There, 'Relia! It's a confounded shame. You shall keep her. I'll make it all right with the old lady somehow. I reckon, as long as the child's safe, she'll be glad to get rid of her to-night. She wouldn't have slept much. Go right into the house, 'Relia, and don't worry."

Aurelia obeyed. She hung over the little creature all night, asleep in her little crib. She watched her every breath. She never thought of sleeping herself—her last night with Myrtie. The seconds were so many grains of gold dust. Her heart failed her when day broke. She washed and dressed Myrtie at the usual time, and gave her her breakfast. Then she sat down with her and waited. The child's sorrow was soon forgotten, and she played about as usual. Aurelia watched her despairingly. She began to wonder at length why they did not come for her. It grew later and later. She would not carry her back herself, she was resolved on that.

It was ten o'clock before any one came; then it was Mrs. Simonds. She had a strange look on her face.

"'Relia," she said, standing in the door and looking at her and Myrtie, "you 'ain't heard what's happened to our house this mornin', hev you?"

"No," said Aurelia, awed.

"Old Mis' Sears is dead. Had her third shock: she's had two in the last three years. She was took soon after Mr. Simonds got home. We got a doctor right off, but she died 'bout an hour ago."

"Oh," said Aurelia, "I've been a wicked woman."

"No you ain't, Aurelia; don't you go to feeling so. There's no call for the living to be unjust to themselves because folks are dead. You did the best you could. An' now you're glad you can keep the child; you can't help it. I thought of it myself the first thing."

"Oh, I was such a wicked woman to think of it myself," said Aurelia. "If I could only have done something for the poor old soul! Why didn't you call me?"

"I told Mr. Simonds I wouldn't; you'd had enough."

There was one thing, however, which Aurelia found to do—a simple and touching thing, though it probably meant more to her than to most of those who knew of it.

On the day of the funeral the poor old woman's grave was found lined with fragrant herbs from Aurelia's garden—thyme and lavender and rosemary. She had cried when she picked them, because she could not help being glad, and they were all she could give for atonement.

"Evelina's Garden"

Harper's New Monthly, June 1896

In the south a high arbor-vitae hedge separated Evelina's garden from the road. The hedge was so high that when the school children lagged by, and the secrets behind it fired them with more curiosity than those between their battered book covers, the tallest of them by stretching up on tiptoe could not peer over. And so they were driven to childish engineering feats, and would set to work and pick away sprigs of the arbor-vitae with their little fingers, and make peep holes—but small ones, that Evelina might not discern them. Then they would thrust their pink faces into the hedge, and the enduring fragrance of it would come to their nostrils like a gust of aromatic breath from the mouth of the northern woods, and peer into Evelina's garden as through the green tubes of vernal telescopes.

Then suddenly hollyhocks, blooming in rank and file, seemed to be marching upon them like platoons of soldiers, with detonations of color that dazzled their peeping eyes; and, indeed, the whole garden seemed charging with its mass of riotous bloom upon the hedge. They could scarcely take in details of marigold and phlox and pinks and London-pride and cock's-combs, and prince's feathers waving overhead like standards.

Sometimes also there was the purple flutter of Evelina's gown; and Evelina's face, delicately faded, hung about with softly drooping gray curls, appeared suddenly among the flowers, like another flower uncannily instinct with nervous melancholy.

Then the children would fall back from their peep-holes, and huddle off together with scared giggles. They were afraid of Evelina. There was a shade of mystery about her which stimulated their childish fancies when they heard her discussed by their elders. They might easily have conceived her to be some baleful fairy entrenched in her green stronghold, withheld from leaving it by the fear of some dire penalty for magical sins. Summer and winter, spring and fall. Evelina Adams never was seen outside her own domain of old mansion-house and garden, and she had not set her slim lady feet in the public highway for nearly forty years, if the stories were true.

People differed as to the reason why. Some said she had had an unfortunate love affair, that her heart had been broken, and she had taken upon herself a vow of seclusion from the world, but nobody could point to the unworthy lover who had done her this harm. When Evelina was a girl, not one of the young men of the village had dared address her. She had been set apart by birth and training and also by a certain exclusiveness of manner, if not of nature. Her father, old Squire Adams, had been the one man of wealth and college learning in the village. He had owned the one fine old mansion-house, with its white front propped on great Corinthian pillars, overlooking the village like a broad brow of superiority.

He had owned the only coach and four. His wife during her short life had gone dressed in rich brocades and satins that rustled loud in the ears of the village women, and her nodding plumes had dazzled the eyes under their modest hoods. Hardly a woman in the village but could tell—for it had been handed down like a folklore song from mother to daughter—just what Squire Adams's wife wore when she walked out first as bride to meeting. She had been clad all in blue.

"Squire Adams's wife, when she walked out bride, she wore a blue satin brocade gown, all wrought with blue flowers of a darker blue, cut low neck and short sleeves. She wore long blue silk mitts wrought with blue, blue satin shoes, and blue silk clocked stockings. And she wore a blue crape mantle that was brought from over seas, and a blue velvet hat, with a long blue ostrich feather curled over it—it was so long it reached her shoulder, and waved when she walked; and she carried a little blue crape fan with ivory sticks." So the women and girls told each other when the Squire's bride had been dead nearly seventy years.

The blue bride attire was said to be still in existence, packed away in a cedar chest, as the Squire had ordered after his wife's death. "He stood over the woman that took care of his wife whilst she packed the things away, and he never shed a tear, but she used to hear him a-goin' up to the north chamber nights when he couldn't sleep, to look at 'em," the women told.

People had thought the Squire would marry again. They said Evelina, who was only four years old, needed a mother, and they selected one and another of the good village girls. But the Squire never married. He had a single woman, who dressed in black silk, and wore always a black wrought veil over the side of her bonnet, come to live with them, to take charge of Evelina. She was said to be a distant relative of the Squire's wife, and was much looked up to by the village people, although she never did more than interlace, as it were, the fringes of her garments with theirs. "She's stuck up," they said, and felt, curiously enough, a certain pride in the fact when they met her in the street and she ducked her long chin stiffly into the folds of her black shawl by way of salutation.

When Evelina was fifteen years old this single woman died, and the village women went to her funeral, and bent over her lying in a last helpless dignity in her coffin, and stared with awed freedom at her cold face. After that Evelina was sent away to school, and did not return, except for a yearly vacation, for six years to come. Then she returned, and settled down in her old home to live out her life, and end her days in a perfect semblance of peace, if it were not peace.

Evelina never had any young school friend to visit her; she had never, so far as any one knew, a friend of her own age. She lived alone with her father and three old servants. She went to meeting, and drove with the Squire in his chaise. The coach was never used after his wife's death, except to carry Evelina to and from school. She and the Squire also took long walks, but they never exchanged aught but the merest civilities of good days and nods with the neighbors whom they met, unless indeed the Squire had some matter of business to discuss. Then Evelina stood aside and waited, her fair face drooping gravely aloof. She was very pretty, with a gentle high-bred prettiness that impressed the village folk, although they looked at it something askance.

Evelina's figure was tall, and had a fine slenderness; her silken skirts hung straight from the narrow silk ribbon that girt her slim waist; there was a languidly graceful bend in her long white throat; her long delicate hands hung inertly at her sides among her skirt folds, and were never seen to clasp anything; her softly clustering fair curls hung over her thin blooming cheeks, and her face could scarce be seen, unless, as she seldom did, she turned and looked full upon one. Then her dark blue eyes, with a little nervous frown between them, shone out radiantly; her thin lips showed a warm red, and her beauty startled one.

Everybody wondered why she did not have a lover, why some fine young man had not been smitten by her while she had been away at school. They did not know that the school had been situated in another little village, the counterpart of the one in which she had been born, wherein a fitting mate for a bird of her feather could hardly be found. The simple young men of the countryside were at once attracted and intimidated by her. They cast fond sly glances across the meeting house at her lovely face, but they were confused before her when they jostled her in the doorway and the rose and lavender scent of her lady garments came in their faces. Not one of them dared accost her, much less march boldly upon the great Corinthian-pillared house, raise the brass knocker, and declare himself a suitor of the Squire's daughter.

One young man there was, indeed, who treasured in his heart an experience so subtle and so slight that he could scarcely believe in it himself. He never recounted it to mortal soul, but kept it as a secret sacred between himself and his own nature, but something to be scoffed at and set aside by others.

It had happened one Sabbath day in summer, when Evelina had not been many years home from school, as she sat in the meeting-house in her Sabbath array of rose-colored satin gown, and white bonnet trimmed with a long white feather and a little wreath of feathery green, that of a sudden she raised her head and turned her face, and her blue eyes met this young man's full upon hers, with all his heart in them, and it was for a second as if her own heart leaped to the surface, and he saw it, although afterward he scarce believed it to be true.

Then a pallor crept over Evelina's delicately brilliant face. She turned it away, and her curls falling softly from under the green wreath on her bonnet brim hid it. The young man's cheeks were a hot red, and his heart beat loudly in his ears when he met her in the doorway after the sermon was done. His eager, timorous eyes sought her face, but she never looked his way. She laid her slim hand in its cream-colored satin mitt on the Squire's arm; her satin gown rustled softly as she passed before him, shrinking against the wall to give her room, and a faint fragrance which seemed like the very breath of the unknown delicacy and exclusiveness of life came to his bewildered senses.

Many a time he cast furtive glances across the meeting-house at Evelina, but she never looked his way again. If his timid boy eyes could have seen her cheek behind its veil of curls, he might have discovered that the color came and went before his glances, although it was strange how she could have been conscious of them; but he never knew.

And he also never knew how, when he walked past the Squire's house of a Sunday evening, dressed in his best, with his shoulders thrust consciously back, and the windows in the westering sun looked full of blank cold to his furtive eyes, Evelina was always peeping at him from behind a shutter, and he never dared go in. His intuitions were not like hers, and so nothing happened that might have, and he never fairly knew what he knew. But that he never told, even to his wife when he married; for his hot young blood grew weary and impatient with this vain courtship, and he turned to one of his villagemates, who met him fairly halfway, and married her within a year.

On the Sunday when he and his bride first appeared in the meeting-house Evelina went up the aisle behind her father in an array of flowered brocade, stiff with threads of silver, so wonderful that people all turned their heads to stare at her. She wore also a new bonnet of rose-colored satin, and her curls were caught back a little, and her face showed as clear and beautiful as an angel's.

The young bridegroom glanced at her once across the meeting-house, then he looked at his bride in her gay wedding finery with a faithful look.

When Evelina met them in the doorway, after meeting was done, she bowed with a sweet cold grace to the bride, who courtesied [*sic*] blushingly in return, with an awkward sweep of her foot in the bridal satin shoe. The bridegroom did not look at Evelina at all. He held his chin well down in his stock with solemn embarrassment, and passed out stiffly, his bride on his arm.

Evelina, shining in the sun like a silver lily, went up the street, her father stalking beside her with stately swings of his cane, and that was the last time she was ever seen out at meeting. Nobody knew why.

When Evelina was a little over thirty her father died. There was not much active grief for him in the village; he had really figured therein more as a stately monument of his own grandeur than anything else. He had been a man of little force of character and that little had seemed to degenerate since his wife died. An inborn dignity of manner might have served to disguise his weakness with any others than these shrewd New Englanders, but they read him rightly. "The Squire wa'n't ever one to set the river a-fire," they said. Then, moreover, he left none of his property to the village to build a new meeting-house or a town-house. It all went to Evelina.

People expected that Evelina would surely show herself in her mourning at meeting the Sunday after the Squire died, but she did not. Moreover, it began gradually to be discovered that she never went out in the village street nor crossed the boundaries of her own domains after her father's death. She lived in the great house with her three servants—a man and his wife, and the woman who had been with her mother when she died. Then it was that Evelina's garden began. There had always been a garden at the back of the Squire's house, but not like this, and only a low fence had separated it from the road. Now one morning in the autumn the people saw Evelina's manservant, John Darby, setting out the arbor-vitae hedge, and in the spring after that there were ploughing and seed-sowing extending over a full half-acre, which later blossomed out in glory.

Before the hedge grew so high Evelina could be seen at work in her garden. She was often seen stooping over the flower beds in the early morning when the village was first astir, and she moved among them with her watering pot in the twilight—a shadowy figure that might, from her grace and her constancy to the flowers, have been Flora herself.

As the years went on, the arbor-vitae hedge got each season a new growth and waxed taller, until Evelina could no longer be seen above it. That was an annoyance to people, because the quiet mystery of her life kept their curiosity alive, until it was in a constant struggle, as it were, with the green luxuriance of the hedge.

"John Darby had ought to trim that hedge," they said. They accosted him in the street: "John, if ye don't cut that hedge down a little it'll all die out." But he only made a surly grunting response, intelligible to himself alone, and passed on. He was an Englishman, and had lived in the Squire's family since he was a boy.

He had a nature capable of only one simple line of force, with no radiations or parallels, and that had early resolved itself into the service of the Squire and his house. After the Squire's death he married a woman who lived in the family. She was much older than himself, and had a high temper, but was a good servant, and he married her to keep her to her allegiance to Evelina. Then he bent her, without her knowledge, to take his own attitude toward his mistress. No more could be gotten out of John Darby's wife than out of John Darby concerning the doings at the Squire's house. She met curiosity with a flash of hot temper, and he with surly taciturnity, and both intimidated.

The third of Evelina's servants was the woman who had nursed her mother, and she was naturally subdued and undemonstrative, and rendered still more so by a ceaseless monotony of life. She never went to meeting, and was seldom seen outside the house. A passing vision of a long white-capped face at a window was about all the neighbors ever saw of this woman.

So Evelina's gentle privacy was well guarded by her own household, as by a faithful system of domestic police. She grew old peacefully behind her green hedge, shielded effectually from all rough bristles of curiosity. Every new spring her own bloom showed paler beside the new bloom of her flowers, but people could not see it.

Some thirty years after the Squire's death the man John Darby died; his wife a year later. That left Evelina alone with the old woman who had nursed her mother. She was very old, but not feeble, and quite able to perform the simple household tasks for herself and Evelina. An old man, who saved himself from the almshouse in such ways, came daily to do the rougher part of the garden work in John Darby's stead. He was aged and decrepit; his muscles seemed able to perform their appointed tasks only through the accumulated inertia of a patiently toilsome life in the same tracks. Apparently they would have collapsed had he tried to force them to aught else than the holding of the ploughshare, the pulling of weeds, the digging around the roots of flowers, and the planting of seeds.

Every autumn he seemed about to totter to his fall among the fading flowers; every spring it was like Death himself urging on the resurrection; but he lived on year after year, and tended well Evelina's garden, and the gardens of other maiden-women and widows in the village. He was taciturn, grubbing among his green beds as silently as a worm, but now and then he warmed a little under a fire of questions concerning Evelina's garden. "Never see none sech flowers in nobody's garden in this town, not sence I knowed 'nough to tell a pink from a piny," he would mumble. His speech was thick; his words were all uncouthly slurred; the expression of his whole life had come more through his old knotted hands of labor than through his tongue. But he would wipe his forehead with his shirt sleeve and lean a second on his spade, and his face would change at the mention of the garden. Its wealth of bloom illumined his old mind, and the roses and honeysuckle and pinks seemed for a second to be reflected in his bleared old eyes.

There had never been in the village such a garden as this of Evelina Adams's. All the old blooms which had come over the seas with the early colonists, and stared as it were their own colony of flora in the new country, flourished there. The naturalized pinks and phlox and hollyhocks and the rest, changed a little in color and fragrance by the conditions of a new climate and soil, were all in Evelina's garden, and no one dreamed what they meant to Evelina; and she did not dream herself, for her heart was always veiled to her own eyes, like the face of a nun. The roses and pinks, the poppies and heart's-ease, were to this maiden-woman, who had innocently and helplessly outgrown her maiden heart, in the place of all the loves of life which she had missed. Her affections had forced an outlet in roses; they exhaled sweetness in pinks, and twined and clung in honeysuckle vines. The daffodils, when they came up in the spring, comforted her like the smiles of children; when she saw the first rose, her heart leaped as at the face of a lover.

She had lost the one way of human affection, but her feet had found a little single side-track of love, which gave her still a zest in the journey of life. Even in the winter Evelina had her flowers, for she kept those that would bear transplanting in pots, and all the sunny windows in her house were gay with them. She would also not let a rose leaf fall and waste in the garden soil, or a sprig of lavender or thyme. She gathered them all, and stored them away in chests and drawers and old china bowls—the whole house seemed laid away in rose leaves and lavender. Evelina's clothes gave out at every motion that fragrance of dead flowers which is like the fragrance of the past, and has a sweetness like that of sweet memories. Even the cedar chest where Evelina's mother's bridal array was stored had its till heaped with rose leaves and lavender.

When Evelina was nearly seventy years old the old nurse who had lived with her her whole life died. People wondered then what she would do. "She can't live all alone in that great house," they said. But she did live there alone six months, until spring, and people used to watch her evening lamp when it was put out, and the morning smoke from her kitchen chimney. "It ain't safe for her to be there alone in that great house," they said.

But early in April a young girl appeared one Sunday in the old Squire's pew. Nobody had seen her come to town, and nobody knew who she was or where she came from, but the old people said she looked just as Evelina Adams used to when she was young, and she must be some relation. The old man who had used to look across the meeting-house at Evelina, over forty years ago, looked across now at this young girl, and gave a great start, and his face paled under his gray beard stubble. His old wife gave an anxious, wondering glance at him, and crammed a peppermint into his hand. "Anything the matter, father?" she whispered; but he only gave his head a half-surly shake, and then fastened his eyes straight ahead upon the pulpit. He had reason to that day, for his only son, Thomas, was going to preach his first sermon therein as a candidate. His wife ascribed his nervousness to that. She put a peppermint in her own mouth, and sucked it comfortably. "That's all 'tis," she thought to herself. "Father always was easy worked up," and she looked proudly up at her son sitting on the haircloth sofa in the pulpit, leaning his handsome young head on his hand, as he had seen old divines do. She never dreamed that her old husband sitting beside her was possessed of an inner life so strange to her that she would not have known him had she met him in the spirit. And, indeed, it had been so always, and she had never dreamed of it. Although he had been faithful to his wife, the image of Evelina Adams in her youth, and that one love-look which she had given him, had never left his soul, but had given it a guise and complexion of which his nearest and dearest knew nothing.

It was strange, but now, as he looked up at his own son as he arose in the pulpit, he could seem to see a look of that fair young

Evelina, who had never had a son to inherit her beauty. He had certainly a delicate brilliancy of complexion, which he could have gotten directly from neither father nor mother; and whence came that little nervous frown between his dark blue eyes? His mother had blue eyes, but not like his; they flashed over the great pulpit Bible with a sweet fire that matched the old memory in his father's heart.

But the old man put the fancy away from him in a minute; it was an old one, which his stern common sense always overcame. It was impossible that Thomas Merriam should resemble Evelina Adams; indeed, people always called him the very image of his father.

The father tried to fix his mind upon his son's sermon, but presently he glanced involuntarily across the meeting-house at the young girl, and again his heart leaped and his face paled; but he turned his eyes gravely back to the pulpit, and his wife did not notice. Now and then she thrust a sharp elbow in his side to call his attention to a grand point in their son's discourse. The odor of peppermint was strong in his nostrils, but through it all he seemed to perceive the rose and lavender scent of Evelina Adams's youthful garments. Whether it was with him simply the memory of an odor, which affected him like the odor itself, or not, those in the vicinity of the Squire's pew were plainly aware of it. The gown which the strange young girl wore was, as many an old woman discovered to her neighbor with loud whispers, one of Evelina's, which had lain away in a sweet smelling chest since her old girlhood. It had been somewhat altered to suit the fashion of a later day, but the eyes which had fastened keenly upon it when Evelina first wore it up the meeting-house aisle could not mistake it. "It's Evelina Adams's lavender satin made over," one whispered, with a sharp hiss of breath, in the other's ear.

The lavender satin, deepening into purple in the folds, swept in a rich circle over the knees of the young girl in the Squire's pew. She folded her little hands, which were encased in Evelina's cream-colored silk mitts, over it, and looked up at the young minister, and listened to his sermon with a grave and innocent dignity, as Evelina had done before her. Perhaps the resemblance between this young girl and the young girl of the past was more one of mien than aught else, although the type of face was the same. This girl had the same fine sharpness of feature and delicately bright color, and she also wore her hair in curls, although they were tied back from her face with a black velvet ribbon, and did not veil it when she drooped her head, as Evelina's used to do.

The people divided their attention between her and the new minister. Their curiosity goaded them in equal measure with their spiritual zeal. "I can't wait to find out who that girl is," one woman whispered to another.

The girl herself had no thought of the commotion which she awakened. When the service was over, and she walked with a gentle maiden stateliness, which seemed a very copy of Evelina's own, out of the meeting-house, down the street to the Squire's house, and entered it, passing under the stately Corinthian pillars, with a last purple gleam of her satin skirts, she never dreamed of the eager attention that followed her.

It was several days before the village people discovered who she was. The information had to be obtained, by a process like mental thumb-screwing, from the old man who tended Evelina's garden, but at last they knew. She was the daughter of a cousin of Evelina's on the father's side. Her name was Evelina Leonard; she had been named for her father's cousin. She had been finely brought up, and had attended a Boston school for young ladies. Her mother had been dead many years, and her father had died some two years ago, leaving her with only a very little money, which had now all gone, and Evelina Adams had invited her to live with her. Evelina Adams had herself told the old gardener, seeing his scant curiosity was somewhat awakened by the sight of the strange young lady in the garden, but he seemed to have almost forgotten it when the people questioned him.

"She'll leave her all her money, most likely," they said, and they looked at this new Evelina in the old Evelina's perfumed gowns with awe.

However, in the space of a few months the opinion upon this matter was divided. Another cousin of Evelina Adams's came to town, and this time an own cousin: a widow in fine black bombazine, portly and florid, walking with a majestic swell, and, moreover, having with her two daughters, girls of her own type, not so far advanced. This woman hired one of the village cottages, and it was rumored that Evelina Adams paid the rent. Still, it was considered that she was not very intimate with these last relatives. The neighbors watched, and saw, many a time, Mrs. Martha Loomis and her girls try the doors of the Adams house, scudding around angrily from front to side and back, and knock and knock again, but with no admittance. "Evelina she won't let none of 'em in more'n once a week," the neighbors said. It was odd that, although they had deeply resented Evelina's seclusion on their own accounts, they were rather on her side in this matter, and felt a certain delight when they witnessed a crestfallen retreat of the widow and her daughters. "I don't s'pose she wants them Loomises marchin' in on her every minute," they said.

The new Evelina was not seen much with the other cousins, and she made no acquaintances in the village. Whether she was to inherit all the Adams property or not, she seemed, at any rate, heiress to all the elder Evelina's habits of life. She worked with her in the garden, and wore her old girlish gowns, and kept almost as closely at home as she. She often, however, walked abroad in the early dusk, stepping along in a grave and stately fashion, as the elder Evelina had used to do, holding her skirts away from the dewy road-side weeds, her face showing out in the twilight like a white flower, as if it had a pale light of its own.

Nobody spoke to her; people turned furtively after she had passed and stared after her, but they never spoke. This young Evelina did not seem to expect it. She passed along with the lids cast down over her blue eyes, and the rose and lavender scent of her garments came back in their faces.

But one night when she was walking slowly along, a full half-mile from home, she heard rapid footsteps behind, and shrank a little closer to the wall, that whoever it was might have room to pass, and the young minister, Thomas Merriam, came up beside her and spoke.

"Good-evening," said he, and his voice was a little hoarse through nervousness.

Evelina started, and turned her fair face up toward his. "Good-evening," she responded, and courtesied [*sic*] as she had been taught at school, and stood closer to the wall, that he might pass; but Thomas Merriam paused also.

"I—" he began, but his voice broke. He cleared his throat angrily, and went on. "I have seen you in meeting," he said, with a kind of defiance, more of himself than of her. After all, was he not the minister, and had he not the right to speak to everybody in the congregation? Why should he embarrass himself?

"Yes, sir," replied Evelina. She stood drooping her head before him, and yet there was a certain delicate hauteur about her. Thomas was afraid to speak again. They both stood silent for a moment, and then Evelina stirred softly, as if to pass on, and Thomas spoke out bravely. "Is your cousin, Miss Adams, well?" said he.

"She is pretty well, I thank you sir."

"I've been wanting to—call," he began; then he hesitated again. His handsome young face was blushing crimson.

Evelina's own color deepened. She turned her face away. "Cousin Evelina never sees callers," she said, with grave courtesy; "perhaps you did not know. She has not for a great many years."

"Yes, I did know it," returned Thomas Merriam; "that's the reason I haven't called."

"Cousin Evelina is not strong," remarked the young girl, and there was a savor of apology in her tone.

"But—" stammered Thomas; then he stopped again. "May I— has she any objections to—anybody's coming to see you?"

Evelina started. "I am afraid Cousin Evelina would not approve," she answered, primly. Then she looked up in his face, and a girlish piteousness came into her own. "I am very sorry," she said, and there was a catch in her voice.

Thomas bent over her impetuously. All his ministerial state fell from him like an outer garment of the soul. He was young, and he had seen this girl Sunday after Sunday. He had written all his sermons with her image before his eyes, he had preached to her, and her only, and she had come between his heart and all the nations of the earth in his prayers. "Oh," he stammered out, "I am afraid you can't be very happy living there the way you do. Tell me—"

Evelina turned her face away with sudden haughtiness. "My cousin Evelina is very kind to me, sir," she said.

"But—you must be lonesome with nobody—of your own age—to speak to," persisted Thomas, confusedly.

"I never cared much for youthful company. It is getting dark; I must be going," said Evelina. "I wish you good evening, sir."

"Sha'n't I—walk home with you?" asked Thomas, falteringly.

"It isn't necessary, thank you, and I don't think Cousin Evelina would approve," she replied, primly; and her light dress fluttered away into the dusk and out of sight like the pale wing of a moth.

Poor Thomas Merriam walked on with his head in a turmoil. His heart beat loud in his ears. "I've made her mad with me," he said to himself, using the old rustic school boy vernacular, from which he did not always depart in his thoughts, although his ministerial dignity guarded his conversations. Thomas Merriam came of a simply homely stock, whose speech came from the emotions of the heart, all unregulated by the usages of the schools. He was the first for generations who had aspired to college learning and a profession, and had trained his tongue by the models of the educated and polite. He could not help, at times, the relapse of his thoughts, and their speaking to himself in the dialect of his family and his ancestors. "She's 'way above me, and I ought to ha' known it," he further said, with the meekness of an humble but fiercely independent race, which is meek to itself alone. He would have maintained his equality with his last breath to an opponent; in his heart of hearts he felt himself below the scion of the one old gentle family of his native village.

This young Evelina, by the fine dignity which had been born with her and not acquired by precept and example, by the sweetly formal diction which seemed her native tongue, had filled him with awe. Now, when he thought she was angered with him, he felt beneath her lady-feet, his nostrils choked with a spiritual dust of humiliation.

He went forward blindly. The dusk had deepened; from either side of the road, from the mysterious gloom of the bushes, came the twangs of the katydids, like some coarse rustic quarrelers, each striving for the last word in a dispute not even dignified by excess of passion.

Suddenly somebody jostled him to his own side of the path. "That you, Thomas? Where you been?" said a voice in his ear.

"That you, father? Down to the post-office."

"Who was that you was talkin' with back there?"

"Miss Evelina Leonard."

"That girl that's stayin' there—to the old Squire's?"

"Yes." The son tried to move on, but his father stood before him dumbly for a minute. "I must be going, father. I've got to work on my sermon," Thomas said, impatiently.

"Wait a minute," said his father. "I've got something to say to ye, Thomas, an' this is as good a time to say it as any. There ain't anybody 'round. I don't know as ye'll thank me for it—but mother said the other day that she thought you'd kind of an idea—she said you asked her if she thought it would be anything out of the way for you to go up to the Squire's to make a call. Mother she thinks you can step in anywheres, but I don't know. I know your book-learnin' and your bein' a minister has set you up a good deal higher than your mother and me and any of our folks, and I feel as if you were good enough for anybody, as far as that goes; but that ain't all. Some folks have different startin'-points in this world, and they see things different; and when they do, it ain't much use tryin' to make them walk alongside and see things alike. Their eyes have got different cants, and they ain't able to help it. Now this girl she's related to the old Squire, and she's been brought up different, and she started ahead, even if her father did lose all his property. She 'ain't never eat in the kitchen, nor been scart to set down in the parlor, and satin and velvet, and silver spoons, and cream-pots 'ain't never looked anything out of the common to her, and they always will to you. No matter how many such things you may live to have, they'll always get a little the better of ye. She'll be 'way above 'em; and you won't, no matter how hard you try. Some ideas can't never mix; and when ideas can't mix, folks can't."

"I never said they could," returned Thomas, shortly. "I can't stop to talk any longer, father. I must go home."

"No, you wait a minute, Thomas. I'm goin' to say out what I started to, and then I sha'n't ever bring it up again. What I was comin' at was this: I wanted to warn ye a little. You mustn't set too much store by little things that you think mean consider'ble when they don't. Looks don't count for much, and I want you to remember it, and not be upset by 'em."

Thomas gave a great start, and colored high. "I'd like to know what you mean, father," he cried, sharply.

"Nothin'. I don't mean nothin', only I'm older'n you, and it's come in my way to know some things, and it's fittin' you should profit by it. A young woman's looks at you don't count for much. I don't s'pose she knows why she gives 'em herself half the time; they ain't like us. It's best you should make up your mind to it; if you don't, you may find it out by the hardest. That's all. I ain't never goin' to bring this up again."

"I'd like to know what you mean, father." Thomas's voice shook with embarrassment and anger.

"I ain't goin' to say anything more about it," replied the old man. "Mary Ann Pease and Arabella Mann are both in the settin'-room with your mother. I thought I'd tell ye, in case ye didn't want to see 'em, and wanted to go to work on your sermon."

Thomas made an impatient ejaculation as he strode off. When he reached the large white house where he lived he skirted it carefully. The chirping treble of girlish voices came from the open sitting-room window, and he caught a glimpse of a smooth brown head and a high shell comb in front of the candle-light. The young minister tiptoed in the back door and across the kitchen to the back stairs. The sitting-room door was open, and the candle-light streamed out, and the treble voices rose high. Thomas, advancing through the dusky kitchen with cautious steps, encountered suddenly a chair in the dark corner by the stairs, and just saved himself from falling. There was a startled outcry from the sitting-room, and his mother came running into the kitchen with a candle.

"Who is it?" she demanded, valiantly. Then she started and gasped as her son confronted her. He shook a furious warning fist at the sitting-room door and his mother, and edged toward the stairs. She followed him close. "Hadn't you better jest step in a minute?" she whispered. "Them girls have been here an hour, and I know they're waitin' to see you." Thomas shook his head fiercely, and swung himself around the corner into the dark crook of the back stairs. His mother thrust the candle into his hand. "Take this, or you'll break your neck on them stairs," she whispered.

Thomas, stealing up the stairs like a cat, heard one of the girls call to his mother—"Is it robbers, Mis' Merriam? Want us to come an' help tackle 'em?"—and he fairly shuddered; for Evelina's gentle-lady speech was still in his ears, and this rude girlish call seemed to jar upon his sensibilities.

"The idea of any girl screeching out like that!" he muttered. And if he had carried speech as far as his thought, he would have added, "when Evelina is a girl!"

He was so angry that he did not laugh when he heard his mother answer back, in those conclusive tones of hers that were wont to silence all argument: "It ain't anything. Don't be scared. I'm coming right back." Mrs. Merriam scorned subterfuges. She took always a silent stand in a difficulty, and let people infer what they would. When Marry Ann Pease inquired if it was the cat that had made the noise, she asked if her mother had finished her blue and white counterpane.

The two girls waited a half-hour longer, then they went home. "What do you s'pose made that noise out in the kitchen?" asked Arabella Mann of Mary Ann Pease, the minute they were out-of-doors.

"I don't know," replied Mary Ann Pease. She was a broad-back young girl, and looked like a matron as she hurried along in the dusk.

"Well, I know what I think it was," said Arabella Mann, moving ahead with sharp jerks of her little dark body.

"What?"

"It was him."

"You don't mean—"

"I think it was Thomas Merriam, and he was tryin' to get up the back stairs unbeknownst to anybody, and he run into something."

"What for?"

"Because he didn't want to see us."

"Now, Arabella Mann, I don't believe it! He's always real pleasant to me."

"Well, I do believe it, and I guess he'll know it when I set foot in that house again. I guess he'll find out I didn't go there to see him! He needn't feel so fine, if he is the minister; his folks ain't any better than mine, an' we've got 'nough sight handsomer furniture in our parlor."

"Did you see how the tallow had all run down over the candles?"

"Yes, I did. She gave that candle she carried out in the kitchen to him, too. Mother says she wasn't never any kind of housekeeper."

"Hush! Arabella; here he is coming now."

But it was not Thomas; it was his father, advancing through the evening with his son's gait and carriage. When the two girls discovered that, one tittered out quite audibly, and they scuttled past. They were not rivals; they simply walked faithfully side by side in pursuit of the young minister, giving him as it were an impartial choice. There were even no heart-burnings between them; one always confided in the other when she supposed herself to have found some slight favor in Thomas's sight; and, indeed, the young minister could scarcely bow to one upon the street unless she flew to the other with the news.

Thomas Merriam himself was aware of all this devotion on the part of the young women of his flock, and it filled him with a sort of angry shame. He could not have told why, but he despised himself for being the object of their attention more than he despised them. His heart sank at the idea of Evelina's discovering it. What would she think of him if she knew all those young women haunted his house and lagged after meeting on the chance of getting a word from him? Suppose she should see their eyes upon his face in meeting-time, and decipher their half unconscious boldness, as he had done against his will. Once Evelina had looked at him, even as the older Evelina had looked at his father, and all other looks of maidens seemed to him like profanations of that, even although he doubted it. Full it had seemed to him of that tender maiden surprise and wonder, of that love that knows not itself, and sees its own splendor for the first time in another's face, and flees at the sight. It had happened once when he was coming down the aisle after the sermon and Evelina had met him at the door of her pew. But she had turned her head quickly, and her soft curls flowed over her red cheek, and he doubted ever after if he had read the look aright. When he had gotten the courage to speak to her, and she had met him with the gentle coldness which she had learned of her lady aunt and her teacher in Boston, his doubt was strong upon him. The next Sunday he looked not her way at all. He even tried faithfully from day to day to drive her image from his mind with prayer and religious thoughts, but in spite of himself he would lapse into dreams about her, as if borne by a current of nature too strong to be resisted. And sometimes, upon being awakened from them, as he sat over his sermon with the ink drying on his quill, by the sudden outburst of treble voices in his mother's sitting-room below, the fancy would seize him that possibly these other young damsels took fond liberties with him in their dreams, as he with Evelina, and he resented it with a fierce maidenliness of spirit, although he was a man. The thought that possibly they, over their spinning or their quilting, had in their hearts the image of himself with fond words upon his lips and fond looks in his eyes, filled him with shame and rage, although he took the same liberty with the delicately haughty maiden Evelina.

But Thomas Merriam was not given to undue appreciation of his own fascination, as was proved by his ready discouragement in the case of Evelina. He had the knowledge of his conquests forced upon his understanding until he could no longer evade it. Every day were offerings laid upon his shrine, of pound-cakes and flaky pies, and loaves of white bread, and cups of jelly, whereby the culinary skill of his devotees might be proved. Silken purses and beautiful socks

knitted with fancy stitches, and holy bookmarks for his Bible, and even
a wonderful bedquilt, and a fine linen shirt with hem-stitched bands,
poured in upon him. He burned with angry blushes when his mother,
smiling meaningly, passed them over to him. "Put them away, mother;
I don't want them," he would growl out, in a distress that was half
comic and half pathetic. He would never taste of the unctuous viands
which were brought to him. "How you act, Thomas!" his mother
would say. She was secretly elated by these feminine libations upon the
altar of her son. They did not grate upon her sensibilities, which were
not delicate. She even tried to assist two or three of the young women
in their designs; she would often praise them and their handiwork to
her son—and in this she was aided by an old woman aunt of hers who
lived with the family. "Nancy Winslow is as handsome a girl as ever I
set eyes on, an' I never see any nicer sewin', Mrs. Merriam said, after
the advent of the linen shirt, and she held it up to the light admiringly.
"Jest look at that hem-stitchin'!" she said.

"I guess whoever made that shirt calkilated 't would do for a
weddin' one," said old Aunt Betty Green, and Thomas made an
exclamation and went out of the room, tingling all over with shame
and disgust.

"Thomas don't act nateral," said the old woman, glancing
after him through her iron-bound spectacles.

"I dun'no' what's got into him," returned his mother.

"Mebbe they foller him up a leetle too close," said Aunt Betty.
"I dun'no' as I should have ventured on a shirt when I was a gal. I
made a satin vest once for Joshua, but that don't seem quite as p'inted
as a shirt. It didn't scare Joshua, nohow. He asked me to have him the
next week."

"Well, I dun'no'," said Mrs. Merriam again. "I kind of wish
Thomas would settle on somebody, for I'm pestered most to death with
'em, an' I feel as if 'twas kind of mean takin' all these things into the
house."

"They've 'bout kept ye in sweet cake, 'ain't they, lately?"

"Yes; but I don't feel as if it was jest right for us to eat it up,
when 'twas brought for Thomas. But he won't touch it. I can't see as

he has the least idee of any one of them. I don't believe Thomas has ever seen anybody he wanted for a wife."

"Well, he's got the pick of 'em a-settin' their caps right in his face," said Aunt Betty.

Neither of them dreamed how the young man, sleeping and eating and living under the same roof, beloved of them since he entered the world, holding himself coldly aloof from this crowd of half innocently, half boldly ardent young women had set up for himself his own divinity of love, before whom he consumed himself in vain worship. His father suspected, and that was all, and he never mentioned the matter again to his son.

After Thomas had spoken to Evelina the weeks went on, and they never exchanged another word, and their eyes never met. But they dwelt constantly within one another's thoughts, and were ever present to each other's spiritual vision. Always as the young minister bent over his sermon-paper, laboriously tracing out with sputtering quill his application of the articles of the orthodox faith, Evelina's blue eyes seemed to look out at him between the fierce doctrines like the eyes of an angel. And he could not turn the pages of the Holy Writ unless he found some passage therein which to his mind treated directly of her, setting further her graces like a prophecy. "The fairest among women," read Thomas Merriam, and nodded his head, while his heart leaped with the satisfied delight of all its fancies at the image of his love's fair and gentle face. "Her price is far above rubies," read Thomas Merriam, and he nodded his head again, and saw Evelina shining as with gold and pearls, more precious than all the jewels of the earth. In spite of all his efforts in those days, when Thomas Merriam studied the Scriptures he was more nearly touched by those old human hearts which throbbed down to his through the ages, welding the memories of their old loves to his living one until they seemed to prove its eternity, than by the Messianic prophecies. Often he spent hours upon his knees, but arose with Evelina's face before his very soul in spite of all.

And as for Evelina, she tended the flowers in the elder Evelina's garden with her poor cousin, whose own love-dreams had been illustrated as it were by the pinks and lilies blooming around them when they had all gone out of her heart, and Thomas Merriam's half-bold, half-imploring eyes looked up at her out of every flower and stung her heart like bees. Poor young Evelina feared much lest she had offended Thomas, and yet her own maiden decorum had been offended by him, and she had offended it herself, and she was faint with shame and distress when she thought of it. How had she been so bold and shameless as to give him that look in the meeting-house? And how had he been so cruel as to accost her afterward? "She had done right for the maintenance of her own maiden dignity," she told herself, and yet she feared lest she had angered him and hurt him. "Suppose he had been fretted by her coolness?" she thought, and then a great wave of tender pity went over her heart, and she would almost have spoken to him of her own accord. But then she would reflect how he continued to write such beautiful sermons, and prove so clearly and logically the tenets of the faith; and how could he do that with a mind in distress? Scarcely could she herself tend the flower beds as she should, nor set her embroidery stitches finely and evenly, she was so ill at ease. It must be that Thomas had not given the matter an hour's worry, since he continued to do his work so faithfully and well. And then her own heart would be sorer than ever with the belief that his was happy and at rest, although she would chide herself for it.

And yet this young Evelina was a philosopher and an analyst of human nature in a small way, and some slight comfort she got out of a shrewd suspicion that the heart of a man might love and suffer on a somewhat different principle from the heart of a woman. "It may be," thought Evelina, sitting idle over her embroidery with far-away blue eyes, "that a man's heart can always turn a while from love to other things as weighty and serious, although he be just as fond, while a woman's heart is always fixed one way by loving, and cannot be turned unless it breaks. And it may be wise," thought Evelina, "else how could the state be maintained and governed, battles for independence be fought, and even souls be saved, and the gospel carried to the heathen, if men could not turn from the concerns of their own hearts more easily than women? Women should be patient," thought Evelina, "and consider that if they suffer 'tis due to the lot which a wise Providence has given them." And yet tears welled up in her earnest blue eyes and fell over her fair cheeks and wet the embroidery—when the elder Evelina was not looking, as she seldom was. The elder Evelina was kind to her young cousin, but there were days when she seemed to dwell alone in her own thoughts, apart from the whole world, and she seldom spoke either to Evelina or her old servant-man.

Young Evelina, trying to atone for her former indiscretion and establish herself again on her height of maiden reserve in Thomas Merriam's eyes, sat resolutely in the meeting-house of a Sabbath day, with her eyes cast down, and after service she glided swiftly down the aisle and was out of the door before the young minister could much more than descend the pulpit stairs, unless he ran an indecorous race.

And young Evelina never at twilight strolled up the road in the direction of Thomas Merriam's home, where she might quite reasonably hope to meet him, since he was wont to go to the store when the evening stage-coach came in with the mail from Boston.

Instead she paced the garden paths, or, when there was not too heavy a dew, rambled across the fields; and there was also a lane where she loved to walk. Whether or not Thomas Merriam suspected this, or had ever seen, as he passed the mouth of the lane, the flutter of maidenly draperies in the distance, it so happened that one evening he also went a-walking there, and met Evelina. He had entered the lane from the highway, and she from the fields at the head. So he saw her first afar off, and could not tell fairly whether her light muslin skirt might not be only a white flowering bush. For, since his outlook upon life had been so full of Evelina, he had found that often the most common and familiar things would wear for a second a look of her to startle him. And many a time his heart had leaped at the sight of a white bush ahead stirring softly in the evening wind, and he had thought it might be she. Now he said to himself impatiently that this was only another fancy; but soon he saw that it was indeed Evelina, in a light muslin gown, with a little lace kerchief on her head. His handsome young face was white; his lips twitched nervously; but he reached out and pulled a spray of white flowers from a bush, and swung it airily to hide his agitation as he advanced.

As for Evelina, when she first espied Thomas she started and half turned, as if to go back; then she held up her white kerchiefed head with gentle pride and kept on. When she came up to Thomas she walked so far to one side that her muslin skirt was in danger of catching and tearing on the bushes, and she never raised her eyes, and not a flicker of recognition stirred her sweet pale face as she passed him.

But Thomas started as if she had struck him, and dropped his spray of white flowers, and could not help a smothered cry that was half a sob, as he went on, knocking blindly against the bushes. He went a little way, then he stopped and looked back with his piteous hurt eyes. And Evelina had stopped also, and she had the spray of white flowers which he had dropped, in her hand, and her eyes met his. Then she let the flowers fall again, and clapped both her little hands to her face to cover it, and turned to run; but Thomas was at her side, and he put out his hand and held her softly by her white arm.

"Oh," he panted, "I—did not mean to be—too presuming, and offend you. I crave your pardon—"

Evelina had recovered herself. She stood with her little hands clasped, and her eyes cast down before him, but not a quiver stirred her pale face, which seemed turned to marble by this last effort of her maiden pride. "I have nothing to pardon," said she. "It was I, whose bold behavior, unbecoming a modest and well-trained woman, gave rise to what seemed like presumption on your part." The sense of justice was strong within her, but she made her speech haughtily and primly, as if she had learned it by rote from some maiden school-mistress and pulled her arm away and turned to go; but Thomas's words stopped her.

"Not—unbecoming if it came—from the heart," said he, brokenly, scarcely daring to speak, and yet not daring to be silent.

Then Evelina turned on him, with a sudden strange pride that lay beneath all other pride, and was of a nobler and truer sort. "Do you think I would have given you the look that I did if it had not come from my heart?" she demanded. "What did you take me to be—false and a jilt? I may be a forward young woman, who has overstepped the bounds of maidenly decorum, and I shall never get over the shame of it, but I am truthful, and I am no jilt." The brilliant color flamed out on Evelina's cheeks. Her blue eyes met Thomas's with that courage of innocence and nature which dares all shame. But it was only for a second; the tears sprung into them. "I beg you to let me go home," she said, pitifully; but Thomas caught her arms, and pressed her troubled maiden face against his breast.

"Oh, I love you so!" he whispered. "I love you so, Evelina, and I was afraid you were angry at me for it."

"And I was afraid," she faltered, half weeping and half shrinking from him, "lest you were angry with me for betraying the state of my feelings, when you could not return them." And even then she used that gentle formality of expression with which she had been taught by her maiden preceptors to veil decorously her most ardent emotions. And, in truth, her training stood her in good stead in other ways; for she presently commanded, with that mild dignity of hers which allowed of no remonstrance, that Thomas should take away his arm from her waist, and give her no more kisses for that time.

"It is not becoming for any one," said she, "and much less for a minister of the gospel. And as for myself, I know not what Mistress Perkins would say to me. She has a mind much above me, I fear."

"Mistress Perkins is enjoying her mind in Boston," said Thomas Merriam, with the laugh of a triumphant young lover.

But Evelina did not laugh. "It might be well for both you and me if she were here," said she, seriously. However, she tempered a little her decorous following of Mistress Perkins's precepts, and she and Thomas went hand in hand up the lane and across the fields.

There was no dew that night, and the moon was full. It was after nine o'clock when Thomas left her at the gate in the fence which separated Evelina Adams's garden from the field, and watched her disappear between the flowers. The moon shone full on the garden. Evelina walked as it were over a silver dapple, which her light gown seemed to brush away and dispel for a moment. The bushes stood in sweet mysterious clumps of shadows.

Evelina had almost reached the house, and was close to the great althea bush, which cast a wide circle of shadow, when it seemed suddenly to separate and move into life.

The elder Evelina stepped out from the shadow of the bush. "Is that you, Evelina?" she said, in her soft melancholy voice, which had in it a nervous vibration.

"Yes, Cousin Evelina."

The elder Evelina's pale face, drooped about with gray curls, had an unfamiliar, almost uncanny, look in the moonlight, and might have been the sorrowful visage of some marble nymph, lovelorn, with unceasing grace. "Who—was with you?" she asked.

"The minister," replied young Evelina.

"Did he meet you?"

"He met me in the lane, Cousin Evelina."

"And he walked home with you across the field?"

"Yes, Cousin Evelina."

Then the two entered the house, and nothing more was said about the matter. Young Evelina and Thomas Merriam had agreed that their affection was to be kept a secret for a while. "For," said young Evelina, "I cannot leave Cousin Evelina yet a while, and I cannot have her pestered with thinking about it, at least before another spring, when she has the garden fairly growing again."

"That is nearly a whole year; it is August now," said Thomas, half reproachfully, and he tightened his clasp of Evelina's slender fingers.

"I cannot help that," replied Evelina. "It is for you to show Christian patience more than I, Thomas. If you could have seen poor Cousin Evelina, as I have seen her, through the long winter days, when her garden is dead, and she has only the few plants in her window left! When she is not watering and tending them she sits all day in the window and looks out over the garden and the naked bushes and the withered flower stalks. She used not to be so, but would read her Bible and good books, and busy herself somewhat over fine needlework, and at one time she was compiling a little floral book, giving a list of the flowers, and poetical selections and sentiments appropriate to each. That was her pastime for three winters, and it is now nearly done; but she has given that up, and all the rest, and sits there in the window and grows older and feebler until spring. It is only I who can divert her mind, by reading aloud to her and singing; and sometimes I paint the flowers she loves the best on cardboard with water colors. I have a poor skill in it, but Cousin Evelina can tell which flower I have tried to represent, and it pleases her greatly. I have even seen her smile. No, I cannot leave her, nor even pester her with telling her before another spring, and you must wait, Thomas," said young Evelina.

And Thomas agreed, as he was likely to do to all which she proposed which touched not his own sense of right and honor. Young Evelina gave Thomas one more kiss for his earnest pleading, and that night wrote out the tale in her journal. "It may be that I overstepped the bounds of maidenly decorum," wrote Evelina, "but my heart did so entreat me," and no blame whatever did she lay upon Thomas.

Young Evelina opened her heart only to her journal, and her cousin was told nothing, and had little cause for suspicion. Thomas Merriam never came to the house to see his sweetheart; he never walked home with her from meeting. Both were anxious to avoid village gossip, until the elder Evelina could be told.

Often in the summer evenings the lovers met, and strolled hand in hand across the fields, and parted at the garden gate with the one kiss which Evelina allowed, and that was all.

Sometimes when young Evelina came in with her lover's kiss still warm upon her lips the elder Evelina looked at her wistfully, with a strange retrospective expression in her blue eyes, as if she were striving to remember something that the girl's face called to mind. And yet she could have had nothing to remember except dreams.

And once, when young Evelina sat sewing through a long summer afternoon and thinking about her lover, the elder Evelina, who was storing rose leaves mixed with sweet spices in a jar, said, suddenly, "He looks as his father used to."

Young Evelina started. "Who do you mean, Cousin Evelina?" she asked, wonderingly; for the elder Evelina had not even glanced at her, nor even seemed to address her at all.

"Nothing," said the elder Evelina, and a soft flush stole over her withered face and neck, and she sprinkled more cassia on the rose leaves in the jar.

Young Evelina said no more; but she wondered, partly because Thomas was always in her mind, and it seemed to her naturally that nearly everything must have a savor of meaning of him, if her cousin Evelina could possibly have referred to him and his likeness to his father. For it was commonly said that Thomas looked very like his father, although his figure was different. The young man was taller and more firmly built, and he had not the meek forward curve of shoulder which had grown upon his father of late years.

When the frosty nights came Thomas and Evelina could not meet and walk hand in hand over the fields behind the Squire's house, and they very seldom could speak to one another. It was nothing except a "good day" on the street, and a stolen glance, which set them both a-trembling lest all the congregation had noticed, in the meeting house. When the winter set fairly in they met no more, for the elder Evelina was taken ill, and her young cousin did not leave her even to go to meeting. People said they guessed it was Evelina Adams's last sickness, and they furthermore guessed that she would divide her property between her cousin Martha Loomis and her two girls and Evelina Leonard, and that Evelina would have the house as her share.

Thomas Merriam heard this last with a satisfaction which he did not try to disguise from himself, because he never dreamed of there being any selfish element in it. It was all for Evelina. Many a time he had looked about the humble house where he had been born, and where he would have to take Evelina after he had married her, and striven to see its poor features with her eyes—not with his, for which familiarity had tempered them. Often, as he sat with his parents in the old sitting-room, in which he had kept so far an unquestioning belief, as in a friend of his childhood, the scales of his own personality would fall suddenly from his eyes. Then he would see, as Evelina, the poor, worn, humble face of his home, and his heart would sink. "I don't see how I ever can bring her here," he thought. He began to save, a few cents at a time out of his pitiful salary, to at least beautify his own chamber a little when Evelina should come. He made up his mind that she should have a little dressing-table, with an oval mirror, and a white muslin frill around it, like one he had seen in Boston. "She shall have that to sit before while she combs her hair," he thought, with defiant tenderness, when he stowed away another shilling in a little box in his trunk. It was money which he ordinarily bestowed upon foreign missions; but his Evelina had come between him and the heathen. To procure some dainty furnishings for her bridal-chamber he took away a good half of his tithes for the spread of the gospel in the dark lands. Now and then his conscience smote him, he felt shamefaced before his deacons, but Evelina kept her first claims. He resolved that another year he would hire a piece of land, and combine farming with his ministerial work, and so try to eke out his salary, and get a little more money to beautify his poor home for his bride.

Now if Evelina Adams had come to the appointed time for the closing of her solitary life, and if her young cousin should inherit a share of her goodly property and the fine old mansion-house, all necessity for anxiety of this kind was over. Young Evelina would not need to be taken away, for the sake of her love, from all these comforts and luxuries. Thomas Merriam rejoiced innocently, without a thought for himself.

In the course of the winter he confided in his father; he couldn't keep it to himself any longer. Then there was another reason. Seeing Evelina so little made him at times almost doubt the reality of it all. There were days when he was depressed, and inclined to ask himself if he had not dreamed it. Telling somebody gave it substance.

His father listened soberly when he told him; he had grown old of late.

"Well," said he, "she ain't been used to living the way you have, though you have had advantages that none of your folks ever had; but if she likes you, that's all there is to it, I s'pose."

The old man sighed wearily. He sat in his arm chair at the kitchen fireplace; his wife had gone in to one of the neighbors, and the two were alone.

"Of course," said Thomas, simply, "if Evelina Adams shouldn't live, the chances are that I shouldn't have to bring her here. She wouldn't have to give up anything on my account—you know that, father."

Then the young man started, for his father turned suddenly on him with a pale, wrathful face. "You ain't countin' on that!" he shouted. "You ain't countin' on that—a son of mine countin' on anything like that!"

Thomas colored. "Why, father," he stammered, "you don't think—you know, it's all for her—and they say she can't live anyway.

I had never thought of such a thing before. I was wondering how I could make it comfortable for Evelina here."

But his father did not seem to listen. "Countin' on that!" he repeated. "Countin' on a poor old soul, that 'ain't ever had anything to set her heart on but a few posies, dyin' to make room for other folks to have what she's been cheated out on. Countin' on that!" The old man's voice broke into a hoarse sob; he got up, and went hurriedly out of the room.

"Father must be getting childish," Thomas thought, wonderingly. He did not bring up the subject to him again.

Evelina Adams died in March. One morning the bell tolled seventy long melancholy tones before people had eaten their breakfasts. They ran to their doors and counted. "It's her," they said, nodding, when they had waited a little after the seventieth stroke. Directly Mrs. Martha Loomis and her two girls were seen hustling importantly down the road, with their shawls over their heads, to the Squire's house. "Mis' Loomis can lay her out," they said. "It ain't likely that young Evelina knows anything about such things. Guess she'll be thankful she's got somebody to call on now, if she 'ain't mixed much with the Loomises." Then they wondered when the funeral would be, and the women furbished up their black gowns and bonnets, and even in a few cases drove to the next town and borrowed from relatives; but there was a great disappointment in store for them.

Evelina Adams died on a Saturday. The next day it was announced from the pulpit that the funeral would be private, by the particular request of the deceased. Evelina Adams had carried her delicate seclusion beyond death, to the very borders of the grave. Nobody, outside the family, was bidden to the funeral, except the doctor, the minister, and the two deacons of the church. They were to be the bearers. The burial also was to be private, in the Squire's family burial-lot, at the north of the house. The bearers would carry the coffin across the yard, and there would not only be no funeral, but no funeral procession, and no hearse. "It don't seem scarcely-decent;" the women whispered to each other; "and more than all that, she ain't goin' to be seen." The deacons' wives were especially disturbed by this last, as they might otherwise have gained many interesting particulars by proxy.

Monday was the day set for the burial. Early in the morning Thomas Merriam walked feebly up the road to the Squire's house. People noticed him as he passed. "How terrible fast he's grown old lately!" they said. He opened the gate which led into the Squire's front yard with fumbling fingers, and went up the walk to the front door, under the Corinthian pillars, and raised the brass knocker.

Evelina opened the door, and started and blushed when she saw him. She had been crying; there were red rings around her blue eyes and her pretty lips were swollen. She tried to smile at Thomas's father, and she held out her hand with shy welcome.

"I want to see her," the old man said, abruptly.

Evelina started, and looked at him wonderingly. "I—don't believe—I know who you mean," said she. "Do you want to see Mrs. Loomis?"

"No; I want to see her."

"Her?"

"Yes, her."

Evelina turned pale as she stared at him. There was something strange about his face. "But—Cousin Evelina," she faltered—"she didn't want—Perhaps you don't know: she left special directions that nobody was to look at her."

"*I want to see her*," said the old man, and Evelina gave way. She stood aside for him to enter, and led him into the great north parlor, where Evelina Adams lay in her mournful state. The shutters were closed, and one on entering could distinguish nothing but that long black shadow in the middle of the room. Young Evelina opened a shutter a little way, and a slanting shaft of spring sunlight came in and shot athwart the coffin. The old man tiptoed up and leaned over and looked at the dead woman. Evelina Adams had left further instructions about her funeral, which no one understood, but which were faithfully carried out. She wished, she had said, to be attired for her long sleep in a certain rose-colored gown, laid away in rose leaves and lavender in a certain chest in a certain chamber. There were also silken hose

and satin shoes with it, and these were to be put on, and a wrought
lace tucker fastened with a pearl brooch.

It was the costume she had worn one Sabbath day back in her
youth, when she had looked across the meeting-house and her eyes had
met the then young Thomas Merriam's; but nobody knew nor
remembered; even young Evelina thought it was simply a vagary of
her dead cousin's.

"It don't seem to me decent to lay away anybody dressed so,"
said Mrs. Martha Loomis; "but of course last wishes must be
respected."

The two Loomis girls said they were thankful nobody was to
see the departed in her rose-colored shroud.

Even old Thomas Merriam, leaning over poor Evelina, cold
and dead in the garb of her youth, did not remember it, and saw no
meaning in it. He looked at her long. The beautiful color was all faded
out of the yellow-white face; the sweet full lips were set and thin; the
closed blue eyes sunken in dark hollows; the yellow hair showed a line
of gray at the edge of her old woman's cap, and thin gray curls lay
against the hollow cheeks. But old Thomas Merriam drew a long
breath when he looked at her. It was like a gasp of admiration and
wonder; a strange rapture came into his dim eyes; his lips moved as if
he whispered to her, but young Evelina could not hear a sound. She
watched him, half frightened, but finally he turned to her. "I ain't seen
her—fairly," said he, hoarsely—"I ain't seen her, savin' a glimpse of
her at the window, for over forty year, and she 'ain't changed not a
look. I'd have known her anywheres. She's the same as she was when
she was a girl. It's wonderful—wonderful!"

Young Evelina shrank a little. "We think she looks natural,"
she said, hesitatingly.

"She looks just as she did when she was a girl and used to
come into the meetin-house. She *is* jest the same," the old man
repeated, in his eager, hoarse voice. Then he bent over the coffin, and
his lips moved again. Young Evelina would have called Mrs. Loomis,
for she was frightened, had he not been Thomas's father, and had it
not been for her vague feeling that there might be some old story to
explain this which she had never heard. "Maybe he was in love with

poor Cousin Evelina, as Thomas is with me," thought young Evelina, using her own leaping-pole of love to land straight at the truth. But she never told her surmise to any one except Thomas, and that was long afterward, when the old man was dead. Now she watched him with her blue dilated eyes. But soon he turned away from the coffin and made his way straight out of the room, without a word. He turned on the threshold and looked back at her, his face working.

"Don't ye go to lottin' too much on what ye're goin' to get through the folks that have died an' not had anything," he said; and he shook his head almost fiercely at her.

"No, I won't. I don't think I understand what you mean, sir," stammered Evelina.

The old man stood looking at her a moment. Suddenly she saw the tears rolling over his old cheeks. "I'm much obliged to ye for lettin' of me see her," he said, hoarsely, and crept feebly down the steps.

Evelina went back trembling to the room where her dead cousin lay, and covered her face, and closed the shutter again. Then she went about her household duties, wondering. She could not understand what it all meant; but one thing she understood—that in some way this old dead woman, Evelina Adams, had gotten immortal youth and beauty in one human heart. "She looked to him just as she did when she was a girl," Evelina kept thinking to herself with awe. She said nothing about it to Mrs. Loomis or her daughters. They had been in the back part of the house, and had not heard old Thomas Merriam come in, and they never knew about it.

Mrs. Loomis and the two girls staid in the house day and night until after the funeral. They confidently expected to live there in the future. "It isn't likely that Evelina Adams thought a young woman no older than Evelina Leonard could live here alone in this great house with nobody but that old Sarah Judd. It would not be proper nor becoming," said Martha Loomis to her two daughters; and they agreed, and brought over many of their possessions under cover of night to the Squire's house during the interval before the funeral.

But after the funeral and the reading of the will the Loomises made sundry trips after dusk back to their old home, with their best petticoats and cloaks over their arms, and their bonnets dangling by their strings at their sides. For Evelina Adams's last will and testament had been read, and therein provision was made for the continuance of the annuity heretofore paid them for their support, with the condition affixed that not one night should they spend after the reading of the will in the house known as the Squire Adams house. The annuity was an ample one, and would provide the widow Martha Loomis and her daughters, as it had done before, with all the needfuls of life; but upon hearing the will they stiffened their double chins into the kerchiefs with indignation, for they had looked for more.

Evelina Adams's will was a will of conditions, for unto it she had affixed two more, and those affected her beloved cousin Evelina Leonard. It was notable that "beloved" had not preceded her cousin Martha Loomis's name in the will. No pretence of love, when she felt none, had she ever made in her life. The entire property of Evelina Adams, spinster, deceased, with the exception of Widow Martha Loomis's provision, fell to this beloved young Evelina Leonard, subject to two conditions—firstly, she was never to enter into matrimony, with any person whomsoever, at any time whatsoever; secondly, she was never to let the said spinster Evelina Adams's garden, situated at the rear and southward of the house known as the Squire Adams house, die through any neglect of hers. Due allowance was to be made for the dispensations of Providence, for hail and withering frost and long-continued drouth, wherein the said Evelina Adams might, by reason of being confined to the house by sickness, be prevented from attending the needs of the growing plants, and the verdict in such a case was to rest with the minister and the deacons of the church. But should this beloved Evelina love and wed, or should she let, through any wilful neglect, that garden perish in the season of flowers, all that goodly property would she forfeit to a person unknown, whose name; enclosed in a sealed envelope, was to be held meantime in the hands of the executor, who had also drawn up the will, Lawyer Joshua Lang.

There was great excitement in the village over this strange and unwonted will. Some were there who held that Evelina Adams had not been of sound mind, and it should be contested. It was even rumored that Widow Martha Loomis had visited Lawyer Joshua Land and broached the subject, but he had dismissed the matter peremptorily by telling her that Evelina Adams, spinster, deceased, had been as much in her right mind at the time of drawing the will as anybody of his acquaintance.

"Not setting store by relations, and not wanting to have them under your roof, don't go far in law nor common-sense to send folks to the madhouse," old Lawyer Lang, who was famed for his sharp tongue, was reported to have said. However, Mrs. Martha Loomis was somewhat comforted by her firm belief that either her own name or that of one of her daughters was in the sealed envelope kept by Lawyer Joshua Lang in his strong-box, and by her firm purpose to watch carefully lest Evelina prove derelict in fulfilling the two conditions whereby she held the property.

Larger peep-holes were soon cut away mysteriously in the high arbor-vitae hedge, and therein were often set for a few moments, when they passed that way, the eager eyes of Mrs. Martha or her daughter Flora or Fidelia Loomis. Frequent calls they also made upon Evelina, living alone with the old woman Sarah Judd, who had been called in during her cousin's illness, and they strolled into the garden, spying anxiously for withered leaves or dry stalks. They had at every opportunity interviewed the old man who assisted Evelina in her care of the garden concerning its welfare. But small progress they made with him, standing digging at the earth with his spade while they talked, as if in truth his wits had gone therein before his body and he would uncover them.

Moreover, Mrs. Martha Loomis talked much slyly to mothers of young men, and sometimes with bold insinuations to the young men themselves, of the sad lot of poor young Evelina, condemned to a solitary and loveless life, and of her sweetness and beauty and desirability in herself, although she could not bring the old Squire's money to her husband. And once, but no more than that, she touched lightly upon the subject of the young minister, Thomas Merriam, when he was making a pastoral call.

"My heart bleeds for the poor child living all alone in that great house," said she. And she looked down mournfully, and did not see how white the young minister's face turned. "It seems almost a pity," said she, furthermore—"Evelina is a good housekeeper, and has rare qualities in herself, and so many get poor wives nowadays—that some godly young man should not court her in spite of the will. I doubt, too, if she would not have a happier lot than growing old over that garden, as poor Cousin Evelina did before her, even if she has a fine house to live in and a goodly sum in the bank. She looks pindling enough lately. I'll warrant she has lost a good ten pounds since poor Evelina was laid away, and—"

But Thomas Merriam cut her short. "I see no profit in discussing matters which do not concern us," said he, and only his ministerial estate saved him for the charge of impertinence.

As it was, Martha Loomis colored high. "I'll warrant he'll look out which side his bread is buttered on; ministers always do," she said to her daughters after he had gone. She never dreamed how her talk had cut him to the heart.

Had he not seen more plainly than any one else, Sunday after Sunday, when he glanced down at her once or twice cautiously from his pulpit, how weary-looking and thin she was growing. And her bright color was well-nigh gone, and there were pitiful downward lines at the corners of her sweet mouth. Poor young Evelina was fading like one of her own flowers, as if some celestial gardener had failed in his care of her. And Thomas saw it, and in his heart of hearts he knew the reason, and yet he would not yield. Not once had he entered the old Squire's house since he attended the dead Evelina's funeral, and stood praying and eulogizing, with her coffin between him and the living Evelina, with her pale face shrouded in black bombazine. He had never spoken to her since, nor entered the house; but he had written her a letter, in which all the fierce passion and anguish of his heart was cramped and held down by formal words and phrases, and poor young Evelina did not see beneath them. When her lover wrote her that he felt it inconsistent with his Christian duty and the higher aims of his existence to take any further steps toward a matrimonial alliance, she felt merely that Thomas either cared no more for her, or had come to consider, upon due reflection, that she was not fit to undertake the responsible position of a minister's wife. "It may be that in some way I failed in my attendance upon Cousin Evelina," thought poor young Evelina, "or it may be that he thinks I have not enough dignity of character to inspire respect among the older women in the church." And sometimes, with a sharp thrust of misery that shook her out of her enforced patience and meekness, she wondered if indeed her own loving freedom with him had turned him against her, and led him in his later and sober judgment to consider her too light-minded for a minister's wife. "It may be that I was guilty of great indecorum, and almost indeed forfeited my claim to respect for maidenly modesty, inasmuch as I suffered him to give me kisses, and did not almost bring myself to return them in kind. But my heart did so entreat me, and in truth it seemed almost like a lack of sincerity for me to wholly withstand it," wrote poor young Evelina in her journal that time; and she further wrote: "It is indeed hard for one who has so little knowledge to be fully certain of what is or is not becoming and a Christian duty in matters of this kind; but if I have in any manner, through my ignorance or unwarrantable affection, failed, and so lost the love and respect of a good man, and the opportunity to become his help-meet during life, I pray that I may be forgiven—for I sinned not wilfully—that the lesson may be sanctified unto me, and that I may live as the Lord order, in Christian patience and meekness, and not repining." It never occurred to young Evelina that possibly Thomas Merriam's sense of duty might be strengthened by the loss of all her cousin's property should she marry him, and neither did she dream that he might hesitate to take her from affluence into poverty for her own sake. For herself the property, as put in the balance beside her love, was lighter than air itself. It was so light that it had no place in her consciousness. She simply had thought, upon hearing the will, of Martha Loomis and her daughters in possession of the property, and herself with Thomas, with perfect acquiescence and rapture.

Evelina Adams's disapprobation of her marriage which was supposedly expressed in the will, had indeed, without reference to the property, somewhat troubled her tender heart, but she told herself that Cousin Evelina had not known she had promised to marry Thomas; that she would not wish her to break her solemn promise. And furthermore, it seemed to her quite reasonable that the condition had been inserted in the will mainly through concern for the beloved garden.

"Cousin Evelina might have thought perhaps I would let the flowers die when I had a husband and children to take care of," said Evelina. And so she had disposed of all the considerations which had disturbed her, and had thought of no others.

She did not answer Thomas's letter. It was so worded that it seemed to require no reply, and she felt that he must be sure of her acquiescence in whatever he thought best. She laid the letter away in a little rosewood box, in which she had always kept her dearest treasures since her school days. Sometimes she took it out and read it, and it seemed to her that the pain in her heart would put an end to her in spite of all her prayers for Christian fortitude; and yet she could not help reading it again.

It was seldom that she stole a look at her old lover as he stood in the pulpit in the meeting-house, but when she did she thought with an anxious pang that he looked worn and ill, and that night she prayed that the Lord would restore his health to him for the sake of his people.

It was four months after Evelina Adams's death, and her garden was in the full glory of midsummer, when one evening, toward dusk, young Evelina went slowly down the street. She seldom walked abroad now, but kept herself almost as secluded as her cousin had done before her. But that night a great restlessness was upon her, and she put a little black silk shawl over her shoulders and went out. It was quite cool, although it was midsummer. The dusk was deepening fast; the katydids called back and forth from the wayside bushes. Evelina met nobody for some distance. Then she saw a man coming toward her, and her heart stood still, and she was about to turn back, for she thought for a minute it was the young minister. Then she saw it was his father, and she went on slowly, with her eyes downcast. When she met him she looked up and said good-evening, gravely, and would have passed on, but he stood in her way.

"I've got a word to say to ye, if ye'll listen," he said.

Evelina looked at him tremblingly. There was something strained and solemn in his manner. "I'll hear whatever you have to say, sir," she said.

The old man leaned his pale face over her and raised a shaking forefinger. "I've made up my mind to say something," said he. "I don't know as I've got any right to, and maybe my son will blame me, but I'm goin' to see that ye have a chance. It's been borne in upon me that women folks don't always have a fair chance. It's jest this I'm goin' to say: I don't know whether you know how my son feels about it or not. I don't know how open he is with ye. Do you know jest why he quit ye?"

Evelina shook her head. "No," she panted—"I don't—I never knew. He said it was his duty."

"Duty can get to be an idol of wood and stone, an' I don't know but Thomas's is," said the old man. "Well, I'll tell ye. He don't think it's right for him to marry ye, and make you leave that big house, and lose all that money. He don't care anything about it for himself, but it's for you. Did you know that?"

Then Evelina grasped the old man's arm hard with her little fingers.

"You don't mean that—was why he did it!" she gasped.

"Yes, that was why."

Evelina drew away from him. She was ashamed to have Thomas's father see the joy in her face. "Thank you, sir," she said. "I did not understand. I will write to him."

"Maybe my son will think I have done wrong coming betwixt him and his idees of duty," said old Thomas Merriam, "but sometimes there's a good deal lost for lack of a word, and I wanted ye to have a fair chance an' a fair say. It's been borne in upon me that women folks don't always have it. Now ye can do jest as ye think best, but you must remember one thing—riches ain't all. A little likin' for ye that's goin' to last, and keep honest and faithful to ye as long as ye live, is worth more; an' it's worth more to women folks than 'tis to men, an' it's worth enough to them. My son's poorly. His mother and I are worried about him. He don't eat nor sleep—walks his chamber nights. His mother don't know what the matter is, but he let on to me some time since."

"I'll write a letter to him," gasped Evelina again. "Good-night, sir." She pulled her little black silk shawl over her head and hastened home, and all night long her candle burned, while her weary little fingers toiled over pages of foolscap-paper to convince Thomas Merriam fully, and yet in terms not exceeding maidenly reserve, that the love of his heart and the companionship of his life were worth more to her than all the silver and gold in the world. Then the next morning she dispatched it, all neatly folded and sealed, and waited.

It was strange that a letter like that could not have moved Thomas Merriam, when his heart too pleaded with him so hard to be moved. But that might have been the very reason why he could withstand her, and why the consciousness of his own weakness gave him strength. Thomas Merriam was one, when he had once fairly laid hold of duty, to grasp it hard, although it might be to his own pain and death, and maybe to that of others. He wrote to poor young Evelina another letter in which he emphasized and repeated his strict adherence to what he believed the line of duty in their separation, and ended it with a prayer for her welfare and happiness, in which, indeed, for a second, the passionate heart of the man showed forth. Then he locked himself in his chamber, and nobody ever knew what he suffered there. But one pang he did not suffer which Evelina would have suffered in his place. He mourned not over nor realized the grief of her tender heart when she should read his letter, otherwise he could not have sent it. He writhed under his own pain alone, and his duty hugged him hard, like the iron maiden of the old tortures but he would not yield.

As for Evelina, when she got his letter, and had read it through, she sat still and white for a long time, and did not seem to hear when old Sarah Judd spoke to her. But at last she rose up and went to her chamber, and knelt down, and prayed for a long time; and then she went out in the garden and cut all the most beautiful flowers, and tied them in wreaths and bouquets, and carried them out to the north side of the house, where her cousin Evelina was buried, and covered her grave with them. And then she knelt down there and hid her face among them, and said, in a low voice, as if in a listening ear, "I pray you, Cousin Evelina, forgive me for what I am about to do."

And then she returned to the house, and sat at her needle-work as usual; but the old woman kept looking at her, and asking if she were sick, for there was a strange look in her face.

She and old Sarah Judd had always their tea at five o'clock, and put the candles out at nine, and this night they did as they were wont. But at one o'clock in the morning young Evelina stole softly down the stairs with her lighted candle, and passed through into the kitchen; and a half-hour after she came forth into the garden, which lay in full moonlight, and she had in her hand a steaming teakettle, and she passed around among the shrubs and watered them, and a white cloud of steam rose around them. Back and forth she went to the kitchen; for she had heated the great copper wash-kettle full of water; and she watered all the shrubs in the garden, moving amid curling white wreaths of steam, until the water was gone. And then she set to work and tore up the roots with her little hands and trampled with her little feet all the beautiful tender flower-beds; all the time weeping, and moaning softly: "Poor Cousin Evelina! Poor cousin Evelina! Oh, forgive me, poor Cousin Evelina!"

And at dawn the garden lay in ruin, for all the tender plants she had torn up by the roots and trampled down, and all the stronger-rooted shrubs she had striven to kill with boiling water and salt.

Then Evelina went into the house, and made herself tidy as well as she could when she trembled so, and put her little shawl over her head, and went down the road to the Merriams' house. It was so early the village was scarcely astir, but there was smoke coming out of the kitchen chimney at the Merriams'; and when she knocked, Mrs. Merriam opened the door at once, and stared at her.

"Is Sarah Judd dead?" she cried; for her first thought was that something must have happened when she saw the girl standing there with her wild pale face.

"I want to see the minister," said Evelina, faintly, and she looked at Thomas's mother with piteous eyes.

"Be you sick?" asked Mrs. Merriam. She laid a hard hand on the girl's arm, and led her into the sitting-room, and put her into the rocking-chair with the feather cushion. "You look real poorly," said she. "Shan't I get you a little of my elderberry wine?"

"I want to see him," said Evelina, and she almost sobbed.

"I'll go right and speak to him," said Mrs. Merriam. "He's up, I guess. He gets up early to write. But hadn't I better get you something to take first? You do look sick."

But Evelina only shook her head. She had her face covered with her hands, and was weeping softly. Mrs. Merriam left the room with a long backward glance at her. Presently the door opened and Thomas came in. Evelina stood up before him. Her pale face was all wet with tears, but there was an air of strange triumph about her.

"The garden is dead," said she.

"What do you mean?" he cried out, staring at her, for indeed he thought for a minute that her wits had left her.

"The garden is dead," said she. "Last night I watered the roses with boiling water and salt, and I pulled the other flowers up by their roots. The garden is dead, and I have lost all Cousin Evelina's money, and it need not come between us any longer." She said that, and looked up in his face with her blue eyes, through which the love of the whole face of loving women from which she had sprung, as well as her own, seemed to look, and held out her little hands; but even then Thomas Merriam could not understand and stood looking at her.

"Why did you do it?" he stammered.

"Because you would have me no other way, and I couldn't bear that anything like that should come between us," she said, and her voice shook like a harpstring, and her pale face went red, then pale again.

But Thomas still stood staring at her. Then her heart failed her. She thought that he did not care, and she had been mistaken. She felt as if it were the hour of her death, and turned to go. And then he caught her in his arms.

"Oh," he cried, out—breaking with a great sob, "the Lord make me worthy of thee, Evelina."

There had never been so much excitement in the village as when the fact of the ruined garden came to light. Flora Loomis, peeping through the hedge on her way to the store, had spied it first. Then she had run home for her mother, who had in turn sought Lawyer Lang, panting bonnetless down the road. But before the lawyer had started for the scene of disaster, the minister, Thomas Merriam had appeared, and asked for a word in private with him. Nobody ever knew just what that word was, but the lawyer was singularly uncommunicative and reticent as to the ruined garden.

"Do you think the young woman is out of her mind?" one of the deacons asked him, in a whisper.

"I wish all the young women were as much in their minds; we'd have a better world," said the lawyer, gruffly.

"When do you think we can begin to move in here?" asked Mrs. Martha Loomis, her wide skirts sweeping a bed of uprooted verbenas.

"When your claim is established," returned the lawyer, shortly, and turned on his heel and went away, his dry old face scanning the ground like a dog on a scent. That afternoon he opened the sealed document in the presence of witnesses, and the name of the heir to whom the property fell was disclosed. It was "Thomas Merriam, the beloved and esteemed minister of this parish," and young Evelina would gain her wealth instead of losing it by her marriage. And furthermore, after the declaration of the name of the heir was this added: "This do I in the hope and belief that neither the greed of riches nor the fear of them shall prevent that which is good and wise in the sight of the Lord, and with the surety that a love which shall triumph over so much in its way shall endure, and shall be a blessing and not a curse to my beloved cousin Evelina Leonard."

Thomas Merriam and Evelina were married before the leaves fell in that same year, by the minister of the next village, who rode over in his chaise, and brought his wife, who was also a bride, and wore her wedding dress of a pink and pearl shot silk. But young Evelina wore the blue bridal array which had been worn by old Squire Adams's bride, all remodeled daintily to suit the fashion of the times; and as she moved, the folds shook out the fragrance of roses and lavender of the old summers during which it had been laid away, like sweet memories.

"The Revolt of Sophia Lane"

Harper's New Monthly, December 1903

The level of new snow in Sophia Lane's north yard was broken by horse's tracks and the marks of sleigh-runners. Sophia's second cousin, Mrs. Adoniram Cutting, her married daughter Abby Dodd, and unmarried daughter Eunice had driven over from Addison, and put up their horse and sleigh in Sophia's clean, unused barn.

When Sophia had heard the sleigh-bells she had peered eagerly out of the window of the sitting-room and dropped her sewing. "Here's Ellen and Abby and Eunice," she cried, "and they've brought you some wedding-presents. Flora Bell, you put the shawl over your head, and go out through the shed and open the barn. I'll tell them to drive right in."

With that the girl and the woman scuttled—Flora Bell through the house and shed to the barn which joined it; Sophia, to the front door of the house, which she pushed open with some difficulty on account of the banked snow. Then she called to the women in the sleigh, which had stopped at the entrance to the north yard: "Drive right in—drive right in. Flora has gone to open the barn doors. She'll be there by the time you get there."

Then Sophia ran through the house to the kitchen, set the teakettle forward, and measured some tea into the teapot. She moved with the greatest swiftness, as if the tea in so many seconds were a vital necessity. When the guests came in from the barn she greeted them breathlessly. "Go right into the sittin'-room," said she. "Flora, you take their things and put them on the bedroom bed. Set right down by the stove and get warm, and the tea'll be ready in a minute. The water's 'most boilin'. You must be 'most froze." The three women, who were shapeless bundles from their wraps, moved clumsily into the sitting-room as before a spanking breeze of will. Flora followed them; she moved more slowly than her aunt, who was a miracle of nervous speed. Sophia Lane never walked; she ran to all her duties and pleasures as if she were racing against time. She hastened the boiling of the teakettle—she poked the fire; she thrust light slivers of wood into the stove. When the water boiled she made the tea with a rush, and carried the tray with cups and saucers into the sitting-room with a perilous sidewise tilt and flirt. But nothing was spilled. It was very seldom that Sophia came to grief through her haste.

The three women had their wraps removed, and were sitting around the stove. The eldest, Mrs. Ellen Cutting—a stout woman with a handsome face reddened with cold,—spoke when Sophia entered.

"Land! if you haven't gone and made hot tea!" said she.

Sophia set the tray down with a jerk, and the cups hopped in their saucers. "Well, I guess you need some," said she, speaking as fast as she moved. "It's a bitter day; you must be froze."

"Yes, it is awful cold," asserted Abby Dodd, the married daughter, "but I told mother and Eunice we'd got to come to-day, whether or no. I was bound we should get over here before the wedding."

"Look at Flora blush!" giggled Eunice, the youngest and the unmarried daughter.

Indeed, Flora Bell, who was not pretty, but tall and slender and graceful, was a deep pink all over her delicate face to the roots of her fair hair.

"You wait till your turn comes, Sis, and see what you'll do," said Abby Dodd, who resembled her mother, being fat and pink and white, with a dumpy, slightly round-shouldered figure in a pink flannel shirt-waist frilled with lace. All the newcomers were well dressed, the youngest daughter especially. They had a prosperous air, and they made Sophia's small and frugal sitting-room seem more contracted than usual. Both Sophia and her niece were dressed in garments which the visitors would characterize later among themselves, with a certain scorn tinctured with pity, as "fadged up." They were not shabby, they were not exactly poor, but they were painfully and futilely aspiring. "If only they would not trim quite so much," Eunice Cutting said later. But Sophia dearly loved trimming; and as for Flora, she loved whatever her aunt Sophia did. Sophia had adopted her when her parents died, when she was a baby, and had brought her up on a pittance a year. Flora was to be married to Herbert Bennet on the next day but one. She was hurrying her bridal preparations, and she was in a sort of delirium of triumph, of pride, of happiness and timidity. She was the centre of attention to-day. The visitors' eyes were all upon her with a half-kindly half-humorous curiosity.

On the lounge at the side of the room opposite the stove were three packages beautifully done up in white paper and tied with red and green ribbons. Sophia had spied them the moment she entered the room.

The guests comfortably sipped their tea.

"Is it sweet enough?" asked Sophia of Mrs. Cutting, thrusting the white sugar-bowl at her.

"Plenty," replied Mrs. Cutting. "This tea does go right to the spot. I did get chilled."

"I thought you would."

"Yes, and I don't like to, especially since it is just a year ago since I had pneumonia, but Abby thought we must come to-day, and I thought so myself. I thought we wanted to have one more look at Flora before she was a bride."

"Flora's got to go out now to try on her weddin'-dress the last time," said Sophia. "Miss Beals has been awful hurried at the last minute; she don't turn off work very fast, and the dress won't be done till to-night; but everything else is finished."

"I suppose you've had a lot of presents, Flora," said Abby Dodd.

"Quite a lot," replied Flora, blushing.

"Yes, she's had some real nice presents, and two or three that ain't quite so nice," said Sophia, "but I guess those can be changed."

Mrs. Cutting glanced at the packages on the sofa with an air of confidence and pride. "We have brought over some little things," said she. "Adoniram and I give one, and Abby and Eunice each one. I hope you'll like them, Flora."

Flora was very rosy; she smiled with a charming effect, as if she were timid before her own delight. "Thank you," she murmured. "I know they are lovely."

"Do go and open them, Flora," said Eunice. "See if you have any other presents like them."

"Yes, open them, Flora," said Mrs. Cutting, with pleasant patronage.

Flora made an eager little movement toward the presents, then she looked wistfully at her aunt Sophia.

Sophia was smiling with a little reserve. "Yes, go and open them, Flora," said she; "then bring out your other presents and show them."

Flora's drab skirt and purple ruffles swayed gracefully across the room; she gathered up the packages in her slender arms, and brought them over to the table between the windows, where her aunt sat. Flora began untying the red and green ribbons, while the visitors looked on with joyful and smiling importance. On one package was marked "Flora, with all best wishes for her future happiness, from Mr. and Mrs. Adoniram Cutting."

"That is ours," said Mrs. Cutting.

Flora took off the white paper, and a nice white box was revealed. She removed the lid and took out a mass of crumpled tissue-paper. It was in three pieces. When she had set them on the table, she viewed them with admiration but bewilderment. She looked from one to the other, smiling vaguely.

Abby Dodd laughed. "Why, she doesn't know how to put them together!" said she. She went to the table and quickly adjusted the different parts of the present. "There!" said she, triumphantly.

"What a beautiful—teakettle!" said Flora, but still in a bewildered fashion.

Sophia was regarding it with an odd expression. "What is it?" she asked, shortly.

"Why, Sophia," cried Mrs. Cutting, "don't you know? It is an afternoon-tea kettle."

"What's that thing under it?" asked Sophia.

"Why, that's the alcohol-lamp. It swings on that little frame over the lamp and heats the water. I thought it would be so nice for her."

"It's beautiful," said Flora.

Sophia said nothing.

"It is real silver; it isn't plated," said Mrs. Cutting, in a slightly grieved tone.

"It is beautiful," Flora murmured again, but Sophia said nothing.

Flora began opening another package. It was quite bulky. It was marked "Flora, with best wishes for a life of love and happiness, from Abby Dodd."

"Be careful," charged Abby Dodd. "It's glass."

Flora removed the paper gingerly. The present was rolled in tissue-paper.

"What beautiful dishes!" said she, but her voice was again slightly bewildered.

Sophia looked at the present with considerable interest. "What be the bowls for?" said she. "Oatmeal?"

The visitors all laughed.

"Oatmeal!" cried Abby. "Why, they are finger-bowls!"

"Finger-bowls?" repeated Sophia, with a plainly hostile air.

"Yes,—bowls to dip your fingers in after dinner," said Abby.

"What for?" asked Sophia.

"Why, to—to wash them."

"We wash our hands in the washbasin in the kitchen with good hot water and soap," said Sophia.

"Oh, but these are not really to wash the hands in—just to dabble the fingers in," said Eunice, still giggling. "It's the style. You have them in little plates with doilies and pass them around after dinner."

"They are real pretty," said Flora.

Sophia said nothing.

"They are real cut glass," said Mrs. Cutting.

Flora turned to the third package, that was small and flat and exceedingly dainty. The red and green ribbon was tied in a charming bow with Eunice's visiting-card. On the back of the card was written, "Flora, with dearest love, and wishes for a life of happiness, from Eunice." Flora removed the ribbons and the white paper, and opened a flat white box, disclosing six dainty squares of linen embroidered with violets.

"What lovely mats!" said she.

"They are finger-bowl doilies," said Eunice, radiantly.

"To set the bowls on?" said Flora.

"Yes; you use pretty plates, put a doily in each plate, and then the finger bowl on the doily."

"They are lovely," said Flora.

Sophia said nothing.

Abby looked rather aggrievedly at Sophia. "Eunice and I thought Flora would like them as well as anything we could give her," said she.

"They are lovely," Flora said again.

"You haven't any like them, have you?" Abby asked, rather uneasily.

"No, she hasn't," answered Sophia for her niece.

"We tried to think of some things that everybody else wouldn't give her," said Mrs. Cutting.

"Yes, you have," Sophia answered dryly.

"They are all beautiful," said Flora, in a soft, anxiously deprecating voice, as she gathered up the presents. "I keep my presents in the parlor," she remarked further. "I guess I'll put these in there with the rest."

Presently she returned, bringing a large box; she set it down and returned for another. They were large suit-boxes. She placed them on the table, and the visitors gathered round.

"I've had beautiful presents," said Flora.

"Yes, she has had some pretty nice presents," assented Sophia. "Most of them are real nice."

Flora stood beside the table and lifted tenderly from the box one wedding-gift after another. She was full of shy pride. The visitors admired everything. When Flora had displayed the contents of the two boxes, she brought out a large picture in an ornate gilt frame, and finally wheeled through the door with difficulty a patent rocker upholstered with red crushed plush.

"That's from some of his folks," said Sophia. "I call it a handsome present."

"I'm going to have a table from his aunt Jane," remarked Flora.

"Sit down in that chair and see how easy it is," said Sophia, imperatively, to Mrs. Cutting, who obeyed meekly, although the crushed plush was so icy cold from its sojourn in the parlor that it seemed to embrace her with deadly arms and made her have visions of pneumonia.

"It's as easy a chair as I ever sat in," she said, rising hastily.

"Leave it out here and let her set in it while she is here," said Sophia, and Mrs. Cutting sank back into the chair, although she did ask for a little shawl for her shoulders.

Mrs. Cutting had always had a wholesome respect for her cousin Sophia Lane, although she had a certain feeling of superiority by reason of her wealth. Even while she looked about Sophia's poor little sitting-room and recalled her own fine parlors, she had a sense that Sophia was throned on such mental heights above mahogany and plush and tapestry that she could not touch her with a finger of petty scorn even if she wished.

After Flora had displayed her presents and carried them back to the parlor, she excused herself and went to the dressmaker's to try on her wedding-dress.

After Flora had gone out of the yard, looking abnormally stout with the gay plaid shawl over the coat and her head rolled in a thick old worsted hood of Sophia's, Mrs. Cutting opened on a subject about which she was exceedingly curious.

"I'm real sorry we can't have a glimpse of the wedding-dress," said she, ingratiatingly.

Sophia gave an odd sort of grunt in response. Sophia always gave utterance to that nondescript sound, which was neither assent nor dissent, but open to almost any interpretation, when she wished to evade a lie. She was in reality very glad that the wedding-dress was not on exhibition. She thought it much better that it should not be seen in its full glory until the wedding-day.

"Flora has got many good presents," said Sophia, "and few tomfool ones, thanks to me and what I did last Christmas."

"What do you mean, Sophia?" asked Mrs. Cutting.

"Didn't you hear what I did, Ellen Cutting?"

"No, I didn't hear a word about it."

"Well, I didn't know but somebody might have told. I wasn't a mite ashamed of it, and I ain't now. I'd do the same thing over again if it was necessary, but I guess it won't be; I guess they got a good lesson. I dare say they were kind of huffy at the time. I guess they got over it. They've all give Flora presents now, anyhow, except Angeline White, and I guess she will."

"Why, what did you do?" asked Abby Dodd, with round eyes of interest on Sophia.

"Why, I'd jest as soon tell you as not," replied Sophia. "I've got some cake in the oven. Jest let me take a peek at that first."

"Wedding-cake?" asked Eunice, as Sophia ran out of the room.

"Land, no!" she called back. "That was made six weeks ago. Weddin'-cake wouldn't be worth anything baked now."

"Eunice, didn't you know better than that?" cried her mother.

"It's white cake," Sophia's explanatory voice came from the kitchen, whence sweet odors floated into the room. The oven door opened and shut with an exceedingly swift click like a pistol-shot.

"I should think she'd make the cake fall, slamming the oven door like that," murmured Abby Dodd.

"So should I; but it won't," assented her mother. "I never knew Sophia to fail with her cake."

Sophia flew back into the sitting-room and plumped into her chair; she had, indeed, risen with such impetus and been so quick that the chair had not ceased rocking since she left it. "It's done," said she; "I took it out. I'll let it stand in the pan and steam a while before I do anything more with it. Now I'll tell you what I did about Flora's Christmas presents last year if you want me to. I'd jest as soon as not. If I hadn't done what I did, there wouldn't have been any weddin' this winter, I can tell you that."

"You don't say so!" cried Mrs. Cutting, and the others stared.

"No, there wouldn't. You know, Herbert and Flora have been goin' together three years this December. Well, they'd have been goin' together three years more, and I don't know but they'd been goin' together till doomsday, if I hadn't taken matters into my own hand. I ain't never been married myself, and maybe folks think I ain't any right to my opinion, but I've always said I didn't approve of young folks goin' together so long unless they get married. When they're married, and any little thing comes up that one or the other don't think quite so nice, why, they put up with it, and make the best of it, and kind of belittle that and make more of the things that they do like. But when they ain't married it's different. I don't care how much they think of each other, something may come up to make him or her kind of wonder if t'other is good enough to marry, after all. Well, nothin' of that kind has happened with Flora and Herbert Bennet, and I ain't sayin' there has. They went together them three years, and, far as I can see, they think each other is better than in the beginnin'. Well, as I was sayin', it seemed to me that those two had ought to get married before long if they were ever goin' to, but I must confess I didn't see how they were any nearer it than when they started keepin' company."

"Herbert has been pretty handicapped," remarked Mrs. Cutting.

"Handicapped? Well, I rather guess he has! He was young when his father died, and when his mother had that dreadful sickness and had to go to the hospital, he couldn't keep up the taxes, and the interest on the mortgage got behindhand; the house was mortgaged when his father died, and it had to go; he's had to hire ever since. They're comin' here to live; you knew that, I s'pose?"

"Sophia, you don't mean his mother is coming here to live?"

"Why not? I'm mighty glad the poor woman's goin' to have a good home in her old age. She's a good woman as ever was, just as mild-spoken, and smart too. I'm tickled to death to think she's comin', and so's Flora. Flora sets her eyes by his mother."

"Well, you know your own business, but I must say I think it's a considerable undertaking."

"Well, I don't. I'd like to know what you'd have her do. Herbert can't afford to support two establishments, no more than he earns, and he ain't goin' to turn his mother out to earn her bread an' butter at her time of life, I rather guess. No; she's comin' here, and she's goin' to have the south chamber; she's goin' to furnish it. I never see a happier woman; and as for Herbert—well, he has had a hard time, and now things begin to look brighter; but I declare, about a year ago, as far as I could see, it didn't look as if he and Flora ever could get married. One evenin' the poor fellow came here, and he talked real plain; he said he felt as if he'd ought to. He said he'd been comin' here a long time, and he'd begun to think that he and Flora might keep on that way until they were gray, so far as he could help it. There he was, he said, workin' in Edgcomb's store at seven dollars a week, and had his mother to keep, and he couldn't see any prospect of anything better. He said maybe if he wasn't goin' with Flora she might get somebody else. 'It ain't fair to Flora,' said he. And with that he heaves a great sigh, and the first thing I knew, right before me, Flora she was in his lap, huggin' him, and cryin', and sayin' she'd never leave him for any man on the face of the earth, and she didn't ask anything any better than to wait. They'd both wait and be patient and trust in God, and she was jest as happy as she could be, and she wouldn't change places with the Queen. First thing I knew I was cryin' too; I couldn't help it; and Herbert, poor fellow, he fetched a big sob himself, and I didn't think none the worse of him for it. 'Seems as if I must be sort of lackin' somehow, to make such a failure of things,' says he, kind of broken like.

"'You ain't lackin',' says Flora, real fierce like. 'It ain't you that's to blame. Fate's against you and always has been.'

"'Now you look round before you blame the Lord,' says I at that—for when folks say fate they always mean the Lord. 'Mebbe it ain't the Lord,' says I; 'mebbe it's folks. Wouldn't your uncle Hiram give you a lift, Herbert?'

"'Uncle Hiram!' says he; but not a bit scornful—real good-natured.

"'Why? I don't see why not,' says I. 'He always gives nice Christmas presents to you and your mother, don't he?'

"'Yes,' says he. 'He gives Christmas presents.'

"'Real nice ones?'

"'Yes,' said poor Herbert, kind of chucklin', but real good-natured. 'Last Christmas Uncle Hiram gave mother a silver card-case, and me a silver ash-receiver.'

"'But you don't smoke?' says I.

"'No,' says he, 'and mother hasn't got any visitin'-cards.'

"'I suppose he didn't know, along of not livin' in the same place,' says I.

"'No,' says he. 'They were real handsome things—solid; must have cost a lot of money.'

"'What would you do if you could get a little money, Herbert?' says I.

"Bless you! he knew quick enough. Didn't have to study over it a minute.

"'I'd buy that piece of land next your house here,' says he, 'and I'd keep cows and start a milk route. There's need of one here,' says he, 'and it's just what I've always thought I'd like to do; but it takes money,' he finishes up, with another of them heart-breakin' sighs of his, 'an' I ain't got a cent.'

"'Something will happen so you can have the milk route,' says Flora, and she kisses him right before me, and I was glad she did. I never approved of young folks bein' silly, but this was different. When a man feels as bad as Herbert Bennet did that day, if the woman that's goin' to marry him can comfort him any, she'd ought to.

"'Yes,' says I, 'something will surely happen. You jest keep your grit up, Herbert.'

"'How you women do stand by me!' says Herbert, and his voice broke again, and I was pretty near cryin'.

"'Well, we're goin' to stand by you jest as long as you are as good as you be now,' says I. 'The tide'll turn before long.'

"I hadn't any more than got the words out of my mouth before the express drove up to the door, and there were three Christmas presents for Flora, early as it was, three days before Christmas. Christmas presents so long beforehand always make me a little suspicious, as if mebbe folks wanted other folks to be sure they were goin' to have something. Flora she'd always made real handsome presents to every one of them three that sent those that day. One was Herbert's aunt Harriet Morse, one was Cousin Jane Adkins over to Gorham, and the other was Mis' Crocker, she that was Emma Ladd; she's a second cousin of Flora's father's. Well, them three presents came, and we undid them. Then we looked at 'em. 'Great Jehosophat,' says I. Herbert he grinned, then he said something I didn't hear, and Flora she looked as if she didn't know whether to laugh or cry. There Flora she didn't have any money to put into presents, of course, but you know what beautiful fancy-work she does, and there she's been workin' ever since the Christmas before, and she made a beautiful centerpiece and a bureau scarf and a lace handkerchief for those three women, and there they had sent her a sort of a dewdab to wear in her hair! Pretty enough, looked as if it cost considerable—a pink rose with spangles, and a feather shootin' out of it; but Lord! If Flora had come out in that thing anywhere she'd go in Brookville, she'd scared the natives. It was all right where Herbert's aunt Harriet lived. Ayres is a city, but in this town, 'way from a railroad—goodness!

"Well, there was that; and Cousin Jane Adkins had sent her a Japanese silk shawl, all over embroidery, as handsome as a picture; but there was poor Flora wantin' some cotton cloth for her weddin' fix, and not a cent to buy a thing with. My sheets and pillow-cases and table-linen that I had from poor mother was about worn out, and Flora was wonderin' how she'd ever get any. But there Jane had sent that shawl, that cost nobody knew how much, when she knew Flora wanted the other things,—because I'd told her. But Mis' Crocker's was the worst of all. She's a widow with a lot of money, and she's put on a good many airs. I dun'no' as you know her. No, I thought you didn't. Well, she does feel terrible airy. She sent poor Flora a set of chessmen, all red and white ivory, beautifully carved, and a table to keep 'em on. I must say I was so green I didn't know what they were when I first saw 'em. Flora knew; she'd seen some somewhere she'd been.

"'For the land sake! what's them little dolls and horses for?' says I. 'It looks like Noah's ark without the ark.'

"'It's a set of chess and a table,' said Flora, and she looked ready to cry, poor child. She thought, when she got that great package, that she really had got something she wanted that time, sure.

"'Chess?' says I.

"'A game,' says Flora.

"'A game?' says I.

"'To play,' says she.

"'Do you know how to play it, Flora?' says I.

"'No,' says she.

"'Does Herbert?'

"'No.'

"'Well,' says I, and I spoke right out, 'of all the things to give anybody that needs things!'

"Flora was readin' the note that came with it. Jane Crocker said in the note that in givin' her Christmas present this year she was havin' a little eye on the future—and she underlined the future. She was twittin' Flora a little about her waitin' so long, and I knew it. Jane Crocker is a good woman enough, but she's got claws. She said she had an eye on the *underlined* future, and she said a chess set and a table were so stylish in a parlor. She didn't say a word about playin'.

"'Does she play that game?' says I to Flora.

"'I don't know,' says Flora. She didn't; I found out afterward. She didn't know a single blessed thing about the game.

"Well, I looked at that present of poor Flora's, and I felt as if I should give up. 'How much do you s'pose that thing cost?' says I. Then I saw she had left the tag on. I looked. I didn't care a mite. I don't know where she got it. Wherever it was, she got cheated, if I know anything about it. There Jane Crocker had paid forty dollars for that thing.

"'Why didn't she give forty dollars for a Noah's ark and done with it?' says I. 'I'd jest as soon have one. Go and put it in the parlor,' says I.

"And poor Flora and Herbert lugged it into the parlor. She was almost cryin'.

"Well, the things kept comin' that Christmas. We both had a good many presents, and it did seem as if they were worse than they had ever been before. They had always been pretty bad. I don't care if I do say it." There was a faint defiance in Sophia's voice. Mrs. Cutting and her daughters glanced imperceptibly at one another. A faint red showed on Mrs. Cutting's cheeks.

"Yes," repeated Sophia, firmly, "they always had been pretty bad. We had tried to be grateful but it was the truth. There were so many things Flora and I wanted, and it did seem sometimes as if everybody that gave us Christmas presents sat up a week of Sundays tryin' to think of something to give us that we didn't want. There was Lizzie Starkwether; she gave us bed-shoes. She gave us bed-shoes the winter before, and the winter before that, but that didn't make a mite of difference. She kept right on givin' 'em, red and black bed-shoes. There she knits beautiful mittens or wristers, and we both wanted mittens or wristers; but no, we got bed-shoes. Flora and me never wear bed-shoes, and, what's more, I'd told Lizzie Starkwether so. I had a chance to do it when I thought I wouldn't hurt her feelin's. But that didn't make any difference; the bed-shoes come right along. I must say I was mad when I saw them that last time. 'I must say I don't call this a present; I call it a kick,' says I, and I'm ashamed to say I gave them bed-shoes a fling. There poor Flora had been sittin' up nights makin' a white apron trimmed with knit lace for Lizzie, because she knew she wanted one.

"Well, so it went; everything that come was a little more something we didn't want, especially Flora's; and she didn't say anything, but tried to look as if she was tickled to death; and she sent off the nice, pretty things she'd worked so hard to make, and every single one of them things, if I do say it, had been studied over an hour to every minute the ones she got had. Flora always tried not to give so much what she likes as what the one she's givin' to likes; and when I saw what she was gettin' back I got madder an' madder. I s'pose I wasn't showin' a Christian spirit, and Flora said so. She said she didn't give presents to get their worth back, and if they liked what she gave, that was worth more than anything. I could have felt that way if they'd been mine, but I couldn't when they were Flora's, and when the poor child had so little, and couldn't get married on account of it, too. Christmas mornin' came Herbert's rich uncle Hiram's present. It came while we were eatin' breakfast, about eight o'clock. We were rather late that mornin'. Well, the expressman drove into the yard, and he left a nice little package, and I saw the Leviston express mark on it, and I says to Flora, 'This must come from Herbert's uncle Hiram, and I shouldn't wonder if you had got something real nice.'

"Well, we undid it, and if there wasn't another silver card-case, the same style as Herbert's mother had given her the Christmas before. Well, Flora has got some visitin'-cards, but the idea of her carryin' a silver card-case like that when she went callin'! Why, she wouldn't have had anything else that come up to that card-case! Flora didn't say much, but I could see her lips quiver. She jest put it away, and pretty soon Herbert run in—he was out with the delivery wagon from the store, and he stopped a second. He didn't stay long,—he was too conscientious about his employer's time,—but he stayed long enough to tell about his and his mother's Christmas presents from his uncle Hiram, and what do you think they had that time? Why, Herbert had a silver cigarette-case, and he never smokin' at all, and his mother had a cut-glass wine set.

"Well, I didn't say much, but I was makin' up my mind. I was makin' it up slow, but I was makin' it up firm. Some more presents came that forenoon, and not a thing Flora wanted, except some ironin' holders from Cousin Ann Drake, and me a gingham apron from her. Yes, Flora did have another present she wanted, and that was a handkerchief come through the mail from the school-teacher that used to board here—a real nice fine one. But the rest—well, there was a sofa pillow painted with wild roses on boltin'-cloth, and there every sofa we'd got to lay down on in the house was this lounge here. We'd never have a sofa in the parlor, and Minerva Saunders—she sent it—knew it; and I'd like to know how much we could use a painted white boltin'-cloth pillow here? Minerva was rich, too, and I knew the pillow cost enough. And Mis' George Harris, she that was Minnie Beard—she was Flora's own cousin, you know,— what did she send but a brass fire-set—poker and tongs and things,— and here we ain't got an open fireplace in the house, and she knew it. But Minnie never did have much sense; I never laid it up against her.

She meant well, and she's sent Flora some beautiful napkins and table-cloths; I told her that was what she wanted for a weddin'-present. Well, as I was sayin', I was makin' up my mind slow but firm, and by afternoon it was made up. Says I to Flora: 'I wish you'd go over to Mr. Martin's and ask him if I can have his horse and sleigh this afternoon. Tell him I'll pay him.' He never takes any pay, but I always offer. Flora said: 'Why, Aunt Sophia, you ain't goin' out this afternoon! It looks as if it would snow every minute.'

"'Yes, I be,' says I.

"Well, Flora went over and asked, and Mr. Martin said I was welcome to the horse and sleigh—he's always real accommodatin'—and he hitched up himself and brought it over about one o'clock. I thought I'd start early, because it did threaten snow. I got Flora out of the way—sent her down to the store to get some sugar; we were goin' to make cake when I got home, and we were all out of powdered sugar. When that sleigh come I jest bundled all them presents—except the apron and holders and the two or three other things that was presents, because the folks that give 'em had studied up what Flora wanted, and given to her instead of themselves,—an' I stowed them all in that sleigh, under the seat and on it, and covered them up with the robe.

"Then I wrapped up real warm, because it was bitter cold—seemed almost too cold to snow,—and I put a hot soapstone in the sleigh, and I gathered up the reins, an' I slapped 'em over the old horse's back, and I set out.

"I thought I'd go to Jane Crocker's first,—I wanted to get rid of that chess table; it took up so much room in the sleigh I hadn't any place to put my feet, and the robe kept slippin' off it. So I drove right there. Jane was to home: the girl came to the door, and I went into the parlor. I hadn't been to call on Jane for some time, and she'd got a number of new things I hadn't seen, and the first thing I saw was a chess-table and all them little red and white Noah's-ark things, jest like the one she sent us. When Jane come in, dressed in black silk stiff enough to stand alone—though she wa'n't goin' anywheres and it looked like snow,—I jest stood right up. I'd brought in the table and the box of little jiggers, and I goes right to the point. I had to. I had to drive six miles to Ayres before I got through, and there it was spittin' snow already.

"'Good afternoon, Jane,' says I. 'I've brought back your presents.'

"Jane she kind of gasped, and she turned pale. She has a good deal of color; she's a pretty woman; well, it jest slumped right out of her cheeks. 'Mercy! Sophia,' says she, 'what do you mean?'

"'Jest what I say, Jane,' says I. 'You've sent Flora some playthings that cost forty dollars—you left the tags on, so we know,—and they ain't anything she has any use for. She don't know how to play chess, and neither does Herbert; and if they did know, they wouldn't neither of 'em have any time, unless it was Sundays, and then it would be wicked.'

"'Oh, Lord! Sophia,' says she, kind of chokin', 'I don't know how to play myself, but I've got one for an ornament, and I thought Flora—'

"'Flora will have to do without forty-dollar ornaments, if ever she gets money enough to get married at all,' says I, 'and I don't think a Noah's ark set on a table marked up in squares is much of an ornament, anyhow.'

"I didn't say any more. I jest marched out and left the presents. But Jane she came runnin' after me. 'Sophia,' says she—and she spoke as if she was sort of scared. She never had much spunk, for all she looks so up an' comin'—'Sophia,' says she, 'I thought she'd like it. I thought—'

"'No, you didn't, Jane Crocker,' says I. 'You jest thought what you'd like to give, and not what she'd like to have.'

"'What would she like to have?' says she, and she was 'most cryin'. 'I'll get her anything she wants, if you'll jest tell me, Sophia.'

"'I ain't goin' to tell you, Jane,' says I, but I spoke softer, for I saw that she meant well, after all,—'I ain't goin' to tell you. You jest put yourself in her place; you make believe you was a poor young girl goin' to get married, and you think over what little the poor child has got now and what she has to set alongside new things, and you kind of study it out for yourself,' says I. And then I jest said good-by, though she kept callin' after me, and I run out and climbed in the sleigh and tucked myself in and drove off.

"The very next day Jane Crocker sent Flora a beautiful new carpet for the front chamber, and a rug to go with it. She knew Flora was goin' to have the front chamber fixed up when she got married; she'd heard me say so; and the carpet was all worn out.

"Well, I kept right on. I carried back Cousin Abby Adkins's white silk shawl, and she acted awful mad; but she thought better of it as I was goin' out to the sleigh, and she called after me to know what Flora wanted, and I told her jest what I had Jane Crocker. And I carried back Minerva Saunders's boltin'-cloth sofa pillow, and she was more astonished than anything else—she was real good-natured. You know how easy she is. She jest laughed after she'd got over bein' astonished. 'Why,' says she, 'I don't know but it is kind of silly, now I come to think of it. I declare I clean forgot you didn't have a sofa in the parlor. When I've been in there I've been so took up seein' you and Flora, Sophia, that I never took any account at all of the furniture.'

"So I went away from there feelin' real good, and the next day but one there come a nice haircloth sofa for Flora to put in the parlor.

"Then I took back Minnie Harris's fire-set, and she acted kind of dazed. 'Why, don't you think it's handsome?' says she. You know she's a young thing, younger than Flora. She's always called me Aunt Sophia, too. 'Why, Aunt Sophia,' says she, 'didn't Flora think it was handsome?'

"'Handsome enough, child,' says I, and I couldn't help laughin' myself, she looked like sech a baby,—'handsome enough, but what did you think Flora was goin' to do with a poker and tongs to poke a fire, when there ain't any fire to poke?'

"Then Minnie she sort of giggled. 'Why, sure enough, Aunt Sophia,' says she. 'I never thought of that.'

"'Where did you think she would put them?' says I. 'On the parlor mantel-shelf for ornaments?'

"Then Minnie she laughed sort of hysterical. 'Give 'em right here, Aunt Sophia,' says she.

"The next day she sent a clock—that wasn't much account, though it was real pretty; it won't go long at a time,—but it looks nice on the parlor shelf, and it was so much better than the poker and tongs that I didn't say anything. It takes sense to give a present, and Minnie Harris never had a mite, though she's a pretty little thing.

"Then I took home Lizzie Starkwether's bed-shoes, and she took it the worst of all.

"'Don't they fit?' says she.

"'Fit well 'nough,' says I. 'We don't want 'em.'

"'I'd like to know why not,' says she.

"'Because you've given us a pair every Christmas for three years,' says I, 'and I've told you we never wear bed-shoes; and even if we did wear 'em,' says I, 'we couldn't have worn out the others to save our lives. When we go to bed, we go to sleep,' says I. 'We don't travel round to wear out shoes. We've got two pairs apiece laid away,' says I, 'and I think you'd better give these to somebody that wants 'em— mebbe somebody that you've been givin' mittens to for three years, that don't wear mittens.'

"Well, she was hoppin', but she got over it, too; and I guess she did some thinkin', for in a week came the prettiest mittens for each of us I ever laid eyes on, and Minerva herself came over and called, and thanked Flora for her apron sweet as pie.

"Well, I went to all the others in town, and then I started for Ayres, and carried back the dewdab to Herbert's aunt Harriet Morse. I hated to do that, for I didn't know her very well; but I went, and she was real nice. She made me drink a cup of tea and eat a slice of her cake, and she thanked me for comin'. She said she didn't know what young girls liked, and she had an idea they cared more about something to dress up in than anything else, even if they didn't have a great deal to do with, and she had ought to have known better than to send such a silly thing. She spoke real kind about Herbert, and hoped he could get married before long, and the next day she sent Flora a pair of beautiful blankets, and now she's given Flora all her bed linen and towels for a weddin'-present. I heated up my soapstone in her kitchen oven and started for home. It was almost dark, and snowin' quite hard, and she said she hated to have me go, but I said I didn't mind. I was goin' to stop at Herbert's uncle Hiram's on my way home. You know he lives in Leviston, half-way from Ayres.

"When I got there it was snowin' hard, comin' real thick.

"I drew up at the front gate and hitched the horse, and waded through the snow to the front door and rung the bell; and Uncle Hiram's housekeeper came to the door. She is a sort of cousin of his—a widow woman from Ayres. I don't know as you know who she is. She's a dreadful lackada'sical woman, kind of pretty, long-faced and slopin'-shouldered, and she speaks kind of slow and sweet. I asked if Mr. Hiram Snell was in, and she said she guessed so, and asked me in, and showed me into the sittin'-room, which was furnished rich; but it was awful dirty and needed dustin'. I guess she ain't much of a housekeeper. Uncle Hiram was in the sittin'-room, smokin' a pipe and readin'. You know Hiram Snell. He's kind of gruff-spoken, but he ain't bad-meanin'. It's more because he's kind of blunderin' about little things, like most men; ain't got a small enough grip to fit 'em. Well, he stood up when I come in. He knew me by sight, and I said who I was—that I was aunt to Flora Bell that his nephew Herbert Bennet was goin' to marry; and he asked me to sit down, but I said I couldn't because I had to drive a matter of three miles to get home, and it was snowin' so hard. Then I out with that little fool card-case, and I said I'd brought it back.

"'What's the matter? Ain't it good enough?' says he, real short. He's got real shaggy eyebrows, an' I tell you his eyes looked fierce under 'em.

"'Too good,' says I. 'Flora she ain't got anything good enough to go with it. This card-case can't be carried by a woman unless she has a handsome silk dress, and fine white kid gloves, and a sealskin sacque, and a hat with an ostrich feather,' says I.

"'Do you want me to give her all those things to go with the card-case?' says he, kind of sarcastic.

"'If you did, they'd come back quicker than you could say Jack Robinson,' says I, for I was gettin' mad myself.

"But all of a sudden he burst right out laughin'. 'Well,' says he, 'you've got horse-sense, an' that's more than I can say of most women.' Then he takes the card-case and he looks hard at it. 'Why, Mrs. Pendergrass said she'd be sure to like it!' says he. 'Said she'd got one for Herbert's mother last year. Mrs. Pendergrass buys all my Christmas presents for me. I don't make many.'

"'I shouldn't think you'd better if you can't get more sensible ones to send,' says I. I knew I was saucy, but he was kind of smilin', and I laughed when I said it, though I meant it all the same.

"'Why, weren't Herbert's all right?' says he.

"'Right?' says I. 'Do you know what he had last year?'

"'No, I don't,' says he.

"'Well, last year you sent him a silver ash-tray, and his mother a card-case, and this year he had a silver cigarette-case, and his mother a cut-glass wine-set.'

"'Well?'

"'Nothin', only Herbert never smokes, and his mother hasn't got any visitin'-cards, and she don't have much wine, I guess.'

"Hiram Snell laughed again. 'Well, I left it all to Mrs. Pendergrass,' says he. 'I never thought she had brains to spare, but then I never thought it took brains to buy Christmas presents.'

"'It does,' says I,—brains and consider'ble love for the folks you are buyin' for.'

"'Christmas is tomfoolery, anyhow,' says he.

"'That's as you look at it,' says I.

"He stood eyin' me sort of gruff, and yet as if he were sort of tickled at the same time. 'Well,' says he, finally, 'you've brought this fool thing back. Now what shall I give your niece instead?'

"'I don't go round beggin' for presents,' says I.

"'How the devil am I going to get anything that she'll like any better if I don't know?' says he. 'And Mrs. Pendergrass can't help me out any. You've got to say something.'

"'I sha'n't,' says I, real set. 'You ain't no call to give my niece anything, anyway; you ain't no call to give her anything she wants, and you certainly ain't no call to give her anything she don't want.'

"'You don't believe in keepin' presents you don't want?'

"'No,' says I, 'I don't—and thankin' folks for 'em as if you liked 'em. It's hypocrisy.'

"He kind of grunted, and laughed again.

"'It don't make any odds about Flora,' says I; 'and as for your nephew and your sister, you know about them and what they want as well as I do, or you'd ought to. I ain't goin' to tell you.'

"'So Maria hasn't got any cards, and Herbert don't smoke,' says he, and he grinned as if it was awful funny.

"Well, I thought it was time for me to be goin', and jest then Mrs. Pendergrass came in with a lighted lamp. It had darkened all of a sudden, and I could hear the sleet on the window, and there I had three miles to drive.

"So I started, and Hiram Snell he followed me to the door. He seemed sort of anxious about my goin' out in the storm, and come out himself through all the snow, and unhitched my horse and held him till I got nicely tucked in the sleigh. Then jest as I gathered up the reins, he says, speakin' up loud against the wind.

"'When is Herbert and your niece goin' to get married?'

"'When Herbert gets enough money to buy a piece of land and some stock and start a milk route,' says I. Then off I goes."

Sophia paused for a climax. Her guests were listening, breathless.

"Well, what did he give Herbert?" asked Mrs. Cutting.

"He gave him three thousand dollars to buy that land and some cows and put up a barn," said Sophia, and her audience drew a long simultaneous breath.

"That was great," said Eunice.

"And he's made Flora a wedding-present of five shares in the Ayres street-railroad stock, so she should have a little spendin'-money," said Sophia.

"I call him a pretty generous man," said Abby Dodd.

"Generous enough," said Sophia Lane, "only he didn't know how to steer his generosity."

The guests rose; they were looking somewhat uncomfortable and embarrassed. Sophia went into the bedroom to get their wraps, letting a breath of ice into the sitting-room. While she was gone the guests conferred hastily with one another.

When she returned, Mrs. Cutting faced her, not unamiably, but confusedly. "Now look here, Sophia Lane," said she, "I want you to speak right out. You needn't hesitate. We all want the truth. Is— anything the matter with our presents we brought today?"

"Use your own judgment," replied Sophia Lane.

"Where are those presents we brought?" asked Mrs. Cutting. She and her daughters all looked sober and doubtful, but not precisely angry.

"They are in the parlor," replied Sophia.

"Suppose you get them," said Mrs. Cutting.

When Sophia returned with the alcohol-lamp and afternoon-tea kettle, the finger-bowls and the doilies, the guests had on their wraps. Abby Dodd and Eunice at once went about tying up the presents. Mrs. Cutting looked on. Sophia got her little shawl and hood. She was going out to the barn to assist her guests in getting their horse out.

"Has Flora got any dishes?" asked Mrs. Cutting, thoughtfully.

"No, she hasn't got anything but her mother's china tea-set," replied Sophia. "She hasn't got any good dishes for common use."

"No dinner-set?"

"No; mine are about used up, and I've been careful with 'em too."

Mrs. Cutting considered a minute longer. "Has she got some good tumblers?" she asked.

"No, she hasn't. We haven't any too many tumblers in the house."

"How is she off for napkins?" asked Eunice, tying up her doilies.

"She ain't any too well off. She's had a dozen give her, and that's all."

The guests, laden with the slighted wedding-gifts, followed Sophia through the house, the kitchen, and the clean, cold wood-shed to the barn. Sophia slid back the heavy doors.

"Well, good-by, Sophia," said Mrs. Cutting. "We've had a nice time, and we've enjoyed seeing Flora's presents."

"Yes, so have I," said Eunice.

"I think she's fared real well," said Abby.

"Yes, she has," said Sophia.

"We shall be over in good season," said Eunice.

"Yes, we shall," assented Abby.

Sophia untied the horse, which had been fastened to a ring beside the door; still the guests did not move to get into the sleigh. A curious air of constraint was over them. Sophia also looked constrained and troubled. Her poor faithful face peering from the folds of her gray wool hood was defiant and firm, but still anxious. She looked at Mrs. Cutting, and the two women's eyes met; there was a certain wistfulness in Sophia's.

"I think a good deal of Flora," said she, and there was a hint of apology in her tone.

Simultaneously the three women moved upon Sophia, their faces cleared; lovely understanding appeared upon them.

"Good-by, Sophia," said Mrs. Cutting, and kissed her.

"Good-by, Cousin Sophia," said the daughters, and they also kissed her.

When they drove out of the snowy yard, three smiling faces turned back for a last greeting to Sophia. She slid together the heavy barn doors. She was smiling happily, though there were tears in her eyes.

"Everybody in this world means to be pretty good to other folks," she muttered to herself, "and when they ain't, it ain't always their fault; sometimes it's other folks'."

PS 648 .N38 F53 1999 v.1 c.1

Fiction by nineteenth
 century women writers

DATE DUE

GAYLORD   PRINTED IN U.S.A.